MODERN TRANSITS

by
LOIS M. RODDEN

To Kay,
my mother -
one helluva lady

First Printing 1978
Eighth Printing 1993
ISBN Number: 0-86690-151-5
Library of Congress Catalog Card Number: 78-56415

Cover Design: Amy Rodden

Published by:
American Federation of Astrologers, Inc.
PO Box 22040, 6535 S. Rural Road
Tempe, Arizona 85285-2040

Printed in the United States of America

ii

FOREWORD

In seven printings *Modern Transits* has steadily gained acceptance by astrologers who report that it is a valuable everyday tool for their personal lives as well as for counseling, and further that it is effective in horary interpretation.

Modern Transits is as pertinent and applicable to daily decisions and practical options as it was in 1974, when the first draft was written for a computer program. Since then, all the transits were checked on some 10,000 actual situations, and with the fourth printing a few aspects were added for people experiencing the phenomena of Pluto's acceleration in Scorpio.

Standing well the tests of time and use, *Modern Transits* is a proven valuable addition to the astrological library.

Lois M. Rodden
January 7, 1993

Books By Lois M. Rodden

Modern Transits
Mercury Method of Chart Comparison
Profiles of Women
Astro Data II (American Book of Charts)
Astro Data III
Astro Data IV
Astro Data V

CONTENTS

I INTRODUCTION

Transit, n. The act of passing over or through; passage; especially, the passage of one heavenly body over the disk of another, or over the meridian. - Transition, n. Passage from one place, condition or action to another; change.

-Funk & Wagnalls Standard Dictionary

Astrologically, the daily transit refers to the longitudinal position of each planet in its daily passage. As each planet reaches a one-degree mathematical relationship to a planet in the natal (radical) chart, there is an effect of a situation, event or attitude.

Transit aspects are read to the natal chart. The effect of a transit to a progressed planet's position is negligible unless that planet is in progressed aspect. Transit-to-transit indications are not pertinent to the individual unless they are in a one-degree aspect to a planet in the natal chart.

The influence of the aspects is not always subjective; it may be objectively demonstrated in the environment, or in a relationship to another person. For example, with a Mars transit, you may have neither energy, temper, zest nor passion, construction nor destruction, but you may see an accident in the street; watch TV violence; contact a lusty, robust friend; find competition and stress in your work environment; or observe someone else who is drinking, hasty or excited.

To a dour pessimist, the easy, leisurely, joyful or festive aspects will make less impression than the stringent oppressive aspects with which he identifies. This person would regard Venus trine Jupiter with suspicion and would key into a simultaneous Mars square Saturn. The innately sensitive person will identify keenly with the aesthetic aspects that fit his temperament; the pragmatist will understand the hard aspects and meet them with vigor; and so on, each to his own nature.

In all astrological aspects there is a Hierarchy of Precedence that tends to be preemptive. The prime determinant is the innate character. The Law of Prece-

1

dence states: *The aspect that fits best into the character will take precedence over the aspect that is foreign to the character.*

If you are inactive generally or at this time in your life, the transits seem to have less effect. If you're not involved in business and finance, the indications of these matters pertain to your personal possessions. If you're not married, the reference to your mate pertains to someone close to you. If you are celibate, the sexual/emotional indications pertain to vigorous social feelings. If you are male, the aspects that refer to "a man" will apply to your own attitude as well as to that of men whom you contact; if you are female, the aspects that refer to "a woman" will apply to your own attitude as well as to that of other women in your life. If you are childless, aspects that refer to children will pertain to the children of others as well as young people in your life.

If you are in the habit of constructive positive action, the planetary energy focuses primarily on your area of activity and interest.

If there are three, four, or more, planets on angular positions in the natal chart, more action will result from the aspects. If there are mainly succeedent planets in the birth chart, the action/reaction is more inclined to express in the environment and in relationships to other people. If there are mainly cadent planets in the birth chart, the result of the aspects is more apt to be passive/subjective in the thinking attitudes.

In any event, we have no way to predict the planets' precise effects. The planets are archetypal symbols of our needs and drives. Each and every definition of aspects, in this or any book, is based on how various people experience this energy, and on how most people feel and act. The influence can be analyzed; the result is highly individual.

Use your discrimination. Read with discernment. How does this influence affect you? Take what belongs to you. Consider how the definition fits your life and your circumstances. The planets do not cause events to happen, but they do show what drives, possibilities and obstacles are present.

Major progressions (secondary directions) are vital indicators of the major changes in your life. No matter how strong the transit aspect is to the Moon, you'll not make a home move unless the natal chart has a 4th-house aspect by major progression. With a transit aspect of Venus/Jupiter, you may go to a wedding, or hear of a friend's marriage, but you will not marry without a major progressed aspect to the 7th and 9th houses, plus appropriate circumstances. Mars by transit may bring bumps and bruises, but it does not necessarily indicate surgery or major accident unless there is a Mars aspect by major progression.

The transit will modify, shape, color, add dimension and *timing* to the major progressed aspects. The transit in itself does not show major progressed events. It does show major *trends and cycles,* particularly in the majestic sweep of the outer planets.

You may be more sensitive to one planet's cycle than to that of another. We have innumerable examples of people who are Saturn-sensitive, Uranus-sensitive, Mercury-sensitive, etc. This means that the transit motion of that planet is particularly significant to the flux and motion of their lives. They "feel" it. Their personal key planet is often the one in their natal first house, the ruler of the first house, or the planet in the closest natal relationship to the Ascendant.

There will always be simultaneous and contradictory aspects. This is true of life; in the midst of doing hard work, you go to a charming party. In the midst of a repressive period, you get a break of buoyant freedom. During a relaxed vacation time, you have a sudden pragmatic problem that requires decision and incentive. These contradictory aspects do not cancel each other out, but operate primarily through the Law of Precedence, secondarily as incidental factors.

The transit indications can mark a situation or attitude for its entire duration, or it may bring a short period or a single event that follows the description.

When there are few or no aspects we often get the feeling that nothing's happening, and during these times we settle into little more than routine, or even inertia.

Under the Law of Precedence, after character, natal chart, and major progressed indications, there is a hierarchy of importance in the transits themselves.

The transit Moon moves thirteen degrees eleven minutes mean motion per day. Its influence is so fleeting as to be indiscernible in terms of an obvious effect, though it can mark time and mood.*

The Sun and inner planets Mercury and Venus tend to have a two-day influence in their one degree to partile. As such they act as a trigger to heavier indicators, but in themselves are significators of the everyday experiences we all share in our daily goals, communications and social exchanges.

As Mars averages four days in its one degree to partile, it acts as a stronger energizer to action.

The Jupiter transit influence averages twenty-five days. As it circles the natal chart once in twelve years, it marks off periods of peace and reward, followed by an urge to grow and expand.

The Saturn cycle of twenty-nine years is famous as the great marker of time in our ambitions and accomplishments. The transit aspect influence is approximately two months, but it casts a long shadow.

The outer planets Uranus, Neptune and Pluto move so slowly that their transit influence ranges from one to three years. They can set so important a shading to the cycle that they color the outcome of the major influences. Together with Saturn, they influence the trend and direction of the life as a whole.

Generally speaking, the aspects of slow-moving outer planets, particularly when in "hard" aspects (conjunction, opposition and square) tend to eclipse the indicators of lesser dynamics.

In each planet chapter a more detailed description is given of the cycle and

---

*The influence of the natal, progressed and transit Moon will be covered in a later study, and is not included in this book.

time of aspect. Technically we consider the one degree to partile as an effective boundary. With actual examples this orb is questionable. Many people are markedly aware of the aspect two degrees or *more* before partile, or do not complete the situation, event or attitude until two degrees or more post-partile. This is particularly true of the slower-moving planets.

Out of a study of our transits we gain a complex multi-dimensional picture of the influences that surround us. The nature of the planets themselves is impersonal. The planets don't make decisions or moral judgments; we do. The planets are not compulsive; we are. The planets do not determine will, integrity or love; we do. We always have alternatives, and out of choice we weave the fabric of our lives.

The flexibility of laws is without limitation. There is no inevitability.

Agni Yoga

⇔ ⇔ ⇔ ⇔ ⇔

Coordinate Transit Patterns by Age

Age

Age	
6	Jupiter opposite Jupiter
7	Uranus semisextile Uranus, Saturn square Saturn
10	Uranus semisquare Uranus, Saturn trine Saturn
12	Jupiter conjunct Jupiter
14	Neptune semisextile Neptune, Uranus sextile Uranus, Saturn opposite Saturn
18	Jupiter opposite Jupiter
20	Saturn trine Saturn
21	Neptune semisquare Neptune, Uranus square Uranus
22	Saturn square Saturn
24	Jupiter conjunct Jupiter
28	Neptune sextile Neptune, Uranus trine Uranus
29	Saturn conjunct Saturn
30	Jupiter opposite Jupiter
31	Uranus sesquisquare Uranus
36	Jupiter conjunct Jupiter
37	Saturn square Saturn
40	Saturn trine Saturn
42	Uranus opposite Uranus, Jupiter opposite Jupiter
44	Neptune square Neptune
45	Saturn opposite Saturn
47	Jupiter conjunct Jupiter
50	Saturn trine Saturn

Age

51	Uranus sesquisquare Uranus
51	Saturn square Saturn
53	Jupiter opposite Jupiter
56	Neptune trine Neptune, Uranus trine Uranus
59	Jupiter conjunct Jupiter, Saturn conjunct Saturn
63	Neptune sesquisquare Neptune
63	Uranus square Uranus
65	Jupiter opposite Jupiter
66	Saturn square Saturn
69	Saturn trine Saturn
70	Uranus sextile Uranus
71	Jupiter conjunct Jupiter
73	Uranus semisquare Uranus
74	Saturn opposite Saturn
77	Jupiter opposite Jupiter, Uranus semisextile Uranus
79	Saturn trine Saturn
81	Saturn square Saturn
83	Jupiter conjunct Jupiter
84	Neptune opposite Neptune, Uranus conjunct Uranus
88	Saturn conjunct Saturn
89	Jupiter opposite Jupiter

Planets are notated by mean motion. In individual lives, the timing of age will vary by more or less, often bringing strong transit patterns to coordinate timing. (Jupiter noted in conjunction, opposition; Saturn in conjunction, opposition, square and trine; Uranus and Neptune in conjunction, opposition, square, trine, semisquare, sesquisquare and semisextile.)

II TRANSIT SUN

The Sun transits the horoscope once a year (365 days 6 hours) and returns to the degree of the natal Sun on each birthday. The Sun is the only transit body to make the same aspects every year on the same day, with a slight variation each year up to leap year. It will conjunct and oppose each planet once; square, trine, sextile, semisquare and sesquisquare every planet twice.

As the transit Sun moves at fifty-nine minutes eight seconds daily mean motion, it has a two-day influence of one degree applying and one degree separating to partile. Due to circumstantial facility or resistance, the effect of the transit definition may be felt a day earlier or later than the orb allowed.

As the Sun is the prime significator of ego identity, all Sun aspects mark days that stand out as being important.

Sun conjunct Sun: Happy Birthday! This is your astrological New Year, so reevaluate your past year and set your resolutions for the year ahead. Reaffirm your own identity; be the center of your environment. Know that your value and importance lie within your own integrity and goals.

Sun opposite Sun: Reevaluate your major relationships and goals today. You may encounter attitudes and actions in your own life that need improvement. Resolve your decisions on goals that are not being accomplished to your satisfaction, and face up to the qualities within yourself of which you may not be proud.

Sun square Sun: This should be a busy day when you can wade through any obstacles to a presentation of your goals and abilities. If you are not conducting yourself with integrity you could be overbearing in a rash attempt to gain your own ends. Stop and evaluate; are you being true to yourself?

Sun trine Sun: Present yourself with integrity and assurance and you can be proud of your goals and abilities. Your character and command can be a source of strength that others will admire and to which they will relate. Any decisions on major relationships or goals that you initiate today have the force to be carried through to completion, so be sure they are of value.

Sun sextile Sun: You have the ability to keep command of your own pride and integrity while being accommodating to others with your goals and actions. Any decision on major relationships or goals at this time tends to be impermanent and inconclusive; rather a transition that can lead to another opportunity.

Sun semisquare Sun: Ease up a little! You may feel depleted from a variety of efforts with your goals and presentation. If others are not deferring to you or paying proper attention to your authority, reevaluate your own integrity and keep your dignity.

Sun sesquisquare Sun: Sudden changes tend to throw your major goals and relationships off balance. Handle all unexpected data or new situations with dignity and integrity, and you can gain respect.

Sun conjunct Moon: This is an excellent day to accomplish domestic goals that can be helpful to your future, or to prepare career work in a home environment. You can carry the role of authority with your family and home with emotional stability, poise, vitality and command.

Sun opposite Moon: A domestic or family situation that causes you a division of interests may require your presence and authority. Be responsive to the fluctuating demands of those who need you as you adapt your plans to include your personal goals.

Sun square Moon: Busy family and domestic matters require adaptability to overcome obstacles of temperament, instability and discontent. You could feel moody, isolated, and be frustrated in your goals; make the effort to respond to the needs of others with empathy to keep your command.

Overexertion or overexposure could tax your health and deplete your reserves of competence.

Sun trine Moon: This is your day to rest, read, relax, pamper yourself. Soak in a hot tub, enjoy simple pleasures and renew your own center with the family, or with warm comfortable people. Those who care are tenderly supportive.

Public matters tend to go smoothly as people relate to you with respect.

Sun sextile Moon: There can be an opportunity to improve your domestic goals and relationships if your mood is sensitive. Extend your empathy to care for those who need your help, and they will be responsive.

Sun semisquare Moon: Complete the odds and ends of domestic needs and personal care, and handle minor frictions in the home with adaptability rather than moody frustration.

Sun sesquisquare Moon: You may feel at odds with your domestic goals and relationships, as plans tend to fluctuate. Be adaptable and responsive to inconsistencies in others, lest temperament and mood deplete your energy and command.

Sun conjunct Mercury: Set goals of what you wish to do and make plans for the future. Talk to people about your aims, write that important letter, call that person who is vital to you. It's a favorable day for buying, selling, trading, and pursuit of objectives.

Be alert, you could meet someone new, try something for the first time, or have a new experience.

Sun opposite Mercury: Circumstances may require maximum effort to accomplish your objectives and a need to organize and stabilize your thoughts and plans. In communications with people of importance it is difficult to establish your position with clarity and integrity, as the most vital thoughts could remain unspoken.

Paperwork, studies or verbal matters can seem an endless duress; keep at it and wade through in order to relax later with satisfying leisure for visiting, a movie or book.

Sun square Mercury: In communications under trying circumstances, it may be very difficult to maintain your pride and position. The other person seems to be holding the authority role and not giving you any help to make understanding easier.

If someone reneges on a contract, or your plans are changed, try to be gracious and revise your efforts to get around the obstacles.

Sun trine Mercury: In public speaking or private communication you can express yourself with authority and integrity that others will respect. Objective plans coordinate smoothly, and short trips are agreeable. News can be helpful to your goals, and the plans you make for the future are encouraging.

Sun sextile Mercury: In communications a gracious compliance will gain you more opportunity of understanding than will touchy pride or unspoken objectives.

With a little effort you can make agreeable contracts, short trips or errands.

Sun semisquare Mercury: You may break appointments or change plans. Distractions cause you to lose your train of thought, and you may have irritating differences of opinion. Traffic seems impossible when you are traveling. Instead of being indecisive, adapt to a new schedule and you may find it to be more interesting than you expected.

Sun sesquisquare Mercury: Inconsistent communications with various people tend to lack understanding. You can't imagine why certain persons said what they did or what they could be talking about. The person you really want to talk to doesn't answer the phone, and the news or call you do get is not what you'd expected. Better keep your mouth shut on matters of importance unless you have enough time to talk it all the way through to agreement.

Sun conjunct Venus: Make yourself and your surroundings attractive. Seek your loved ones for happiness and be content with easy, relaxed fun. Meet with the people you like best as you're serene, poised and pleasant company.

You can soft-sell your goals and easily gain agreement with gentle men who wish to please you.

Sun opposite Venus: You may feel limp, bored and lonely. You're in the mood for romance or for comfortable social exchanges, but either the right person is lacking, or your friends seem insensitive. Your self-assurance may be jarred by a less-than-enthusiastic reception. Rather than being overemotional and touchy, extend yourself to be courteous and gracious to others. Look in the mirror; are you overdressed? Be moderate in food or drink.

Sun square Venus: Your feelings are not geared to work today; you may feel emotional, distracted and touchy. Though lazy and longing for sensual pleasures, it's not the best day to entertain or meet a friend or lover, as social plans tend to have obstacles. Even when you try to be pleasant, you're on the defensive or at a disadvantage. It's a better time to seek quiet ease and stabilize yourself. Avoid overindulgence in good food, drink, or emotional scenes.

Sun trine Venus: You feel relaxed, at peace with the world, not too ambitious about work or social affairs, but agreeable and compliant to friends or lover. There is contentment and harmony with loved ones; others are responsive and kind to you. Festivities go well as you are charming and pleasant. In work matters there's no great pressure, and you can easily soft-sell yourself.

Sun sextile Venus: In romantic or social situations you have the opportunity to create or to renew harmony with gracious compliance and courtesy. Touchy sensitivity will leave you feeling lonely and distracted, but the effort to be pleasant will lead to warmer relationships.

Sun semisquare Venus: A little friction with a friend or loved one could distress or disturb your peace of mind. You could resent that person and feel inclined to overemotional scenes. Try serenity and graciousness through that touchy moment, to keep the harmony.

Social affairs could be mildly boring or not entirely to your advantage. The right person is missing or not paying you the proper attention.

Sun sesquisquare Venus: You may feel mildly disagreeable, tired and touchy; you'd rather withdraw into yourself than meet social obligations. There can be a disturbance with a friend or loved one that gives you an emotional upset. You're not apt to present yourself well under pressure; subdue sudden erratic feelings until you can regain your own serenity and be pleasant.

Sun conjunct Mars: Your vitality and energy are vigorous and aggressive, and you can feel your strength and personal power. Action, accomplishment and decision are yours to work with constructively, but be careful of overdrinking or overassertion that could lead to strife. You have impact in a vital relationship with a man.

Sun opposite Mars: Your work and action may demand maximum energy, skill and self-control under pressure. Run no unnecessary risks, as a cut, blow, burn or injury is possible at this time. Forcing issues is a mistake, but if a fight is thrust on you, stand up for your own integrity to demand constructive answers to a problem. You may have a direct and hostile encounter with a vital person.

Sun square Mars: If you work through the obstacles and problems that require decision and action you can make constructive and aggressive strides forward. Bossiness, arrogance, or temper will get you into arguments and fights that you regret. Take care with mechanical objects and tools, hostile animals, or competitive men, that you don't rashly invite trauma. Direct your energy into constructive goals.

Sun trine Mars: This is a vital and alert time when you feel confident, industrious and energetic. Your sex energy and vitality are keen, you are courageous and well-equipped to make daring decisions, assume leadership and take command. Assert yourself and meet competitive challenges boldly; you can win.

If any surgery is required, this is a good time, as your recuperative vitality is high.

Sun sextile Mars: Some strife and challenge may be invigorating today. Not foolhardy, but courageous decisions and efficient action will be productive and give you satisfaction. It's an opportune time to push for your own desires and goals.

Sun semisquare Mars: An action or desire may be blocked by someone's resistance or change of plans. This could be irritating and bring resentment or a blunt clash. Think it through before you decide on a rash action that is hasty or misdirected.

Sun sesquisquare Mars: Scattered activities and pressures can make you irritable and grouchy with restless, inconsistent energy. Jump into action to finish those dozen petty jobs that need doing but are a bore.

Use machinery, tools and sharp objects with great care to not be inattentive or careless. Avoid that sudden impulse to tell somebody off.

Sun conjunct Jupiter: This is a good day to meet with professional people who give you good will and credit. Don't rest on your laurels, go after what you want with optimistic conviction. Be generous, open and jovial, and this can be a lucky day. Someone will surely give you benefit, favors, gifts or an indulgence.

Expand your goals, broaden your tolerance and your philosophy with the faith that you can get what you want from the wealth of life. Take freedom and joy as your own with a moral consideration of values and honor. Don't settle for any less than your own worth; you won't be content with second-rate or second-best.

Formal occasions can be elegant, so dress well and retain your dignity.

Sun opposite Jupiter: Reviewing your own achievements can show you what steps of growth you have made. Be grateful for your capacities, have faith in yourself and your goals with a reevaluation of your own worth based on moral values.

Expand only where you must, as overoptimism could be costly in time, energy, hope or faith. Certain expenses may be necessary; delay a few days if possible to find better quality at a lower price.

A formal or conventional occasion could be elegant and require your best manners and deportment; dress well and retain your dignity, even if things seem a bit dull.

Sun square Jupiter: Matters on which you feel optimistic and confident today may be overrated. That purchase is overpriced. At the formal occasion you may be overdressed; or you could overeat, overdrink, or put on too much show. If you're on a diet, today is very trying; if you're on a budget, today it can be demolished.

Educational, professional and financial matters require formality and effort. You could be restless and discontent from wanting more out of life than you're getting just now. Question your own moral judgment and values, and strive for modesty, humility and gratitude for what you have.

Sun trine Jupiter: Seek favors or advancement from superiors or those with wealth and power as you easily gain benefit, credit and good will. In professional and public appearances you can display poise, dignity and elegance. Prepare or present material for publication or for your further education. See your minister or lawyer if the need is current, or begin legal action if needed.

Purchases are highly satisfactory and give you much pleasure for a long time.

Your relaxed hours can be deeply content in familiar surroundings with people who are close and dear to you.

Sun sextile Jupiter: There are more opportunities to advance your profession, career and standing with a moral consideration of values, faith and loyalty, than there are with overexpansion or overoptimism.

You can make contacts with important people in key positions to advance your legal or business conditions, academic or religious interests.

In shopping, you can find the purchase you want; the price may be high but you can afford it. In personal matters there is greater contentment in moderation than in self-indulgence.

Sun semisquare Jupiter: You may vacillate between restless moderation and self-indulgence, with an irritable urge to be free of routine. A matter could arise where you discuss considerations of values and feel indecisive about your course of honor.

In professional or social matters watch your deportment as you could feel a mild resentment at lengthy formalities and are tempted to be rude.

You could find the purchase you want, but wait a day or two to shop around for a better price.

Sun sesquisquare Jupiter: You could be disappointed if overoptimistic plans fall through. Matters that have been going so well suddenly seem to break up with inconsistent luck that is frustrating. You may discuss considerations of values and find that your own position of honor is none too stable.

In professional or financial matters and in public appearances keep a formal dignity, and in personal matters observe moderation. Indulgence can be costly.

Sun conjunct Saturn: You may be called upon to assume a new responsibility or to reevaluate old obligations seriously with your present sense of duty. You're apt to feel and act more stable, down to earth, sober and practical, so it is an excellent time to efficiently attend to business and to handle situations that require organization and planning, concentration and persistence. You can carry authority and management in your work and career and in administrative matters.

Your goals and security are aided by old and stable friends, or you can be of assistance to older, conservative people.

Sun opposite Saturn: This could be a trying day, as it seems that circumstances demand the maximum of your discipline and responsibility to cope with tedious or anxious problems.

Your energy tends to be depleted, a cold may be lurking if you get overtired, you could need dental work, and do be careful of falls or bruises. You may find yourself depressed and suspicious of deception from someone who could use you unfairly; beware of persons who may let you down.

In important decisions you could fear failure, but if you try to avoid a responsibility your loss is greater and you may hurt another. Your best course is to dig in — finish all the tedious and necessary tasks, meet each problem with a maturity or persistence, stability and dignity. And get to bed early.

Sun square Saturn: Responsibilities can seem heavy and disappointing now. You may have just cause to be suspicious or to worry, as a man in your life may cancel an important appointment or not honor an agreement. Other people may cause you work or concern, or tedious time-consuming effort. Work requires methodical planning and organization, concentration and persistence. You may feel pessimistic and dull. Your authority can be challenged by those who are less important.

Your best course is to knuckle down and plow into the work load, to gain the satisfaction of a job well done. Handle your responsibilities with dignity and efficiency.

Be careful of falls and bruises, getting overtired could invite a cold; and if you need dental work, get it done.

Sun trine Saturn: You should find it easier to assume responsibility just now and to honor your commitments and duties to others who need you. Settle matters of a practical nature to advance your career in a prudent and methodical way.

Superiors are likely to notice your sound, reliable and industrious traits. Routine, monotonous work can be handled productively as it is easier to work within the rules and to cooperate with authority. Your ideas are efficient, and your efforts well organized, so you can give enduring form to the ambitions that you advance.

Make decisions that are expedient to your own safety, rather than selfish, and you can be a tower of strength.

Sun sextile Saturn: There are better opportunities to advance your ambitions with reliability, practicality and efficiency than there are with selfish demands or suspicion. If another is unfair or lets you down, shoulder your own responsibilities. Attending to duties will give you a feeling of worth. You are capable of patience and self-discipline and of drawing on your reserves of stability and strength of character.

Sun semisquare Saturn: A variety of responsibilities and concerns could leave you tired and strained, irked by your limitations and small frustrations.

You may feel unsure of a person who could use you unfairly, and vaguely incompetent or inefficient. Consider this a challenge to your self-control and do not give in to the urge to throw responsibility out the window. When the work areas are met and the problems are solved, the pressure will ease.

Sun sesquisquare Saturn; Your sense of worth may be in for a rude shock today as some person or situation is likely to make you feel unneeded or unwanted. You are likely to be reminded of all your shortcomings and limitations. Another person could be a worry to you, and you could be tired, suspicious and miserable.

Get in and get all those scattered jobs done; tackle the problem area with persistence and honesty; take on the responsibilities with discipline; observe your own duties and you can build a stable security for tomorrow.

Sun conjunct Uranus: You could be unstable and distracted with a taut nervous tension. It's hard to concentrate on immediate affairs as new matters keep popping up. Sudden calls, changes of schedule, unexpected events or people may bombard you. Your own reactions tend to be independent, erratic or detached.

The people you're with today are unusual, unconventional, or different from your customary associates, or you may find yourself in new situations. It can be a stimulating day that opens some new doors of activity or ideas for you.

Sun opposite Uranus: You tend to be nervous, tense, distracted and unstable as matters unexpectedly seem to turn upside down. Sudden situations could demand the maximum of ingenuity and command to cope with, and your tendency may be to make a declaration of independence and tell everyone to "go jump in the lake."

Don't relinquish your judgment entirely by burning bridges behind you, as erratic, impatient actions could damage your reputation in a way of which you'd not be proud. Handle your high tension by looking for more inventive solutions to change your condition to a better position of personal insight and command. That position is *not* secured, and that person in your life is volatile just now.

Sun square Uranus: You could feel tight with tension today, as sudden changes in your affairs, or unexpected obstacles, require that you make an effort to cope on a different level. Rather than erratic or detached independence, use your inventive ingenuity to handle new situations, and it can be a stimulating day.

You may see or hear from someone from the past that causes you some excitement or feelings of disturbance, as well as being in situations where you meet new people.

Sun trine Uranus: New situations and sudden changes in your affairs can be exciting and stimulating. Your ability to cope with insight and brilliance gains the respect of others, and you can easily make daring or innovative moves that advance your position in their viewpoint.

You may see or hear from someone from the past with whom you make a contact of greater clarity as you're both able to appreciate the changes that you've made.

Sun sextile Uranus: Meeting new people, going into different situations and having changes of plans can be stimulating and interesting today. You carry a certain nervous verve that can strike sparks and you are able to stimulate your environment and other people. It's a matter of your choice whether to use that spark to ignite challenge or to impress others with your unusual command and capacity.

Sun semisquare Uranus: New people you meet today will size you up to see how you handle yourself. You can impress them and handle new situations by being modestly proud of your own independent identity, but it's not the day to make separate demands, as you'll be upstaged. If you are perverse, erratic, nervous and rashly independent you'll handle new data poorly.

Sun sesquisquare Uranus: The events of today could leave you scattered in a dozen pieces unless you hold to your own separate identity. Nervous tension could cause you to feel detached from, and independent of, the people around you.

An old friend or a new acquaintance may throw you a curve that triggers instability. You can handle these inconsistencies by drawing on your insight, poise, and ingenuity, to have a stimulating day.

Sun conjunct Neptune: This is an ideal time to take a day off, if possible, to float in daydreams and ease, to have a vacation, or to seek a renewal of deep serenity in still harmony.

Conditions of pressure or duress could give you anxiety that's not at all unfounded, as there is a person or situation in your life that is unsure, insecure, or actually deceptive. Some condition that you envision is unrealistic or exaggerated, and any plans or schemes that are presented may not work out just now.

Be considerate of others, helpful, courteous, sympathetic and acquiescent.

Sun opposite Neptune: It may be necessary for you to acquiesce to others without allowing yourself to be pulled into their exaggerations or dramatics. Though sensitive to that person's needs, don't allow your sympathies to pull you down.

Someone may be late or cancel an appointment that you'd looked forward to, causing you disappointment and let-down. Some matter you'd wanted could be ideal, exactly what you'd envisioned, and you still have the feeling of vague discontent or anxiety. Regard all plans, schemes and propositions with a grain of salt, as they could be unrealistic.

Sun square Neptune: This is a low-tone day where you may feel dreamy, indecisive and impractical. As someone needs your acquiescent consideration, give it graciously in order to feel mellow. Don't let yourself be let down by keying in to that person's emotional dramatics, and regard with caution any promotional schemes or sensational visions.

Sun trine Neptune: Today you can feel calm, mellow and dreamy. By contemplating the spiritual or mystical values you can be unselfish, forgiving

14

and considerate. Music or art could touch you deeply, or a movie or play catch your imagination. Promotional schemes or plans for a more thoughtful relationship present some ideal possibilities. If they are impractical or unrealistic you'll find yourself bored and inattentive, as your discrimination gives you more insight today.

Sun sextile Neptune: By acquiescing to the needs of another with thoughtful consideration, you have the opportunity to have a more ideal relationship than you'd gain with evasion or exaggeration.

As you're keenly sensitive to music, drama and aesthetics, you can gain mellow ease and renewal with a few quiet hours.

Sun semisquare Neptune: As ideal as certain matters seem today, there can be an undercurrent of anxiety; a person or situation is unreal, exaggerated, or actually deceptive.

You may feel somewhat vague, scattered, mystical, or confused. Your environment could have a dream-like quality that is strange and disturbing. The best way to keep your feet on the ground is by thoughtful, considerate actions to others.

Sun sesquisquare Neptune: Strange and inconsistent circumstances could give you a feeling of unreality. Some condition seems to be perfect, ideal, but you may be tinged with a vague anxiety that all this is a dream. If you feel confused, keep your feet on the ground by thoughtful consideration of others.

Sun conjunct Pluto: Today your powers of leadership are amplified, and you are able to sway others to cooperate in matters of mutual benefit. Only those persons hiding their covert insubordination will give you passive resistance by cancelling appointments or leaving your presence. In matters where the group is working as a team for a common goal, you exert a force of command that molds and directs your environment.

Sun opposite Pluto: You may be required to cooperate under the duress of "take it or leave it" by persons who have willfully challenged your leadership. Resist the temptation to manipulate others by passive resistance, but give the extent of your ability to yield without compromising your own integrity. If your goals are for the benefit of all concerned you can advance your own coc-mand with dignity.

Sun square Pluto: Other persons may push you to the maximum today by forcing you into collusion or agreement with their force of will. You could feel compromised, manipulated, or frustrated by your inability to take command. Try to work out ways to cooperate for the good of all concerned rather than force issues, as any ultimatum you issue will backfire.

Sun trine Pluto: You can easily elicit the helpful cooperation of others today, as they will acknowledge your position of importance or leadership. People will center around you or look to you for command. Your authority carries force and dignity, giving you self-confidence and a feeling of power. Any problem of passive resistance or insubordination comes out where you can deal with it openly for the good of all concerned.

Sun sextile Pluto: You have the opportunity to be agreeable and cooperative with others today. If you secretly feel that they are imposing or manipulating, it is still to your best interests to hold your position of leadership without forcing issues. Express your authority indirectly in group situations and you'll gain greater respect than you would with ultimatums.

Sun semisquare Pluto: In matters where you want or expect cooperation it may not come through today, and you feel that your position of control has been undermined. Be alert for a change of possibility, as some alternative plan may come up that brings out a hidden potential.

Sun sesquisquare Pluto: You can find excellent cooperation today as long as you go along with the crowd; it's not the time to push your own authority or to issue ultimatums. Another person could be trying to manipulate you; let him do so but keep your own motives hidden for now.

III TRANSIT MERCURY

As Mercury is never more than twenty-eight degrees away from the Sun it will transit the horoscope once a year. Approximately every one hundred days Mercury has an apparent retrograde motion that lasts roughly twenty days. By daily mean motion of one degree twenty-three minutes Mercury will conjunct and oppose each planet once; square, trine, sextile, semisquare and sesquisquare every planet twice. However, due to the change of station, Mercury may repeat a specific aspect three times. When moving at mean motion Mercury has a two-day influence of one degree applying and one degree separating to partile, but Mercury can move as fast as two degrees twelve minutes per day, making a one-day aspect and, when slowing to change station, holds an aspect orb for approximately ten days.

The faster the motion, the less discernible is the transit effect; the slower the motion, the more intense is the transit influence. A Mercury aspect on the change of station deserves prime consideration and may have an obvious effect in a two-degree orb.

As Mercury is the significator of the thought process that is influential to plans and decisions it has importance to everyday communications and decisions, understandings and agreements; transportation, travels and errands.

Mercury conjunct Sun: You may think of and discuss your own integrity today, talk about your own work and goals, or have the general conversation center on a specific area of your expertise. Clarify your objectives and act upon that decision.

Mercury opposite Sun: Though not in agreement with the plans, goals and objectives of another, you may be reluctant to state your position on the matter. Listen until all the information is in. Get your own reports and communications completed and then discuss your ideas.

Mercury square Sun: In discussion today you are not in any position to state your own goals and objectives to gain understanding or support. People are not giving you any particular credit, so defer to their plans and discuss their interests.

Mercury trine Sun: You can easily present and advance your goals today, as others will defer to your judgment and command. Discuss your position for supportive understanding. Have a quiet, relaxed evening with easy conversation, a good book, TV, or a friendly game that takes no great mental effort.

Mercury sextile Sun: You can gain an understanding of your position with calm discussion that respects the opinions of another, better than with insistence on your interests.

Mercury semisquare Sun: Your objectives today may be subject to changes of plan. An incident of misunderstanding can be due to lack of communication. Get all the facts before you act.

Mercury sesquisquare Sun: If there is a breakdown in communication today, you can gain better understanding by making your own objectives known and finding out what the other person's ideas are.

Mercury conjunct Moon; You may talk more than usual, as your mind is full of ideas and you want to express your feelings and attitudes. You can gain more information at a class or public function, and short trips can give you a variety of fluctuating conversations.

Your best visits will be with women and children, as you feel close in making plans together and nesting.

Mercury opposite Moon: As much as you'd like to talk it out to express your feelings and attitudes, it seems that you can't get together with that person to complete a conversation. Make every effort to get your communications clearly defined, as misunderstandings could lead to harassed moodiness.

A variety of short trips, calls, public contacts and domestic errands pull you in several directions, to where it's difficult to settle down in one spot. Complete all the little details in plans and pull yourself together at home.

Mercury square Moon: You could feel harassed and critical with misunderstandings and lack of appreciation. Your thoughts tend to fluctuate over such a variety of moods that you may jump from one subject to another.

If you're tired and don't feel well, your judgment could be touchy and out of perspective, so that you feel sorry for yourself. There can also be temperament, nagging or illness in your domestic environment that requires your empathy or care.

Clear up the needed errands and scattered activities so that you can quietly settle down at home.

Mercury trine Moon: If you feel tired, depleted or moody, this is the time to let go, relax, take it easy and take care of yourself. There will be someone there who'll nurture you with tenderness and gentle empathy. Contact your family or a dear woman; they'll help you.

Plans to make domestic changes for greater comfort work out smoothly; negotiations are agreeable; with short trips you can meet companionable people.

Mercury sextile Moon: You can gain more understanding and empathy for your feelings and attitudes by talking them out than by moody temperament.

That person will listen to you with responsiveness, but if you jump from one subject to another the conversation can get out of perspective. There are matters that need to be cleared up, and now is an opportune time.

Mercury semisquare Moon: You may feel tired, scattered and indecisive, irritable and moody. You don't mean to present yourself as insensitive but you may talk too much or make a blunder.

Relax and pull yourself together; get a rest and freshen up, and nest with compatible people.

Mercury sesquisquare Moon: You could feel tired, scattered and harassed to the point of disassociation by errands, domestic temperament and inconsistent demands on your reserves. No one appreciates you, and you're pulled into a dozen pieces by jumpy moods.

Take one job at a time; stick to one subject at a time. Keep your moods to yourself but relate to that other person's needs. When you can settle down in your own comfortable nest you can relax and regain your serenity.

Mercury conjunct Mercury: Review all communications; if made clear now they will be on a better note of understanding for the future. Attend to deeds or contracts and catch up on neglected correspondence and calls.

Any tests, exams, pending letters or news should come through with satisfactory results.

Mercury opposite Mercury: Communications may be difficult and demanding just now, as you feel that it is impossible to say what you really think. It's better that you don't so as not to disturb another.

Make the effort to be understanding and review your own clarity before speaking out of turn. Take only the calls, contracts and correspondence that cannot be avoided; try to put off until later all important decisions.

Mercury square Mercury: You may feel tired of the mental work and demands of communications that lack understanding. There are obstacles in short trips, or you may be late to prior commitments that you're reluctant to keep. Be careful of losing or forgetting papers or contracts.

Mercury trine Mercury: This is an excellent time for travels to be satisfactory for good accommodations and no delays. Public speaking or private communications are satisfactory, as you say what you mean clearly and convincingly and gain understanding.

Mercury sextile Mercury: Take the opportunity that comes up for a short trip as it may lead to further avenues of information that can be helpful. Send that letter, take that exam, or make the call that could prove productive with later results.

Mercury semisquare Mercury: Running short errands and a variety of calls and people to talk to could make you feel a little scattered just now. Calm down, it will all get done by taking one thing at a time.

Mercury sesquisquare Mercury: Communications can be disturbing and unfulfilling with lack of understanding. Avoid unnecessary phone calls, exams, or short trips. If they must be done, try to be discreet, as whatever you write or say could be a cause of regret.

Mercury conjunct Venus: Visit or have company; call the people you like and to whom you want to talk. Express yourself with serenity and you'll gain understanding. A helpmate is comforting.

If you read a novel or see a movie, it's likely to be a love story, and you could feel sentimental or emotional.

Mercury opposite Venus: A misunderstanding with a friend or loved one could leave you feeling lonely and neglected. Extend yourself to be pleasant in social situations even if you're touchy, and someone there will give you comfort and approval.

Mercury square Venus: If you feel critical or touchy you could be ungracious. Work through any obstacles that are present in your communications with friends and loved ones, and be polite with impersonal contacts.

Mercury trine Venus: This can be a placid time when you can easily go along with the plans of pleasant companions. From your actions of friendliness and courtesy, others will love you and take care of you.

Mercury sextile Venus: This is a more opportune day to maintain pleasant casual social relationships than to get into emotional discussions. You can smooth matters over to keep peace.

Mercury semisquare Venus: Your friend or loved one may be vacillating between compliance and restlessness. Smooth things over to avoid touchy emotions.

Mercury sesquisquare Venus: Misunderstandings with a friend or loved one can cause disruptions or strain. Better talk it out to be sure you both know what the plans are. There can be unexpected social changes. A little courtesy and compliance will smooth things into better results.

Mercury conjunct Mars: Your mind and speech tend to be sharp, aggressive, combative and pragmatic. Tackle mental and intellectual challenges instead of needling someone into a fight.

You, or someone in your environment, could have a fever, injury or operation. Avoid impulsive haste or impatient, rash combat; use that virile, satirical energy constructively.

Get some physical exercise, a sexual exchange, or put in overtime and run errands. Be careful in traffic.

Mercury opposite Mars: Your reason and your impulse are at odds today, and the result could be hasty impulsive action that you later regret. You could be crude, blunt, horny, satirical and biting. Outspoken opinions can irritate others and bring conflict.

Be reasonable; make an effort to use that virile energy constructively in physical exercise, meeting sexual challenge, running errands and putting in overtime, or you can run head-on into a fight, trauma or frustration. Someone in your environment is lusty, impetuous or hostile.

Mercury square Mars: Do you have a chip on your shoulder? You could

20

have a short fuse on anger and impatience that hampers your judgment. Better not get into that critical fight; you may get a hostile rejection or insult. There can be obstacles to your lusty, vigorous energy, with disagreeable conflicts.

Be careful in traffic of red lights, speeding tickets, or rumpled fenders.

Put your incisive energy into constructive accomplishment by tackling the mental and intellectual challenge of paperwork, games or debates. Get some physical exercise or outlet, run errands or get a tough competitive job done.

Mercury trine Mars: You're in top form with sharp, incisive mental vigor that can give constructive results to intellectual work or games. Physical energy can be expended with lusty pleasure in sex, exercise, or in getting a tough job done.

You, or someone in your environment, may be opinionated, aggressive, sexy, or may have a fever or trauma. Competitive challenge is stimulating, and you can hold your own or win unless you're drinking, as that dulls your expertise.

Mercury sextile Mars: If you, or others in your environment, are competitive, grouchy, lusty or opinionated, or have a fever or injury, you'll do better to be firm with pragmatic judgment than to get into a bickering discussion. Make up your mind and act upon your decision.

It's an opportune time to sign contracts or to have repairs done.

Mercury semisquare Mars: If you, or others in your environment, are restless and irritable, a fight, insult or critical rejection is possible, particularly if you're drinking. Better use your energy constructively with mental or intellectual challenge, or put it into physical outlets.

Take care of car repairs, trips and errands but be careful, as traffic may be indecisive, and the delays make you impatient.

Mercury sesquisquare Mars: Restless, inconsistent activities and irritability can scatter your energies. Take care of those odd jobs one at a time, of car repairs, estimates, short trips and errands, mental and intellectual work. Be careful of crazy traffic.

A sudden incident of trauma, criticism, insult or competition could require your discussion and decision. Be firm and reasonable (without drinking) and you can stabilize your environment into constructive results.

Mercury conjunct Jupiter: Your thinking can expand with good judgment and a self-confident, optimistic outlook. The practical knack of making things go well can aid in writing, teaching, making contracts, and traveling. You're making tolerant decisions.

A business, financial or legal matter just now is very fortunate. Talk things over with a professional person who is helpful.

Mercury opposite Jupiter: Your optimistic expectations could override your sensible judgment, and you count on more than you get. A business, financial or legal matter just now could be overrated and costly.

Formal red-tape matters are a bore, and people around you don't satisfy your intellectual needs. Do maintain the formalities that you must, and don't speak out of turn.

Mercury square Jupiter: Your judgment on business, financial or legal matters may be overexpansive; make that big expense only if you're sure you can afford it. Great expectations or a blind trust is unwise; neither count on promises nor offer more than you can deliver.

Formal functions are a bore; it's a better day to seek contentment with good old friends to discuss life and philosophy, or have a cheerful game.

Whatever you do today has a tendency to go to extremes.

Mercury trine Jupiter: Be happy, buoyant, optimistic and expansive; everything's going your way. Have faith that your decisions will turn out well, and others will be kind and generous.

Travels, business, financial or legal matters, and formal contracts are favorable.

Mercury sextile Jupiter: There are opportunities to expand your professional position with business, finance, teaching or travel, by expressing yourself with serene optimism and assurance. In formal situations you'll have a better time by acting in moderation than by going to extremes.

Mercury semisquare Jupiter: You may vacillate between optimistic contentment and a restless dissatisfaction. Don't count on promises, spend more than you can afford, offer more than you can deliver, or go to extremes. A calm moderation will show better judgment and stabilize your environment pleasurably.

Mercury sesquisquare Jupiter: You may be hoping for more than you have just now, as promises seem unstable and you have a restless dissatisfaction. Inconsistent activities require your courteous attention, but you'd rather relax in a serene environment. Do so, after the disruptions of the day, to renew your faith and contentment.

Mercury conjunct Saturn: Write, plan and organize methodical detail work. Catch up on bills, correspondence, filing and tedious duties. Analyze your career situation and work to see if you're operating as efficiently as possible.

You're not at your best in public speaking or appearances, and critical people can be depressing. If you feel tired and pessimistic, or if news and talk are discouraging, you may feel the need to be alone in your own safe harbor.

Mercury opposite Saturn: News or communications can be depressing or disappointing. Others may demand your understanding, and it takes your patience and effort, as you're more inclined to skepticism, pessimism or depression. Your daily routine can seem tedious or bleak, and you're not very good company. You may be right in wanting to be alone to pull yourself and your own affairs in order.

Mercury square Saturn: You may feel tired, discouraged and beset by tedious problems. Avoid business deals or signing papers, as the matters will be delayed, lost or disappointing. You could get tied up in duty meetings or impositions and miss the appointment you'd rather keep. You tend to be critical, ungracious, sarcastic or pessimistic.

22

Your best course is to keep your mouth shut and your opinions to yourself. Keep busy on a work task that will totally absorb your critical, exacting, analytical mental outlook.

Mercury trine Saturn: Now you can make expedient decisions and act on more efficient plans to accomplish all that needs to be done. It's a good time for quiet study, finishing up details on writing and paperwork, and matters that need concentration.

In communication and correspondence you'll be more discreet to wisely keep any critical opinions to yourself. Some news or new information can be useful.

Mercury sextile Saturn: You have the opportunity now to analyze your activities to devise methods of greater efficiency. Detail work that is often tedious is more interesting and gives a greater sense of achievement than usual.

News or communications will be of matters that you can efficiently improve by serious and intelligent plans.

Mercury semisquare Saturn: Work details can be tedious and irritating today, as sudden changes in plans require that you adapt to new responsibilities or impositions. You may be indiscreet or critical in your opinions and none too gracious. News or talk with others can be upsetting. Try to keep a steady, even keel and cope with minor problems reasonably.

Mercury sesquisquare Saturn: Sudden changes in plans may seem like depressing setbacks, and you're inclined to be critical, ungracious or pessimistic. Keep working at it; the news can be more favorable if you apply your methodical efficiency to keep the lines of communication open.

Mercury conjunct Uranus: You may talk to someone whom you've not seen for some time, or discuss new information and unusual subjects. A new person you meet can be interesting though not indicated to be a stable or enduring influence in your life.

Short trips can put you in a location that is not customary, and you may be separated from those with whom you're usually in close contact.

The change of pace is stimulating, but nervous tension can make you jumpy or disturb your sleep.

Mercury opposite Uranus: Sudden news or unexpected situations can give you an erratic nervous disturbance. Both you and other people tend to be unstable, with actions ranging from mild tension to hysterics.

If your thinking is at variance with others', you may be brusque, tactless, flippant, independent or perverse. Meet unusual situations with some degree of reason; if you blow up just now you'll only make things worse.

The people with whom you're usually close are acting crazy, and new people you meet are unreliable.

Mercury square Uranus: You could meet with someone on an unexpected basis, where new information is stimulating or even explosive to prior attitudes.

You, or someone in your environment, may be having an attack of unreasonable perverse independence in reaching out for erratic changes. A person

23

with whom you're usually close may be detached, nervous, or doing something new and exciting. Circumstances are out of context with your usual patterns just now; a new situation may endure for a short while before gradually getting back to normal.

Mercury trine Uranus: New plans, ideas and people can be interesting; a change of pace is timely as long as you're reasonable. If you do feel like making sudden, drastic changes, ease off a little. Some new data or information is pending that will change the picture. Your situation may be out of context with your usual patterns and will soon be back to normal.

You could see or hear from an old friend who is changing or doing something different.

Mercury sextile Uranus: Be flexible to plans, ideas and people, as they can range from being mildly unstable to highly erratic. By taking new information with a reasonable adaptability you'll find more opportunities for interesting activity than you will with perverse independence.

Mercury semisquare Uranus: You could feel a little nervous temperament or a mildly restless independence. A sudden incident with new plans, ideas or people could upset you, and you tend to react with independent perversity. Don't make rash decisions just now; be reasonable, shift to a change of pace that will absorb your interest.

Mercury sesquisquare Uranus: A sudden incident could throw you into an attitude that ranges from mild nervous temperament to explosive independence. You, or someone in your environment, can get into an unusual situation or be in an unstable period of change. Look at the plans, ideas and people around you and make reasonable decisions about how to build better patterns.

Mercury conjunct Neptune: Your mind tends to drift into imagination, exaggeration or lack of focus. You could feel like isolating yourself from a world that is either harsh or moving too fast. If there is gossip, scandal or deception in the air, you'd be sensitive to it and you may dramatize or be drawn into strange, unreal situations. You may sleep more and have vivid dreams or retire from activities to relax.

Wine or drugs have an extremely dopey effect. Better go to an amusement park, consult a psychic, see a movie, or read science fiction. Talk over your dreams and promotional plans.

Mercury opposite Neptune: You cannot indulge in daydreams now as you must bring yourself back into focus to communicate with people or deal with situations that are dramatic, imaginative, idealistic, mystical or elusive.

You are vulnerable to error, imposition, confusion or deception, so be cautious in your dealings, wary of exaggeration, and double-check your own work. Someone may renege, cancel or let you down; keep your own feet on the ground to uphold your competence.

You could go to an amusement park, visit a psychic, see a movie, read science fiction, or talk over promotional schemes; balance your judgment by discounting most of it.

24

Mercury square Neptune: Communications could be elusive and frustrating due to evasion, misconceptions or exaggeration. A person or situation that is dramatic, idealistic, mystical, anxious or deceptive may be hard to grasp or understand, and your tendency is to slip off into daydreams.

You could get lost in traffic, forget appointments, make errors in correspondence, or feel vaguely drained. Wine or drugs have an extremely dopey effect.

Discount half the things you hear just now, but do appreciate those imaginative, considerate persons who are at least partly real.

A movie, psychic or science fiction story could catch your fancy and may well be surprisingly accurate.

Mercury trine Neptune: Though your communications are not strongly assertive, you easily catch the imagination and compliance of others, who are not only pleased to go along with you but may offer more than you'd anticipated.

Any errors you make just now through laziness, acquiescence or incompetence will be forgiven; and if you act with consideration and hospitality you can gain the adoration of one who'll idolize you.

A matter you'd dreamed of may come easily to pass; if you are deceptive or exaggerating, it will dissolve, but with the integrity of working for your ideals you can gain more than you'd imagined. A little trip, vacation or favorable outing can give you relaxation and pleasure.

Mercury sextile Neptune: You can spend this time to greater advantage in gentle consideration, quietly going along with whatever turmoils and exaggerations another may have, than with counter-dramatics or anxiety.

If you've made an error or forgotten an appointment, been lazy or incompetent, now is the time to correct this, as you'll not only clear up misconceptions but gain greater respect for your ethics.

Someone in your environment may be drinking, dopey or a little strange; discount all exaggerations and regard communications with discrimination.

Mercury semisquare Neptune: Your activities may vacillate between a lazy, retiring, daydreaming quiet and a restless anxiety. Certain matters seem vague, unrealistic or exagerated, and there may be moments of drama, confusion and incompetence, when you don't know what's happening. You could get lost, be late, or forget, and are subject to error, imposition, deception and let-down.

Discount all exaggerations in yourself and others, keep your own feet on the ground and take it easy. Maintain your own ethics on an even keel by not acquiescing to strange impulses.

Mercury sesquisquare Neptune: A breakup of communication could lead to misconceptions and unrealistic anxiety. You could feel imposed upon, confused, or out of context with reality. Someone may renege or let you down, and it all seems vaguely unstable.

Discard the exaggerations, avoid double entendre and play it straight; clear up the drama, gossip, scandal or deception that's in the air to gain more reasonable communications. Don't let it build up but talk it out to gain understanding.

Mercury conjunct Pluto: With cooperative plans and communications you can be helpful to others for your own good and for that of the whole group. With forceful extremes of attitude you could overdo. There is a situation where you must extend yourself to be understanding or accommodating, to negotiate or conciliate factions.

In talk or studies, news or short trips you can get to the root of matters, cut through and discard nonessentials. Keep your reservations to yourself and maintain a politic position.

Mercury opposite Pluto: Being forceful and outspoken could alienate people, particularly in group situations. Meet others halfway in your opinions, with compromise for better solutions. Someone in your environment is strong-willed or has a powerful control, but you can gain an equitable cooperation by keeping your reservations to yourself. A blunt encounter just now is not politic as it would breed enmity.

Mercury square Pluto: In your plans and communications there is frustration in wanting to force your ideas through the obstacles; you can't seem to get through to understanding. That strong-willed person is not cooperating or has gone underground in passive resistance. You can't seem to marshall your forces, and ultimatums from yourself or from another create an impasse.

You're not expressing yourself well in group situations and you may find there is a division of factions.

It's more politic to lie low, keep your opinions to yourself, and do some deep thinking about how much compromise you can give to keep unity. Compulsive decisions of force to get your own way are destructive.

Mercury trine Pluto: In your affairs you can grasp the situation, get to the root of things, and prove your point. With forceful communications you can easily get cooperation to further your goals. Don't sit back but insist on your plans. Compromise, be reasonable but adamant.

If a matter falls through with someone who is coercive, another will step up to fill the gap.

Mercury sextile Pluto: You'll gain better cooperation with communications of compromise and understanding than you will with compulsive demands for your plans. Keep your reservations and willful opinions to yourself, and there's more opportunity to persuade others. Lie low and go along with a strong-willed person or yield to the group policy.

Mercury semisquare Pluto: Communications can vacillate between cooperative agreement and passive resistance. A person or situation requires your compromise, and you may be undecided about whether to force your opinions or go along with the policy. Find strength in your own realities, lie low, and wait for more information to get to the root of the matter.

Mercury sesquisquare Pluto: Your plans are subject to revisions and compromise to another person's policy. Because of delay, compulsion or pressure you feel like withdrawing in passive resistance. You do better to approach communications on a detached level, as attitudes are in a state of flux. Be prepared to renegotiate for better cooperation.

A sudden phone call or news could require that you reexamine your own position or change your plans.

IV   TRANSIT VENUS

As Venus is never more than forty-eight degrees away from the Sun it will transit the horoscope once a year. Every eighteen months Venus has an apparent retrograde motion that lasts roughly forty-two days.

By daily mean motion of one degree twelve minutes Venus will conjunct and oppose each planet once in a year; square, trine, sextile, semisquare and sesquisquare every planet twice. However, due to the change of station, Venus may repeat a specific aspect three times. When moving at mean motion, Venus has a two-day influence of one degree applying and one degree separating to partile.

Venus never exceeds one degree fifteen minutes daily motion but, when slowing to change of station, holds an aspect orb for approximately fifteen days. The slower the motion, the more intense is the transit influence. A Venus aspect on the change of station deserves prime consideration, as the effect may extend to a discernible two-degree orb.

As Venus is the significator of the social/emotional responses, it is important to our relationships with family, friends and loved ones; and to artistic and cultural affairs.

Venus conjunct Sun: This is an excellent day to pursue artistic interests: paint, decorate, polish, and beautify yourself and your environment. Family, friends and loved ones give you favors and approval; and social affairs are comfortably relaxed. You can go along with an easy, unruffled poise that adds serenity to your activities.

Venus opposite Sun: Under emotional pressure today you could feel wistful, lonely or unappreciated. Your tendency may be to withdraw in passive compliance. You'll have a better time by beautifying yourself and your environment and by extending yourself to be gracious, even if the social circumstances are awkward.

Venus square Sun: Bad manners, emotional conflict and turmoils create obstacles to the serene satisfaction you long for today. Too much good food or drink, or emotional scenes, would wipe you out. Rather than self-gratifying touchiness or the path of least resistance, make an effort to smooth out your affairs with gracious command.

Venus trine Sun: People around you are pleasant, agreeable and kind. As you feel easygoing and amiable you're apt to quit work early to relax or attend a low-pressure social activity.

Artistic interests or cultural exchanges are smooth. You can dress or present yourself in a way that is particularly attractive.

Venus sextile Sun: If there is a situation potentially disturbing to your emotional equilibrium, you'll make better opportunities for friendship and approval by being cheerful and pleasant than by making scenes. Smooth over touchy social exchanges to keep harmony.

Venus semisquare Sun: Several different social exchanges can vary from easy harmony to touchy moments. There's contentment in quiet relaxation but accompanied by lonely longings; there's fun in mixing with people but accompanied by a possible friction or hurt feelings. Keep it easygoing, observe etiquette and cheerful compliance.

Venus sesquisquare Sun: Unexpected changes in social situations can bring in tension that ruffles your serenity. If a friend or loved one is rude, independent or touchy, you can smooth out the situation graciously with easygoing good humor.

Venus conjunct Moon: As you are sensitive to the feelings of others you are drawn to people you meet today, and they respond to you. It's a good time for dealing with, and seeking favors from, the general public; and a warm close day to nest with the family or with a dear woman.

Venus opposite Moon: A conflict between domestic and social obligations could leave you feeling dissatisfied with a moody sensitivity. Adapt to the emotional mood of others graciously to gain the best social response.

Venus square Moon: You tend to have a moody touchiness today that makes family and love relationships difficult. You could feel tired or "crampy."

Nagging or emotional scenes are destructive. You may do better to go home and brood alone about your poor self until you can pull yourself into a serenity that considers the feelings of others.

Venus trine Moon: In public or social situations you can go along with a low-key ease as you move in pleasant or attractive surroundings but, to gain greater contentment, nest quietly with dear ones in a placid home environment. Someone in the family is helpful and nurturing. Let down and relax.

Venus sextile Moon: There's more opportunity for easy contentment in quiet, low-key, friend and family situations than in public social pressures. A cheerful acquiescence to another cultivates a harmonious response.

Venus semisquare Moon: An emotional pressure or social friction just now could give you a moody touchiness. With vacillation in your feelings you could be tired and unsure of what you want. If you nag your loved ones, they'll respond with irritation. When you settle down at home relax quietly to pull yourself together.

Venus sesquisquare Moon: Public pressures or inconsistent activities with family could leave you scattered, moody or touchy. Social plans tend to break up in disruptive patterns that you hadn't expected. Nagging or emotional scenes are highly destructive. Be adaptable, go with the tide and, when you can, settle into your own nest quietly.

Venus conjunct Mercury: As you have a friendly and cheerful attitude you meet with persons whom you like and can talk to easily. Communications clear the air, and even if you don't reach any decisive conclusions you'll feel better to talk it out with an easy, low-key, relaxed exchange.

Short trips and errands tend to put you into pleasant surroundings.

Venus opposite Mercury: Emotional conflicts and sensitivity can make discussion difficult, and if there is a scene, rational communication may break down entirely. You'll do best to not speak of your true feelings just now, as touchy misunderstandings would result. You may have news or visitors that require your compliant courtesy and tact. Be polite and withhold any reactive opinions to keep harmony.

Attend to short trips or errands that are necessary, and if the surroundings or accommodations are less than pleasant, reserve your comments.

Venus square Mercury: There may be obstacles to communication in social situations, where an effort is required to gain understanding of the other person's feelings on the matter.

If you express yourself in a touchy or emotional way, there can be controversy and criticism; you may be told to shut up. Clear up differences of opinion with courtesy and tact.

On short trips and errands be polite to keep harmony.

Venus trine Mercury: In social or emotional situations you can express yourself with a calm serenity that brings harmony and attracts an affectionate response. Friends and loved ones are helpful and agreeable, and there can be great pleasure in visiting, entertainment, art, music, short trips and errands.

A gift, favor or approval may come to you to further your cheerful contentment.

Venus sextile Mercury: If your social plans are not going exactly as you've wished, you can smooth matters more easily with calm graciousness than with touchy responses. Someone you like will give you approval, if you keep the lines of communication open with understanding.

Venus semisquare Mercury: Emotional vacillation would create friction with a friend or loved one just now. Controversy or criticism is touchy, as you don't have all the facts, and misunderstandings are worrisome. Keep your shakey feelings discreetly to yourself and act with courtesy until you can talk it out reasonably.

Venus sesquisquare Mercury: Inconsistent and hectic social exchanges can be an emotional strain. Very careful communications are required to keep from slipping into a sudden misunderstanding that would be regarded with criticism. Think before speaking emotionally and hang onto your fragile peace.

Venus conjunct Venus: You are drawn to people who are gentle, compliant and gracious, perhaps weak in character but certainly considerate and affectionate to you.

Your own attitude is placid, easygoing, relaxed and mellow. In social situations you can have great fun with friendliness and gaiety. Romantic situations easily arise, as you are appealing and attractive.

Venus opposite Venus: In social situations it may be necessary to mix with, and be pleasant to, people with whom you're not usually close. By extending yourself with courtesy and warmth you can have more fun and keep your poise. It doesn't help to be touchy or have your nose out of joint.

You may have some emotional pressure within yourself or be concerned about a loved one. If circumstances should separate you from the person you want to be with, do call so as to not allow any feeling barriers to arise.

Venus square Venus: If there are emotional barriers between you and your loved ones at this time, make the effort to clear them up with honest and tender consideration, not with touchy scenes. Be supportive of your friends and lover, and in social engagements be careful not to offend others.

Venus trine Venus: Social events and outings can go smoothly but are not too exciting. An easy and comfortable day with dear and familiar people is much more enjoyable than a "dress-up" occasion. Any little present-time conflicts will iron out easily. If reconciliations are in order, now is the best time, as you feel mellow and placid.

Venus sextile Venus: In social situations there are more opportunities to build friendship, gain approval and appreciation by being comforting, pleasant and gracious than with touchy feelings. If someone seems weak or is not your usual choice of companion, be tolerant and considerate; you may find that you like this person better than before.

Venus semisquare Venus: The social plans you make for today may not work out quite as you'd hoped. Better be placid and adaptable to the possibility of some touchy moments. You could feel muted, quiet and disagreeable, so try to be considerate of others to keep harmony.

Venus sesquisquare Venus: As your social plans are subject to unexpected changes and a variety of people, there may be hectic moments when you feel nervous, emotional or scattered. Muster your own poise and relax; if you try too hard you're apt to be clumsy and make others uncomfortable. Go with the tide, be gracious and you can have fun.

Venus conjunct Mars: As your emotional nature tends to temperament you could be volatile, impulsive, quickly aroused and ready to mix into either fun or a fight.

If your affectional life is drab, you'll be ready to make an effort now to stir things up; by all means do so but with a light touch.

Social affairs take a little extra time and energy to dress attractively and to generate sparks in another. If you should get into overexcitement and excess, make a fast retreat to keep matters friendly and harmonious.

Venus opposite Mars: Your passionate longing for more fun, companionship, affection and self-satisfaction could lead you to hasty or impulsive excess.

If you're having an active sex life, your erotic arousal is at a peak, and you can gain lusty satisfaction by pleasing your partner. If your affectional life is drab, you could feel frustrated or bored and critical of companions who don't satisfy your temperament.

In social situations make an effort to be friendly and vivacious with a light touch and you'll have a good time, but you could later regret a wild adventure or a volatile affair with an inappropriate person.

Venus square Mars: If there are obstacles to your social or sexual satisfactions, your tendency now is to impatient, aggressive action. If you can keep calm, honest and direct you can break down barriers to constructively build a more vital relationship, but if you're frustrated, brooding and mad you may impulsively destroy your chances of harmony.

A critical rejection is possible just now. Impulsive temperament or lusty demands can create volatile situations. Take it easy.

You could put that energy into a rip-roaring party that takes all your effort and skill, or mix with music and dancing, or have a rousing competitive game with good friends.

Venus trine Mars: As you have an easygoing, relaxed zest, you can go along with present activities amicably. Social and artistic ventures are fun, and there could be a spur-of-the-moment party or get-together with people you enjoy. Others are responsive and give you approval, affection, compliments and compliance.

Venus sextile Mars: Social and affectional exchanges are opportune when you initiate action with a light touch that is casual and easygoing. Be friendly, cordial and amicable, and others will relax and respond with warmth, care or favors.

Venus semisquare Mars: You may feel a little grouchy, with volatile impatience. There could be a mix-up or change of plans that is irritating, or someone displays a spark of emotional temperament. Calm down and keep it smooth. If you put a little effort into cheerful comraderie, the friction will ease off.

Venus sesquisquare Mars: Your emotions and desires tend to be erratic and inconsistent just now, shifting from nervous impatience to volatile excitement to a detached calm.

Sudden social changes, or people that you don't usually see, require adjustment on your part. Romantic or sex attractions don't work out well; a "first date" may be the last.

If you push matters or jump into compulsive excess you could regret it later. Calm down, take it easy. Shift to a different social environment that is less volatile. Observe courtesy, self-control and temperance, and your tension will ease.

Venus conjunct Jupiter: As you feel expansive, this is a good time for an elegant outing or for the gracious hospitality of formal entertainment. People come into your atmosphere who are important in their field, wealthy, generous and approving of you. You can have social exchanges with educated or professional people.

Artistic or cultural pursuits can be pleasurable; and shopping purchases can add elegance and beauty to your life.

A trip at this time would include the pleasure of seeing friends and a party or engagement.

There could be a gift or bonus or, at the least, a favor or kindness given you. As your own attitude is more tolerant, you can make up any disagreements smoothly.

Quiet reflection or time spent with dear familiar ones in a comfortable atmosphere gives serenity and peace.

Venus opposite Jupiter: By extending yourself to be gracious, tolerant and hospitable you can expand your social life with elegance and show. There may be a big party, an extravagant date, or a formal occasion, where you must observe protocol and deportment. Be careful not to overindulge, overdress or show off; with moderation you can still have a flamboyant good time.

In shopping the tendency is to overspend; in business you may count on more than you get; philosophical discussions about life and love may get a little pretentious; travels or public appearances may drag on with formalities. However, a cheerful and serene enthusiasm can carry you through graciously.

There can be a gift, bonus, favor or kindness that is not as much as you expected or felt you deserved; strive for modesty, calm and gratitude.

Venus square Jupiter: Restless, flamboyant self-indulgence can lead to excesses where you don't count the cost. You could easily overindulge, overspend, or grab for extravagant self-satisfactions. Misplaced confidence and poor judgment bring disturbing emotional profusion.

With a little moderation and calm, observe the proprieties of courtesy and hospitality. You don't really have to be the center of the stage or stir up excitement. There's enough in your life to appreciate with modesty and gratitude.

Be discreet. Draw on your own philosophical serenity to handle temperament in yourself and others.

Venus trine Jupiter: If there is an emotional profusion of feeling over a situation in your life, you can relax with calm optimism now, as matters are smoothing out to more abundant satisfactions. Dear friends or loved ones will give you warmth, comfort, gifts, favors or approval. People of wealth, education or professional status regard you with favor. Artistic or cultural, business or financial activities have a flair and elegance. Social exchanges tend to be gracious with an observation of formalities.

Appreciate the feelings of tolerance, content and optimism that renew your faith in the goodness of life.

Venus sextile Jupiter: There are better opportunities for warmth, comfort, approval, gifts or favors at this time, if you keep an optimistic serenity than if you display emotional temperament or overindulge. An artistic or cultural, business or financial situation may tend to be excessive, costly, over-formal, or run on too long. Be patient and courteous.

Social exchanges, dates or parties are more fun with a little discretion and moderation. A gracious tolerance clears up any prior disagreements.

Venus semisquare Jupiter: Social or business activities can vacillate from relaxed calm that is serene and joyful to optimistic excitement at expansive possibilities, to disappointment and let-down on a matter for which you had misplaced expectations. Educational or professional contacts can be disturbing or indecisive.

A restless urge for self-indulgent pleasures could lead to unwise excess or poor judgment. With faith and serenity observe moderation while you question your own philosophy of values.

Venus sesquisquare Jupiter: Expanded social activities can be inconsistent and overrated. Instead of the fun you'd anticipated, affairs tend to be lengthy, over-formal, too costly, or boring. Erratic or flamboyant self-indulgence or great expectations are unwise and fruitless. Sudden expenses or extravagance can be a loss.

With contemplative serenity, poise and courtesy, matters are more apt to change for the better and are certainly more enjoyable.

Venus conjunct Saturn: In your affections you may feel lonely, limited or sad and you long to cling to the dear ones who are safe and secure. There is great contentment in being in a safe harbor with people who are serene and steady, and pleasure in simple old-fashioned values and familiar routines. Problems in your emotional environment can be met with gentle persistence and humility. With a sense of calm discipline you can give up social fun for the sake of duty.

You may incorporate social exchanges with your business, or work with people with whom you have an emotional relationship. Your work gives you a serene feeling of pleasure in its steady routine. Artistic or cultural pursuits can be productive and well-organized. There can be satisfaction in painting, cleaning, sorting, and beautifying your surroundings.

Give yourself a beauty treatment with care of your skin, hair, glasses, teeth, nails and personal effects.

Venus opposite Saturn: Social obligations or business entertainment may be a strain, as you feel unloved, unattractive and out of place. You may be exhausted with the emotional pressure demanded by the duties of family, friends and loved ones. Your tendency could be to act humorless, grouchy, rude and awkward; you wonder why you have to be pleasant to anyone, anyhow. Try to be gracious until you can get back into the secure and familiar surroundings that give you the serenity of routine.

Romantic involvements may be discouraging, as the price is too high; you may be reluctant to take on the level of responsibility that a loved one needs, and either you or another could be gloomy, depressed, cold, worried or selfish.

Work to keep steady values, care for those persons for whom you have a social or moral responsibility with patience, loyalty, and maturity.

Take care of personal needs; care for your skin, hair, nails, glasses, teeth and general appearance. If painting, cleaning, sorting and organizing are necessary, get it done.

Venus square Saturn: There could be jealousy, cold feelings or hardheartedness with your loved ones that cause you grief, loneliness and loss. A person may disappoint you with indifference or criticism. Your emotional environment could be highly strained, and nothing seems to go smoothly at home or on the job.

If possible avoid parties or emotional encounters, as they could be more work than fun, or could leave you feeling slighted, empty or regretful. Try to keep steady in order to wade through obstacles that threaten your security. Your organization and planning work best at the little detail duties that improve the comfort of your familiar surroundings.

Venus trine Saturn: This is a fine time to make duty calls, visit elderly people, or mix into social situations connected with your work. You have more graciousness and patience with boring situations and people. You can handle any problem and responsibility that come up with diplomacy, charm and efficiency.

A party at this time tends to be well-organized but more decorous than festive. Familiar and routine social exchanges, such as playing cards, watching TV with your family, or dining with old friends, are comfortable and pleasurable. There is serenity and security in your safe harbor and in calm self-discipline.

Other people are helpful in your organizations to improve the beauty and comfort of your surroundings. Get the kids to clean the garage; ask your secretary to straighten the files; have your mate help you paint the porch, or ask your service representative for advice on a maintenance problem.

Venus sextile Saturn: There is contentment and security in keeping a calm and steady course of observation of duty and responsibility. Touchy or cold behavior can leave you lonely and sorry.

Social obligations or business entertainment tend to be decorous but not too much fun. Steady routine work can give you the pleasure and satisfaction of getting caught up and improving the beauty and harmony of your environment.

You have the opportunity to cement better social and emotional relationships by gracious and patient courtesy. If you've made a prior error correct it now.

Venus semisquare Saturn: You could vacillate between serenity and discouragement. It seems that your friends or loved ones are not treating you with the appreciation or care you need or deserve. Business entertaining, parties or emotional encounters could be a strain that leaves you drained. It's a better time to settle into a safe harbor with a secure person.

A romance just now could be more of a worry or a bore than a pleasure.

A quiet work time can be satisfactory. If appointments are broken or there are changes in work procedure, you are able to adjust with efficiency if you patiently maintain your pace.

Venus sesquisquare Saturn: Unexpected changes in your social and emotional relationships can be discouraging. A sudden coldness, indifference or criticism could come up when you least expect it, catching you at an awkward time. Your tendency is to react with a touchy independence.

A party or romance at this time is not inclined to go as you'd anticipated and is none too stable.

If you can cope on an even keel of self-discipline you can stay in control of the situation and turn it to your advantage. Take responsibility in a mature and gracious way to methodically get around obstacles in timing and temperament.

Artistic and cultural pursuits: painting, cleaning and sorting; and personal upkeep can reestablish your stability. In business presentations a certain nervous verve can be attractive.

Venus conjunct Uranus: Social activities can bring unusual or "far-out" people into your life, who are here today and gone tomorrow. Some unexpected matter can be interesting or exciting. You may see an old friend or lover from the past, who is stimulating for a brief visit.

You or someone in your environment may be exhibiting emotional independence or unconventional conduct that can key you up to nervous tension. Meet new situations with sparkle and verve but act with discretion.

Venus opposite Uranus: Social affairs can be stimulating or even bring a high pitch of excitement. Someone unusual or unexpected can be attentive, alluring or provocative, but don't count on anything enduring. That person will either renege or be unreliable — or you suddenly lose interest.

You, or others in your environment, are being emotionally independent, perverse, crass or indiscreet.

Be gracious and agreeable in social situations; your nervous verve is attractive, and by extending yourself you can gain attention and interest. However, if you make crazy moves that are emotionally unstable, matters are not apt to conclude well and may even be disastrous.

Venus square Uranus: An unusual party or a sudden change in social matters can be interesting and stimulating, if you keep some measure of calm and discretion. With restless or perverse rebellion you could jump into a crazy, unstable and destructive affair or cut off the people who are dearest to you with emotional independence that leads to estrangement.

Meet social changes or your own emotional pitch with self-control; this is a poor time for erratic decisions that are contrary to your own interests.

Venus trine Uranus: Changes in your social and emotional activities can best be handled with poise, calm and discretion. As your feelings can be somewhat volatile, you may be attracted to new people, mixing in unusual combinations or going to places that are different from your customary environment.

Though a romance or affair could begin easily now, it tends to be more exciting than enduring.

Cultural, artistic or decorating ideas can have an originality that attracts attention.

Venus sextile Uranus: New situations or changes in your social life can be interesting and diverting, if you relax and enjoy them. The opportunity of a new romance could be provocative but is not really appropriate; the flirtation is more fun than the consummation.

Unusual social exchanges with people who are not your customary companions are more enjoyable in the long run if you act with discretion and poise.

Venus semisquare Uranus: A restless, unstable independence can mar the serenity of your emotional life. You are, or someone in your environment is, having changes of heart or nervous, touchy indecision. As you could easily be at odds with people who are dear to you, sudden, little unexpected obstacles could bring a volatile reaction.

Relax and calm down, take it easy. New people or unprecedented situations do not set stable patterns just now. Handle your social affairs with discretion.

Venus sesquisquare Uranus: Your social life may be inconsistent, with sudden changes that tend to throw you off balance. New people or unprecedented situations tend to occur only this once, so relax and handle matters with poise rather than with nervous or erratic, volatile emotions.

Venus conjunct Neptune: You can easily be drawn into strange situations of intrigue, drama or confusion, or go into an environment that is enchanting, theatrical or vaguely unreal. If you feel vulnerable, nostalgic or lazy you may withdraw in a dreamy introversion or follow a line of compliant nonresistance.

As you're emotionally sensitive you or someone in your environment could be having a poignant love story, if only in the movie you watch. You could feel compassion or anxiety for one of your dear ones who is weak and defenseless.

There can be a social occasion that is delightful or a gift or favor.

Venus opposite Neptune: You may well be vulnerable to error or confusion, if not deception, as someone may renege, let you down, or be acting in a way that causes you anxiety. Someone in your environment is weak or defenseless, incompetent, exaggerating, or actually lying.

Your romantic life can be subject to disappointment and a vague discontent, as you long for more tenderness or a little enchantment. Don't count on promises or flights of fancy.

Give your calm consideration rather than dramatics. A dreamy seclusion is satisfactory, where you can withdraw in quiet introversion without hassle.

Venus square Neptune: Your sensitivity can easily make you vulnerable to intrigue, drama, confusion or actual deception. Your tendency may be to exaggerate with emotional theatrics or to flee in mute seclusion to nurse your hurt.

Someone may renege, abandon you or let you down, be evasive, conceaing, or impossible to figure out. Don't count on flights of fancy.

Draw on your inner serenity and make the effort to be considerate and tender to anyone who is weak and defenseless or incompetent. Pursue artistic or aesthetic interests and decorating, shop with discretion, seek easygoing social exchanges. Romance, theatrics, or strange situations and people can be unreal just now.

Venus trine Neptune: Someone in your life is tender and considerate, giving you love and approval. If you feel vulnerable and touchy with an exaggerated sensitivity, you can easily regain your serenity by reaching out to those persons who do care for you.

A social occasion could be delightful, if somewhat strange or theatrical. There could be a gift or favor that you hadn't anticipated.

When you act with compassion to one who is weak, defenseless or anxious, your loving support will gain deep appreciation.

Venus sextile Neptune: You can gain greater satisfaction from actions of consideration and tenderness to others than from touchy evasion or hypersensitive dramatics.

Someone in your life is vague, weak, unrealiable or scheming. If you feel vulnerable or confused withdraw to seclusion to regain your own inner serenity.

Venus semisquare Neptune: You may feel emotionally indecisive, vaguely restless or anxious but unsure of what it is you long for. If you are hypersensitive to real or imagined rejection, deception or imposition you may wish to seclude yourself in mute introversion. A romance or social occasion could give you a mild discontent as it seems lacking.

Hold onto your poise and consideration to keep a harmonious calm.

Venus sesquisquare Neptune: A strange, sudden or unexpected breakup in your social plans could shatter your peace and leave you feeling nervous and anxious, rejected or betrayed. Don't exaggerate; you can turn matters to your advantage if you resist intrigue or theatrics, behave with courtesy and consideration, and relate to those persons who do truly care for you.

Venus conjunct Pluto: In social contacts there may be a need to conform to the timing or standards of others. Make that compromise graciously for the sake of peace and good manners but isolate your own feelings from compulsive reactions.

If there are any hidden or festering areas in your love life they could come out now with an emotional impact that marks a turning point. By completing a social, artistic or relationship commitment you can have more peace, beauty and comfort.

In group situations you can take command with good-natured ease and sway others with your gentle charm and appeal.

Venus opposite Pluto: A social event may require your maximum cooperation to proceed smoothly to everyone's satisfaction. Unless you're ready to quit, make a gracious compromise for the sake of peace and good manners. The more you extend yourself for the love of others, the more approval and harmony will surround you.

If a loved one is pushing for emotional impact, isolate your own feelings from compulsive reactions. This is not the time to yield to manipulative tactics. Social, artistic or relationship commitments are not ready to be completed as they require more interchange and effort.

In group situations you may be aware of the undercurrents and diversity of social strata. Don't take sides; keep your feelings to yourself with a serene, politic compliance.

Venus square Pluto: Your social life could have some emotional impact where you feel manipulated, uncooperative and ungracious. You may have to lie low and conform to the timing and standards of others just now. Don't push —it can work out later. Compromise for the sake of peace and good manners; if you work through the obstacles you'll be able to express your own feelings later in private.

In group situations a diverse cultural range of people may not appreciate your charms, unless you make an effort to relate on their level.

Venus trine Pluto: For your own serenity and to keep control of social situations, give your gracious cooperation to your loved ones. Matters are gradually moving to a turning point that will bring out any hidden areas in yourself or in your social, artistic or relationship involvements that need to be cleansed and healed. New patterns at this time can be to your advantage if they're based on loving cooperation for the good of all concerned.

A romance can have depth and intensity, sweeping force and intimacy.

Group situations can be a pleasure when you yield and fit into the team with quiet, serene compliance.

Venus sextile Pluto: Your social life will go much more smoothly with gracious cooperation than with manipulative tactics. If a friend or loved one is subtly imposing, compromise for now to keep peace.

Though you may feel like completing an artistic or emotional involvement, it's not yet time to do so until more loose ends are tied up. If a new romance is ventured, you may not be ready for the impact and intensity it would involve.

In group situations, if you're not entirely compatible or agreeable, be gracious and compliant, and matters will go more smoothly for all concerned.

Venus semisquare Pluto: You may feel restless and indecisive in social situations. If you feel manipulated or imposed upon, your tendency could be to react with impulsive or compulsive force.

Your friends and loved ones may vacillate between compliance and resistance, causing you irritation and impatience. Cooperate with those persons you do care for to keep unity and harmony.

Venus sesquisquare Pluto: Sudden changes in your social situation could trigger a compulsive reaction that is ungracious and unwise. An unexpected imposition or emotional conflict in your environment could be upsetting.

Relax: you can turn this to a better level of cooperation and unity by acquiescing to the timing and standards of another. Be gracious and helpful, and tensions will ease.

V   TRANSIT MARS

Mars transits the horoscope in one year ten months twenty-two days. Every twenty-four to twenty-six months Mars has an apparent retrograde period of sixty to eighty days. In its two-year cycle Mars will conjunct and oppose each planet once; square, trine, sextile, semisquare and sesquisquare every planet twice. However, due to the change of station, Mars may repeat a specific aspect three times.

At daily mean motion of thirty-three minutes twenty-eight seconds Mars has a four-day influence of one degree applying and one degree separating to partile, going through one sign in approximately eight weeks. At the maximum rate of motion of forty-six minutes a day Mars has a three-day orb. When slowing to change of station, Mars holds the aspect orb for twenty-five days.

When Mars is in aspect during the slower motion to change of station, the influence extends to a discernible two-degree orb limit. The urge to action in the manner of the planet aspected is intensified.

As Mars is the significator of undifferentiated energy, the most appropriate expression of Mars is constructive action and positive assertion. Without a monitor Mars tends to rash destruction, hostility and trauma.

Mars conjunct Sun: With energy and drive you can accomplish objective goals, assert your own opinions, and make practical decisions. As your attitude tends to be positive, you may initiate action toward a constructive achievement and you can stimulate others to follow your desires.

Exercise or physical exertion brings a sense of well-being. Competition or challenge is stimulating.

If there is impulse, force, strife or trauma in your environment, you can meet it directly and take command.

Mars opposite Sun: Challenge, competition or objective problems seem to be thrust upon you and to require your energy and exertion. Trauma or fever, strong attitudes, assertive opinions and self-willed people can cause conflict and blunt encounters. By meeting this with positive, courageous direct practicality you can be sure and decisive. Avoid rash changes or impulsive hostilities, as they can lead to unpleasant scenes but, if there is a demand, meet it with zest and take command.

Mars square Sun: Lusty, aggressive, competitive energy can trigger you to crude actions and rash behavior. Face courageously the decisions that will influence your future goals as you may encounter obstacles of anger, trauma, hostility and challenge, particularly from vital men.

Consider the feelings of others in the action you take as you could antagonize them needlessly and cause yourself a great deal of trouble. Look for physical outlets for your energy in exercise, competitive games, cleaning and repairs; rather than in drinking, fighting, or taking risks. Watch your temper!

Mars trine Sun: Put your drive and energy into activities that will advance your goals. Strike for that position of advancement that you want, as your decisions are commanding and vital.

Your sex drive and vitality are comfortable and satisfying, making this a good time for enjoyable earthy pleasures: a steak, a drink, a competitive game, good partnership exchanges. Put action toward that which you want; you can win!

Mars sextile Sun: With impulsive, decisive action you can cut through obstacles and objective problems to accomplish your goals. You have the energy, zest and decisive drive to initiate progress in constructive achievement. It's a time more opportune to strike for the position that will advance your goals than to rashly mix into bickering, competition or drinking.

Mars semisquare Sun: Rash actions based on impulsive indecision will rob you of satisfactory results or bring small losses and disputes. A minor breakage or trauma could interfere with your objectives. You or another may have flashes of irritation, impatience and antagonism. Meet these vacillations with direct constructive action to further your goals.

Mars sesquisquare Sun: You may feel pressured and grouchy as you wish to push forward your goals, but other people are not being helpful or agreeable. Someone is overaggressive, or a matter is not working out to your satisfaction. As your desires may be rash and ill-advised, tackle only those matters you feel sure to be constructive. Avoid that impulse to tell somebody off or blow your own horn; you'll not help your own cause. Use your energy to check out new approaches to your goals.

Mars conjunct Moon: Use your energy constructively in domestic affairs. Cooking, games or sports at home, or vigorous family activities will ease any moody restlessness.

You or one of the children could have a fever or flu, so guard against the bug. A woman tends to have an uncomfortable menstrual period or could visit the doctor at this time for a functional checkup.

If you are temperamental you could have strife or quarrels with a woman or over a domestic situation, or be impatient with others. Keep an open attitude and care for those who are younger or weaker; engage in activities that need your care.

Women and children are more aggressive, active, loud, or busy with a variety of fluctuating tasks.

Mars opposite Moon: It takes a maximum effort to keep domestic and family relations rolling smoothly and constructively. A variety of fluctuating activities divides your time and pressures you; delays can cause impatience and stress.

A woman can have an aching menstrual period; she or a child can have a fever or flu, a doctor appointment, temperament and volatile moods.

If you are put in a situation where your hands are tied or you're dependent upon others, contain your frustrated irritation. As domestic situations demand adaptability in caring for others, you can manage best with vigorous empathy.

Mars square Moon: As you may find yourself tense and unsettled with volatile mood swings, avoid quarrels, strife with a woman, or impatience with children. Domestic problems take energy and action to solve; tackle them with the adaptability that will better your conditions. Cook, clean and make repairs; care for those who need you.

A woman may have a grouchy menstrual period; she or a child could have a fever or flu, doctor appointment, or critical temperament.

Attack all domestic or mood problems with vigor and zest rather than irritation, and you can make constructive improvements.

Mars trine Moon: You have the energy and adaptability to make smooth, constructive domestic improvements. Repair the lawn mower or oil the squeaky hinge, wax the floor or bake a feast; do something vigorous with the children; or tend your plants and pets; your home will hum with activity and contentment. The dear woman you relate to with tenderness and care will respond with empathy and vitality.

Mars sextile Moon: Your familial and domestic relations will improve considerably if you are tender and considerate, with the empathy to care for those who need you. If you feel moody temperament and impatience, someone will give you the opportunity to have a lift of spirit. You can overcome negative feelings by taking initiative to improve your home environment and relationships.

Help a friend with domestic chores, be hospitable, plan a children's party, take care of doctor appointments, or start your own diet or health improvement plan.

Mars semisquare Moon: A variety of odd jobs and domestic activities can scatter your energy and bring irritable moods. Women tend to be tense and unsettled, perhaps with a touchy menstrual period, and little nagging spats can erupt. Children seem rude or loud, and your patience is short.

Changes of plans may cause tension in the home. Be adaptable and care for others with empathy; the friction will ease off.

Mars sesquisquare Moon: Family and domestic matters tend to be unstable with sudden changes of plans and restless mood swings. Other people seem to be inconsistent and unreliable; they may draw on your empathy and tenderness at a time when you feel impatient and temperamental. You could be caught short by unexpected spats or nagging.

A woman could have an untimely or "crampy" menstrual period, and she or a child could have a sudden fever or flu. The children seem erratic, so keep them out of traffic and direct them into constructive sports or play.

Turn this variety of activity into constructive improvement by taking initiative to clear up all loose ends, and care for those who need you.

Mars conjunct Mercury: With that good vigorous energy you can wade into work and busy activities with zest. As you tend to be firm in your opinions, lively and alert, you may talk rashly before thinking, or interrupt others. If you are restless direct that mental energy into constructive channels of practical paper or math work, intellectual challenge, competitive games, and social exchanges with vital, intelligent people.

There may be news of strife or trauma or a communication that requires pragmatic decision or courageous action.

Mars opposite Mercury: If you find yourself with a mountain of work on errands, details, short trips, paper and study material, wade in methodically to finish it in the order of importance. This is not the time for conceptual thought and insight; demands of abstract discussion can be irritating, and your tendency is to react with dogmatic opinions. Communications tend to be competitive, with a lack of understanding that antagonizes you.

There may be news of strife or trauma, or a communication that requires pragmatic decision or courageous action that may be inconvenient to work into a busy schedule.

Be careful in traffic but do attend to any needed car repairs.

Mars square Mercury: Put your mental effort into work on textbook studies, writing, or talking about constructive subjects. Otherwise you may find yourself impatient, critical and ready to jump into hasty quarrels. Misunderstandings are lurking, as others don't like what you have to say or how you say it.

News can be disturbing. Planned activities have obstacles presented. Short trips are a bother, as traffic is disagreeable. So are you.

Mars trine Mercury: Your mind is sharp and incisive for mental activities of all kinds: paperwork, letter writing, teaching, math, studies and communications. Brainstorming sessions, mental and verbal games are productive and stimulating. Others will acknowledge your intelligence and expertise.

Your decisions tend to be firm and courageous; in conversation you present yourself as being pragmatic, with strong, firm, broad opinions.

A phone call or piece of news is stimulating as it can stir you into enthusiastic action.

Mars sextile Mercury: Mental and intellectual exchanges that take busy effort and challenge are more opportune with courteous but blunt honesty than with critical irritation. If you are restless put your energy into short trips and errands that are planned to be constructive rather than impulsive.

Your help may be needed in giving someone directions, translating or other assistance involving mental work or communication. You may talk more about your own ideas and plans.

There can be a call or news from a pleasant friend about his or her activities and interests.

Mars semisquare Mercury: A restless indecision can lead to blunt retorts or brief spats.

If your activities are scattered with irritating obstacles in short trips and errands, studies or paperwork, you may well become impatient, disagreeable and exhausted.

Plans, news and communications just now are inconclusive. Others are critical. Perhaps you can't make up your mind about a course of action.

Take it easy – wait – yield – get more information before making decisions.

Mars sesquisquare Mercury: Your energy for mental work, errands and short trips may run in fits and starts that make it difficult to concentrate on one thing. Sudden information or a change of plans, and unexpected calls or news break up your train of activity and add stress that is tiring. Others may be obnoxious or lack understanding, and your tendency is to critical irritation.

Traffic is disagreeable, with detours or delays.

Make short-term practical decisions on how to handle one thing at a time with reasonable construction. Adapt your thinking to new data that may not be stable but that aid your education.

Mars conjunct Venus: As you can put energy, drive and zest into social exchanges, a party or festive occasion is exciting. You tend to be busy with interesting, sociable and fun activities. It's a good time to mingle with people, entertain or go out.

Constructive efforts to improve the beauty and comfort of your environment are enjoyable, and you can spark others to help you.

As your feelings, emotions and sex drive are sensitive and responsive, you can receive attention, popularity and favors from romantic partners as well as from pleasant friends.

Any volatile situations tend to smooth out and relax.

Mars opposite Venus: There may be a party or social gathering for which you feel an obligation, even though your tendency is to be critical, touchy, reluctant and ungracious. If you extend the energy and constructive effort into being cheerful and hospitable you'll make a better time for yourself and others.

Separations and delays in your romantic interests can subject you to tremulous feelings or emotional stress. The persons with whom you exchange a social, sexual, or emotional interaction may be unsatisfactory or inappropriate to your needs and temperament just now.

When you can release your tension through a good cry, a fight, an orgasm, or a rowdy party, you'll feel better to let matters smooth out and relax.

Mars square Venus: Fever, trauma, excitable persons and touchy temperament in your environment are obstacles to your serenity and pleasures.

Your social life could include unsatisfactory dates, delays and disappointments that cause frustration. Romantic or sexual attention may come from the wrong person, and the right person is absent, disagreeable, or grouchy. Your sex is better if you get the hostilities out first with an honest fight for which you can make amends. With no sexual outlet you could be irritable, impatient and critical.

Mix with others with vigor, dance or play music, be loud or rambunctious, play in sports or games, or run around on artistic and courtesy errands to release your emotional tension.

Mars trine Venus: This is the time for music, fun, a party, noisy activities, people, or love and romance with good lusty sex relations. If you're not having an active sex life, a flirtation with an attractive potential partner is still exciting. Loved ones of both sexes will give you approval and seek your company, as you impress them with your vitality and charm.

If you should snap at someone with a sudden excitable impulse, you can apologize honestly to smooth out the harmony and gain easier friendly comradery.

You could get a beauty treatment, have your hair done, or make an enjoyable luxury purchase that adds attractive pleasure to your life.

Mars sextile Venus: This is a better time to work out social and emotional differences with vigorous honesty than to indulge in touchy bad temper. There will be an opportunity to resolve sexual and emotional tensions through a party, game or sports, music, dance or loud rambunctious activities. Someone is there to give you supportive approval.

Mars semisquare Venus: If you are undecided in emotional matters, doubt and ambivalence can nag at you. A romantic interest could be a worry, as you're not sure of your own feelings.

Social agreements are unstable with shifting plans. You may have company you hadn't planned on, or a party or outing that's a mild bother, and your tendency is to be none too gracious.

Avoid emotional scenes or excitable extremes. Handle busy activities with calm, and matters will go more smoothly.

Mars sesquisquare Venus: Your social life tends to be inconsistent, with sudden changes of plans and unexpected activities. An old friend or lover who is somewhat disturbing to your peace of mind may call or come into your life. New romantic interests are unstable and don't work out too well.

Erratic, excitable and independent emotions can be volatile. Turn matters to your advantage by holding a detached calm to evaluate new data.

Mars conjunct Mars: There is a potential for a trauma, fight or criticism now. Someone in your environment is certainly angry, lusty, disagreeable or smoldering. If there are old resentments or hostilities, it is better to bring them into the open to be worked out with direct impact.

As your energy level is vigorous, you may use that drive with constructive action in hard physical labor, sports or exercise, barbeques, cooking, cleaning or making repairs, or sexual activity.

Mars opposite Mars: If you are restless and impatient, your tendency may be to strike out at a person who irritates you. There can be critical rejection, hostility, anger, infection or trauma in your environment.

Fast action may be required to sidestep danger or avoid an accident; that constructive use of your energy is better than rash responses.

Go to a violent movie or to the fights; use your physical drive in hard exercise or labor, taking care to handle sharp tools or instruments with care. Engage in competitive sports, actions, games or debates or expend lusty sexual energy with your mate.

Mars square Mars: In your environment there can be tension, trauma or infection, criticism or hostility. Quarrels or fighting could get out of hand, rash or impatient actions could be dangerous, overexertion and bursts of adrenalin could leave you drained and feeling mean.

Use that excessive energy constructively in hard physical labor or making repairs, being careful with tools or instruments. Go to a violent movie or to the fights, engage in competitive sports, athletics, games or debates, and express your sexual passion with an agreeably lusty mate.

Mars trine Mars: As your physical energy is decisive and invigorating, you can handle all the matters that need to get done: cleaning, errands, and shopping. If someone in your environment is hyperactive, noisy, aggressive, drinking, lusty, or has a fever or trauma, you can handle matters firmly.

Games, exercise, sports or debates are stimulating, and in competitive matters your chances of winning are good. Your sexual exchange with your mate is lusty and satisfying.

Mars sextile Mars: Your peak energy may be used more constructively in hard physical exercise and labor, cleaning and errands, repairs, and healthy competition, than in striking out in hostile rebellion.

You can stimulate others to be on your side and to get things done if you don't antagonize them. Meet challenges with finesse.

Mars semisquare Mars: A variety of activities could scatter your energy and require that you cope with alertness and decision. Little accidents and irritations are nagging. Someone may not agree with you, be critical or hostile. Keep a clear head and be firm in your decisions.

Mars sesquisquare Mars: Think twice before any sudden rash action. Someone in your environment may be obnoxious, hostile, or competitive, and you could snap back or be critical. There could be trauma, infection, or sudden flashes of anger.

Keep busy, be decisive, and put your energy into constructive labor, sports, athletics or games, or into agreeable sexual activities.

Mars conjunct Jupiter: Vital, optimistic energy gives you a restless desire for more adventure and freedom, affluence and abundance. If you should feel impatient and hostile, you need to get out to roam. This is the time to shop for the purchases you've wanted, gamble and spend money. You can find good, elegant quality, but watch your tendency to rashly overspend.

See your doctor, lawyer, minister, or make the professional contacts that are due. You are able to assert yourself with decision and dignity.

Put your energy into being helpful to loyal friends; you can spark them to enthusiasm. A philosophical discussion can renew your courage and zest in life.

Mars opposite Jupiter: A restless surge of vital optimistic energy can give you the impulse to get out and roam. If you feel circumstances are holding you back, your tendency may be to go to extremes without counting the cost.

Don't gamble. Shop for the purchases you've wanted but avoid rash spending or impulsive extravagance. In your business and professional contacts you can set matters into motion, but they're not ready to be consummated or completed due to red tape and delays.

Though you may have a philosophical disagreement with another, this is not the time to meet in head-on combat or to proselytize; keep your own courage in practical areas of growth but aim for tolerance.

Mars square Jupiter: Channel that restless surge of vital energy into optimistic goals and growth. If you gamble or are careless, there is danger of financial loss through theft, extravagance, or rash impulse that is unwise. In shopping, count the cost and desirability before the purchase decision. In legal, professional, religious or educational matters use some discretion and moderation, or you could come across as being overbearing and pretentious.

Overindulgence is costly. Spend money only if it's an item you've wanted for some time at a fair price—not on impulse. Philosophize only if you can keep a level of tolerance—not to proselytize.

Mars trine Jupiter: You have a robust, lusty optimism with which you can meet challenge with zest to expand your financial, professional or educational position, have an adventure or trip, or mix into enthusiastic philosophical discussions.

Financial gain, generosity, favors or hospitality may come your way. In shopping you'll find the purchase you wanted and make up your mind decisively.

No one is about to impose on you, as you can tell them exactly how you feel about that and gain their respect in doing so.

Mars sextile Jupiter: You have the opportunity to expand your financial, professional or educational position, have an adventure or trip, or mix into philosophical discussions. This can give you gain and goodwill if you are robust, lusty and decisive, but rash impulse or extravagance would be unwise. Use discretion and moderation rather than overindulgence or pompous pretentions.

Mars semisquare Jupiter: You could have a robust, lusty restlessness with which you scatter your activities. As you vacillate between impatience and optimism you may swing from blunt self-assertion to impulsive extravagance.

When shopping look carefully before buying; in business and professional matters debate the point before rash action. With philosophical discussions or personal decisions use some discretion, moderation and tolerance.

Mars sesquisquare Jupiter: Conditions in your professional and private life are subject to sudden changes, with inconsistent swings from robust enthusiasm to sudden irritation at unexpected setbacks. There are people who are generous with good will and hospitality, and others who are self-indulgent or pretentious.

As your stability and judgment are erratic, use some discretion and moderation rather than restless, impulsive action.

Mars conjunct Saturn: Discipline your energy into constructive action. When you keep in control, do it yourself, or direct others with firmness and command, you can put out a massive amount of hard work and accomplishment. As you are not tender or sentimental just now, but feel a hard-driving, ambitious energy, it's the best time to overcome objective, practical, pragmatic problems and to get jobs done that take calculating decision, time and effort.

Someone in your environment may be hostile, cruel or competitive. If there is a physical injury or pain, cold responses or criticism, you may feel bitter or depressed. As clashes and trauma are occurring around you, you can get involved or you can keep the hard core of your own resolve for self-control.

Mars opposite Saturn: Maximum energy, courage and self-control are needed, as a fight, trauma, physical danger, infection, imposition, injustice or driving hard work is thrust upon you. If you react with hostile depression you could bitterly reject the rational decision and make the situation worse. Use a direct and honest energy to find the most constructive solution; consider your long-range ambitions for secure advancement. Use that cold, hard core of energy to accomplish extra work and overcome setbacks and delays.

Mars square Saturn: An injustice at this time could cause you to feel bitter, resentful and hostile. If you can't take the stress of hard responsibilities you could even be cold, vicious and cruel with a total lack of any empathy for others. In this case you could cut off your nose to spite your face by making rash, destructive decisions.

Physical danger, pain, trauma, clashes and rejection can be in your environment. Use self-discipline and control in your own actions. Even if you're down you're not defeated, as a cold core of hard energy for your own survival will pull you through.

The most constructive action at this time is to put in hard work and extra hours; attack obstacles in your environment for ambitious advancement. As your social and sex lives are not at their best, use your time and effort on objective impersonal goals.

Mars trine Saturn: You have the courage, drive and self-control to handle hard work and extra hours, as your tendency is to put in the detail and care to get the job done carefully and well. As you are determined in your own decisions with a firm core of resolve you are not swayed by empathy or outside considerations.

If there is any hardship, stress, or criticism in your environment, you can handle it with practical efficiency. With directness and courage you can take control, to fight injustice or demand your rights.

With sports or strenuous exercise you combine energy with skill.

Mars sextile Saturn: You can further your projects and ambitions to greater advantage by using practical decisive energy, than by rash, willful attempts to rule or ruin.

If someone in your environment is unjust, mean or critical, keep a cold core of self-discipline. Though you may feel no empathy, there is no need to be cruel. Matters will go much more smoothly if you direct your control into impersonal objective work areas.

Mars semisquare Saturn: If you feel imposed upon and not in control you could react with a cold, mean criticism. Someone in your environment is certainly obnoxious or insulting, or has a clash or trauma. Nagging can be rash, as you're inviting stress that could leave you feeling dragged.

To be constructive use a self-disciplined restraint; work to get all the facts, and direct your energy to combat irritating problems or hardships in your objective environment.

Mars sesquisquare Saturn: Your energy may be scattered by a variety of responsibilities. Sudden problems in your objective environment can bring criticism, rejection, imposition, hostility, or simply unexpected obstacles that take effort and readjustment of your time.

Someone in your life may be obnoxious or disagreeable, have a clash or trauma; your better course just now is to calculate a retreat in order to keep self-control.

Mars conjunct Uranus: You may feel inclined toward drastic and erratic action, or encounter it from others, as you're subject to considerable nervous tension. Your willful, independent energy will cause you explosive restlessness under routine conditions, so must be directed into original directions that are constructive.

New people you meet may be magnetic and virile but are not indicated to be enduring in your life. Old acquaintances who show up turn out to be more stimulating than before. With a sudden hostility you can either break off a relationship bluntly, if it is truly outgrown, or meet it with direct courage to change it for the better.

Unexpected accidents involving appliances could happen, or mechanical and electrical devices could require attention.

Mars opposite Uranus: New or unexpected conditions can subject you to extreme tension and nervous strain. A maximum of energy and will power may be required to handle sudden encounters and disruptions with people. Certain matters you counted on may come through in a way you hadn't anticipated, or may be cancelled and replaced with alternatives.

Someone you've known in the past can call or come into your life, and you find they are different or changed in some way. New people you meet at this time may be magnetically stimulating and virile but are not indicated to be an enduring part of your future.

Unexpected accidents involving electrical or mechanical devices and appliances could happen. Your car battery may need attention. Be prepared for sudden changes that take your time and energy.

Mars square Uranus: New or unexpected conditions can subject you to tension, stress and nervous strain. Your temper may be impatient and volatile with explosive restlessness. With rash energy, eccentricity and self-will, you could have a sudden blunt encounter or take a foolish risk.

Sudden changes or surprises could interfere with your routine in a disagreeable way. Use your energy and decision to handle matters in a more ingeneous way; take a different approach that asserts your independence to make constructive changes. This is not the time to count on anyone nor to take advice.

Take special care in traffic and in handling electrical or mechanical appliances and devices.

Mars trine Uranus: If you feel in need of a change, now is the time to make decisions that are daring, inventive and constructive. New and unexpected occurrences and changes are certainly happening in your environment; and if you build up a nervous tension it can best be expended by going into a different environment, meeting new people, or looking up the most stimulating of your old friends.

As you tend to be magnetic and independent, unusual activities and challenges are exciting; sexual or social intercourse can be dynamic.

Mars sextile Uranus: If you feel tension, stress or restless independence you can handle it most constructively by going into a new or unusual environment, making aggressive contacts with new people, or having stimulating exchanges with old friends. Rather than rash eccentric moves, make decisions that are inventive; change your routine around; do something different and exciting.

Mars semisquare Uranus: New people and sudden changes can bring nervous tension and restless strain. You may feel scattered and irritable, as unexpected stress is disruptive to your routine. Use your energy constructively by taking a different approach that is ingeneous; there may be a detour in your plans.

Mars sesquisquare Uranus: Sudden and unexpected changes are potentially explosive. If there is a hostile independence in you or in another, you could be tense and unsettled with the nervous strain. By detaching yourself from emotional reactions you can use your energy more constructively to handle new data and detours.

Mars conjunct Neptune. You may feel a vague restlessness or anxiety just now. Your imagination can wander down strange paths that are brooding, macabre, sinister or erotic. Any problems around you are complex or dramatic, and you could be drawn into conspiracies or schemes.

Put your energy into acts of consideration to help others, postpone impulsive moves or decisions where you don't know all the facts and are tempted to exaggerate the situation.

Use caution with drugs or alcohol, as your sensitivity to stimulants is keen. Your sex life can be exquisite with the right person; with someone who does not fit your ideals there could be either disinterest or impotence.

As your creative energy is high, you can put your energy into imaginative accomplishments to inspire others.

Mars opposite Neptune: Keep both feet on the ground; something in your life is a little unreal just now. You could encounter a situation that is strange, with schemes, conspiracy, or indiscretion.

A matter you'd anticipated may fall through, or someone may promise something that's a pipe dream. People around you are a little odd or they are exaggerating. Rather than being drawn into fantasies, put your energy into active consideration to help others with practical effort. Get all the facts and avoid concealment of your own motives.

Your response to stimulants is keen, so drugs or alcohol could have an exaggerated effect. If there is insensitivity or deception in your sex life with a person who is not ideal, you may find yourself losing interest; becoming impotent or dissatisfied.

Mars square Neptune: Emotions and desires can be turbulent, and you may feel a strange restlessness or anxiety. Someone in your life is unstable or has complex interwoven problems. Matters you count on may not materialize or may seem to be slipping from your hands.

Keep your own commitments at this time, keep your own feet on the ground and your own imagination on practical resolutions. Be considerate of others and keep busy with action to gain your ideals.

Your sensitivity to stimulants is high, so drugs or alcohol could have an exaggerated effect.

Any psychic advice at this time can be disturbing or unrealistic. Analyze all situations with reason; do not accept delusions.

Mars trine Neptune: There could be a little vacation, outing or idyllic occasion where you are with delightfully strange people: poets, artists, actors, visionaries, psychic or gay friends. Your environment is stimulating, and your sensual response is keen to drugs or alcohol, or sex relations with that person who is right for you. With the people who do not fit your ideals you have a vague disinterest and discontent.

There can be contemplative hours when your imagination and sensitivity can be put to creative use in solving complex problems. As you are fascinating to others you can inspire them with your promotions or dramatics.

Mars sextile Neptune: Your restless dissatisfaction can stir you to seek new opportunities. Though there are animating and interesting experiences, variety and promise of color, excitement and drama, don't count on the promises or start construction on that dream castle—it may be exaggerated.

You are certainly fascinating and daring, imaginative and creative, and may try something you've never done before. Secret plans are fun, like a surprise party. Psychic or gay friends can be stimulating.

Promotional ideas and plans get a vigorous start but are apt to fade with the sunset unless backed with practical effort.

Mars semisquare Neptune: There can be some strange, vague conflicts in your life and in your feelings just now. A certain matter may fall through, leaving you restless and dissatisfied, with turbulent feelings and anxiety. Another matter can be exquisite, a delightful adventure, a surprise party, a visit to a psychic, or contact with imaginative, creative or gay people.

Keep busy with a practical imagination and active consideration for others.

Mars sesquisquare Neptune: There can be changes and sudden upsets just now that seem deceptive and disappointing; someone may renege on an appointment or promise. You may have fitful surges of emotion with vague restlessness and anxiety that detract from steady plans or progress.

Cope with the upsets with consideration of others and a practical application of your own actions; some imaginative construction can be accomplished.

Mars conjunct Pluto: During this last few and next few weeks you can complete a cycle of action or stress with a shift of direction or a different emphasis on your thrust of desire and effort. Specific changes at this time can have far-reaching and long-lasting results. A compelling force seems to drive you ahead in activities that bring out more of your potential.

You rebel against people or situations that you feel to be covert or manipulative, but are more than willing to cooperate with others in matters that are constructive and exhilarating.

In group activities with the club, team, committee or gang, your drive and positive assertion can be productive toward the common goal of mutual constructive benefit.

Mars opposite Pluto: During the last few and next few weeks an inner compelling rebelliousness seems to be pushing you to make a constructive change of direction in the thrust of your desire. However, this cycle of action or stress is not ready to be completed or consummated, and the attempts you make to start a new cycle or program of assertion meet with resistance.

People around you may be finishing certain cycles and making new beginnings, and circumstances demand that you cooperate with them for the good of all concerned.

In group activities with the club, team, committee or gang your maximum positive decision and assertion are productive toward constructive action, though there is a faction or a single strong-willed person who is bluntly uncooperative.

Mars square Pluto: During these last few weeks you may have been working out some heavy changes in yourself in an attempt to put a different emphasis of thrust in your desires. There could be heavy obstacles of stress, rebellion, jealousy and bitchy hostility in you or in your environment that cause a pressure of uncooperative resistance. Other people could be manipulating or insidiously putting you in a position of compromise. Rash or compulsive reactions can be self-destructive. Smoldering temper or ultimatums could be critical, as you'll meet with blunt criticism.

Your best course of action is to put your willful energy into constructive areas, where you can cooperate with a group, club, team, committee or gang to combat objective problems.

In your personal decisions a courageous and direct encounter can bring out covert information to gain a more honest relationship.

Mars trine Pluto: During the past few weeks you may have been using your energy to make constructive changes in your own attitudes and environment, to finish a program or policy, to eliminate discordant or nonessential factors, and to reconstruct your thrust of action to a more positive approach.

An encounter at this time that brings out covert information can transmute your emphasis to a more honest, courageous direction. You have the energy, drive and force to sweep others along with your vital convictions, and you can elicit cooperation easily for reforms, renovations or constructions.

In group activities with the club, team, committee or gang you are given credit for your expertise.

Mars sextile Pluto: If you feel a restless, compelling urge to make a constructive change of direction, you can gain greater force and impetus by cooperating with others than by a rash assertion of resistance. Combined efforts for long-range desires and goals are opportune, as you can get the help you need for reforms or renovations.

It's not the time to finish a program or policy, but discard the nonessentials to make a more positive and courageous emphasis in the thrust of your action.

In group or team activities you can gain credit for your expertise by upholding your vital convictions.

Mars semisquare Pluto: During these past few weeks you may have been working out an indecision in your arena of compromise and cooperation. There are compelling desires for unity that vacillate with willful resistance to any pressure or manipulation. You're not ready to complete a program or policy but need to shift the emphasis of your thrust of action by getting more information and understanding of your own attitude and position.

In group or team efforts cooperate with others for constructive goals but keep your own reservations; there can be covert motives.

Mars sesquisquare Pluto: During these past few weeks there could have been some unexpected changes in your program or policy. The cooperation and unity you desire could have sudden, inconsistent breakups from willful, restless independence that overthrows the existing condition.

These changes can put you in a stronger position if you constructively discard nonessential data and eliminate manipulative people who insidiously put you in a position of compromise.

In group or team activities cooperate with others for the good of the whole. If there are factions, arbitration can be effective; keep your reservations to yourself.

VI   TRANSIT JUPITER

Jupiter transits the horoscope in eleven years ten months fourteen days. Approximately every nine months Jupiter has an apparent retrograde period that lasts close to four months. In its twelve-year cycle Jupiter will conjunct and oppose each planet once; square, trine, sextile, semisquare and sesquisquare every planet twice. An aspect it makes near the change of station may repeat three times.

At daily mean motion of four minutes forty-nine seconds Jupiter has a twenty-five day influence of one degree applying and one degree separating to partile, going through one sign in approximately one year. However, Jupiter can move as fast as fifteen minutes a day, making an aspect orb in eight days. When slowing to retrograde, Jupiter may hold an aspect for approximately two months.

Aspects of Jupiter made on the change of station, particularly the conjunction and opposition, deserve prime consideration, as the influence extends beyond the orb limit to a discernible two degrees, which can extend the time span two or three months before or after the change of station.

With Jupiter we begin to get into a more marked variability of extremes in the lives of people. The innate character and present-time circumstances, as well as the natal harmony or discord of Jupiter, must be taken into consideration.

The overall effect falls into four basic categories. In the first case Jupiter marks a period of serenity and contentment, where the life situation is settled, pressure or strain areas are eased and there is little effect shown in external events.

The second type of example occurs to restless, striving, moving, active people, who have a great surge of growth in the areas for which they have been working. There are numerous examples of long trips, moves, buying and selling of property and businesses, financial and legal matters, and investment capital gains.

The third type is the person reaching for values and for moral and ethical understanding. For them Jupiter marks a period of religious resurgence with the joy of faith and conviction. If this basic type leans more to the intellectual, that need is supplied by increased education or expansion in the academic community.

The fourth type shows the overexpansive use of Jupiter. This can range from mild overoptimism to rampant self-indulgence, irresponsibility, and extravagance without counting the cost to anyone. The person magnifies his or her situation or feelings all out of proportion with an apparent attitude of invulnerability. With arrogance and egotism these persons greedily grab self-satisfactions and rewards, or presume their own superiority in lawlessness.

Most of us express some measure of all four types of effect with periods of quiet content, successful mundane growth, philosophical or educational expansion, and the buoyancy of lush freedom.

The Law of Precedence determines the outcome. The basic character and natal chart indicate primarily how and where we seek areas of growth.

Major progressed aspects show the trend of the year; other transits indicate whether Jupiter is being monitored by serious counter aspects, or is given free reign by easy planetary patterns.

As Jupiter is the significator of expansion, the most appropriate expression of its nature is in healthy, happy growth, faith in God and man, appreciation and wonder in life, and the well of joy in yourself that is a special wisdom.

Jupiter conjunct Sun: This can be a period of contentment and deep appreciation for the goals you have attained. As mundane pressure and strain have eased, you now have the time and enthusiasm to strive for another step of growth.

With an expanded confidence in your goals you can reach out for more freedom, joy and adventure. Your poise and self-assurance can encourage others, attract good will and important patronage. Professional contacts can broaden your authority and advance your position.

With buoyant optimism you tend to aim high and magnify your expectations. You could make a big investment or get a raise, gift, bonus or material benefit. Sales can be lucrative and purchases satisfactory.

As you feel good you're more hospitable, generous, liberal and tolerant. You may enjoy a healthy, robust self-indulgence, with good luck.

You have contact with men who are prestigious, successful, well-educated or professional; they also are magnanimous, honorable and trusting of you.

There can be a formal occasion, where you shine with graciousness and command. In sports, outdoor activities or travel, you get good weather, fine accommodations, good publicity and approval.

Your urge to increase your education or your religious or philosophical understanding can move you to advance your studies to include broader fields and concepts. Moral and ethical considerations are brought to your attention.

Jupiter opposite Sun: Circumstances may require that you broaden your horizon and viewpoint with more education, tolerance and hospitality to increase your authority and position. You can reach out for that better job, that big trip, that new class, or for an expansion of experience, adventure and growth.

However, your expectations may be set too high; if you go to extremes, are overly generous or self-indulgent, you may find your trust and overoptimism misplaced.

In your professional contacts someone may be pompous or pretentious. Legal matters can be a strain with red tape and extended costs. Purchases are too expensive; be careful of overextending your credit or of unwise generosity. Resist financial pressures of loans or investment as you could suffer a loss of faith as well as cash, or bite off more than you could handle.

A social occasion could be formal and lengthy with dull conversation and stuffy people. Your religion or philosophy may require ritual. On a trip you could travel late or long and have to hunt for good accommodations. You may have to wait in long lines.

Do make the effort; as long as you maintain modesty and prudence, and strive to keep your faith and a positive attitude, it can be a time of growth.

Jupiter square Sun: During this period you may want more freedom. You may feel so self-confident and self-sufficient as to be reckless and not count the cost of your actions and decisions. Think twice before biting off more than you can chew, wanting too much, or taking on too many projects, extra expense, excessive eating or drinking; it can lead to overoptimistic expectations, debts or overweight.

In travels there are obstacles to your satisfaction. You may not get the accommodations or hospitality you'd anticipated, or you may have to wait for others or get stuck in long lines. In professional contacts the red tape and formalities may seem endless. Legal proceedings are ill-advised as they tend to be costly and overrated.

Investments, purchases or sales tend to be premature; financial decisions are better postponed for a more advantageous time.

You may find yourself impatient with moral and ethical considerations. As you have a broader view of religious or academic subjects, other people seem to lack understanding.

Practice moderation, strive for tolerance and humility rather than magnification of your own capacities.

Jupiter trine Sun: During this time you tend to magnify your expectations and set great aims. You have self-assurance based on your own command. As you feel so good, optimistic, vigorous and liberal, you tend to broaden your experience and increase your range of activity.

Good luck and advantages can come easily in your business, financial and professional goals. In academic or religious environments you have authority and pleasure. With public speaking, advertising or publications, you are given credit, praise and supportive acknowledgement. You easily gain the trust and magnanimity of loyal, important or successful people. Your social graces and self-confidence give you poise and tolerance.

People in a higher social and economic bracket not only regard you with good will but are eager to help or back you. Investments, purchases or sales are well-timed, and a lucrative business matter may be presented to you.

As you expand your horizons in honorable goals you can move into a period of greater abundance and joyful serenity. With moral and ethical considerations this can be a time of richly rewarding satisfactions.

If circumstances at this time give you a placid inertia, it is still a period of peace and deep contentment.

However, if this past year has been spent in lazy indulgence, where you were putting on a big show and letting other people pay the price, your house may be built on sand. If you are indulgent in self-gratifications, you still have loyal friends, good luck and protection, but you may lose something of value in yourself.

Jupiter sextile Sun: Be alert for opportunities to advance your profession and public standing. You may make an important contact with a person who is prestigious, magnanimous and trusting; or mingle with people in a higher social or economic bracket. Others are helpful and give you their good will and supportive backing.

Activities in church, school or business are advantageous to your authority and goals. You can expand your horizons in public speaking or publications, investment opportunities, sales or purchases. Setbacks dissolve with your cheerful optimism.

If there is an area of freedom-seeking self-indulgence, you still have a measure of protection, good will and forgiveness. The greater joy is in your actions of honor that observe moral and ethical considerations.

Jupiter semisquare Sun: There can be an area in your life or an occasion that is fortunate, with good will, a gift or favor, important patronage, professional or educational experience, an adventure or travel. However, you tend to be unsure of yourself with a restless urge for more freedom or self-satisfaction. Your attitude can vacillate from serene content to an excited buoyancy. In new situations all your poise is required to observe the formalities.

Luxury expenses may be extravagant; a certain purchase could be unsatisfactory and need to be returned or replaced.

Take that step of growth in your religion, philosophy, profession, or experience with appreciation and calm moderation rather than erratic extremes.

Jupiter sesquisquare Sun: There can be high hopes and optimism now, as there is so much promise of changes for the better. Those changes based on honorable promise can open wonderful doors of adventure, travel, public appearances, publication, just and fair legal action, sincere religion or philosophy. But not all promises are honorable and just; in certain of these matters there can be false hope or disappointment as plans fall through. To be protected from overexpectations in agreements, keep your own integrity and weigh decisions carefully for moral judgment rather than self-indulgence.

You can meet some important people at this time; conduct yourself with

57

dignity and self-respect and you will gain their good will.

Jupiter conjunct Moon: This is a mellow and content period, when domestic affairs go smoothly and women and children in your life are companionable and agreeable. Any differences can be reconciled and family relationships are serene. Home improvements give you a happy outlook.

Any financial strain not only eases, but extra income, gifts or favors come with little or no effort on your part. Your attitude and mood tend to be expansive, optimistic, gracious and hopeful, giving you a natural tendency to attract the good will of others.

Business or personal matters from the past may be concluded satisfactorily to begin new patterns of greater growth with faith and self-assurance.

Jupiter opposite Moon: Family relationships and domestic affairs may put a strain on you this month to cope with conditions that are expanding; there can be an increase in the family; more women, children or company in the home; financial extravagance; or more formal affairs that detract from constructive working time.

Business or personal matters from the past may culminate in such a way as to require decisions that push you into a period of growth. You may feel the need to take on more expense, increase your education and experience, or improve your understanding of religion, philosophy, business or travel.

Good money returns are indicated from prior investment, bonuses or extra sources, but expenses or extravagance can also be present.

Jupiter square Moon: Family and domestic matters, such as schooling, food and clothes, visiting relatives or entertaining in the home, may require expense and formal effort at this time. Women and children in your life cause some emotional strain or need your supportive faith, at a time when you'd rather relax and take it easy yourself.

Business and financial matters require expense if not extravagance; take care to buy good quality in order to get your money's worth.

You may feel optimistic about past matters that have been put into motion, but they are not ready to pay off until you put a little more time and effort into these affairs.

Jupiter trine Moon: This is a peaceful and content period when domestic affairs and family relationships go smoothly, any differences are reconciled to harmony, the women and children in your life are cheerful and agreeable. Your own attitude tends to be mildly optimistic, relaxed if not lazy, at peace with yourself and those around you. You can feel confident in your own decisions, hopeful and happy about your future.

Financial decisions may be culminated satisfactorily. Investments are favorable. There is little stress on income, and any bonus or extra money can go into savings or for purchases that are enjoyable rather than necessary. You may stock up on groceries or commodities to your satisfaction.

Academic, religious, or business matters may be smoothly advanced, and travels are delightful.

Jupiter sextile Moon: There are opportunities now to improve your home conditions and domestic life. Do take advantage of these, as women, children, kin and those close to you are helpful financially as well as with their faith and good will. Old differences can be reconciled, and new friends will give you loyalty and pleasure for a long time. It's a time of hope, growth, and joy.

Investments in legal or business matters, commodities, groceries or domestic improvements are advantageous.

You can move happily into a philosophical, educational, and economic period of expansion.

Jupiter semisquare Moon: Family and domestic matters may cause some concern just now as they seem a little unstable. The moods of women and children tend to fluctuate occasionally, and your home is not giving you the goodwill environment you need to support your areas of growth.

Business and financial matters require that you increase your education and experience. Finances may be pressing, as any surplus is eaten up by vacillating needs.

Hold onto your religious and philosophical faith in your own attitudes and care for those who need you.

Jupiter sesquisquare Moon: Your tendency at this time is to break up the existing conditions in your home and domestic affairs; to set up new conditions for the women and children in your life; to move or expand your home; or to put expense into your personal or business interests.

You can grow philosophically by expanding your day-to-day activities, but draw on your wisdom and faith in others before making agitating changes in personal relationships. People may have more loyalty than you give them credit for, and it may be you who is indulgent in your mood.

Jupiter conjunct Mercury: On the whole this period tends to be quiet and fairly content. Your routine is serene, your environment cheerful, and your economic position comfortable.

As you tend to be thoughtful, perhaps even introspective, studies and conversations can focus on evaluation of what you've learned in the past and what you plan for the future. You may think often of religious and philosophical concepts, make moral judgments, and weigh ethical considerations.

It's a period of low-key growth in your poise and tolerance. New people you meet give you their faith and trust, and old acquaintances are dear and familiar. Contacts with a doctor, lawyer, teacher, minister or another professional person can expand your comprehension and encourage your confidence. You hear good news from others and could possibly receive a gift or bonus, a favorable contract, or have a prestigious meeting.

You may travel at this time or make plans for a pending trip. By all means go; part of your expenses could be paid, or else you receive rewarding hospitality and cordial accommodations.

If there is an underlying restlessness, an urge may be stirring within you for a change that would give you more freedom. This may be a time of calm before your next step of expansion.

Jupiter opposite Mercury: You may feel a restless frustration at this time; an urge for more consummate satisfactions. Your serene routine is a bore, and the changes you reach for are disappointing. You can't seem to communicate your introspective thoughts to those people who lack understanding, and your environment lacks the intellectual exchange you long for.

You may spend more time in evaluations of the past and thinking of plans for the future that include more freedom and growth. In philosophical and religious discussions you have difficulty expressing your moral viewpoint. New acquaintances seem inhospitable, and even your dear old friends are acting dumb or indifferent.

It's not a good time to sign papers, engage in litigation or make important decisions in business and financial matters; you tend to get tied up in tedious red tape and formal procedures.

There could be obstacles to travel; delays and awkward accommodations.

Strive to increase your own education and tolerance. Every man has his story; listen and you may learn something.

Jupiter square Mercury: During this time you have an overexpanded optimism that may not be in keeping with the facts. Enthusiasm, serenity and faith in the ultimate outcome are beautiful, but great expectations can lead you to promise more than you can deliver, or count on more than you get.

Academic, financial and legal matters that you start at this time could be overrated and are apt to be delayed in red-tape procedures, take longer than you expect, or not give the return you'd hoped for.

People around you may lack the moral or intellectual comprehension necessary to discuss your interests, or your religion or philosophy; you have to break down communication barriers to gain understanding.

If you take a trip it could lift your spirits but would require effort and expense, and you may have delays or awkward accommodations.

With introspective thought, evaluate the past and make constructive, realistic plans for the future.

Jupiter trine Mercury: As you are hospitable, generous and confident you impress people with your poise, knowledge and tolerance. A formal occasion or public appearance can be elegant and gracious. It's an excellent time for intellectual progress; read, write, teach or advertise, seek publication, handle legal affairs, sign contracts, or make expansive decisions that will pay off in future rewards.

You can be optimistic about business matters, as a bonus, raise, or settlement can ease your mind with satisfactory agreements. Others are helpful, and you easily gain important patronage or clientele.

You can meet interesting and prestigious professional people, and with tolerance and enthusiasm, exchange ideas on religion, philosophy, education, business or finance. Relationships with old friends and familiar acquaintances tend to be serene and enjoyable.

60

Jupiter sextile Mercury: Opportunities for mental and intellectual progress are available; read, write, teach or advertise, and exchange ideas with interesting people on religion, philosophy, business, financial or educational matters. There's a chance of important patronage, a raise, bonus, favor or fortunate news. Formal occasions tend to be gracious, and personal relationships with dear and loyal people give a warm contentment.

If you feel restless for more freedom of expression or self-directed satisfaction, you could overrate the present possibilities; your growth and joy are more opportune with a mellow appreciation of what you have.

Jupiter semisquare Mercury: Your mental activity tends to vary between great expectations and serene optimism. As there is an intermittent vacillation in your growth patterns at this time, you may shift from reckless indulgence to peaceful contemplation, from slipshod communications to philosophical understanding.

Legal, financial or business matters can be annoying as they tend to small delays and red tape. Relationships with friends and old acquaintances can vary from trust and confidence to concern and dismay. In all, this is an unstable period that requires you cope with matters that broaden your education and experience in tolerant understanding.

Jupiter sesquisquare Mercury: This can be a reckless period of variety and change, in which you tend to break up the patterns that hamper your growth and freedom. You have optimism and high hopes for the future that can be realized by holding onto your faith and moral judgment, but if you are overrating big expectations you may not get the return for which you'd hoped.

In writing, speaking, studies, legal matters, and travel, certain expectations may be greater than the realization, but if your expansion is backed up with tolerant judgment, the end result can add to your insight and understanding.

Jupiter conjunct Venus: Though this period seems objectively serene, there may be a profusion of subjective feelings. With magnified sensitivity you long for more peace, harmony, beauty and serenity, love and tenderness.

As you are more sentimental you are responsively touched by others. A social visit with old friends and relatives can be rich with generosity, the formalities of entertaining, and philosophical discussions of life and love, shared experiences and feelings. With consideration you have a warm joy and contentment in the company of dear and familiar people. As you are more aesthetic, artistic interests, fashion, decorating, music or entertainment activities gain a focus of attention.

Your social life is apt to increase with popularity and attention. Professional people or those in a prestigious income or social bracket tend to give you favors, patronage or approval. You may attend a formal function, a party, banquet or wedding.

If you are having a romance, your emotional life can be tremulous with great expectations and profuse feelings. At any harshness or disharmony you'd feel dismayed and sorry. You could walk on air, float on serenity, and exaggerate any poignant tremor. Relax, let it flow. Old friends, family and dear loyal ones will endure. An indulgent relationship, where you take the path of least resistance, will not.

Jupiter opposite Venus: If this period is objectively serene, you'll feel a restless frustration as you long for a more active social life, love and approval.

Your feelings are magnified; you are touched by an emotional and sentimental response to others. You could feel the impulse to immerse yourself in a love affair extravagant with profusion, but your romanticism may be greater than the situation warrants. The right person is not interested or is involved with someone else, and the person who pays you attention is a bore. Old friends and relatives, your mate or lover are not giving you the supportive harmony you need; they are putting on pressures that turn off your sympathies. This is a difficult time for emotional relationships; your loved ones may be touchy, cold, hurt, worried, busy or inappropriate.

You may be trying too hard as you want so much more. Relax—strive for serenity and for the faith and tolerance that will encourage and support others, rather than for self-centered indulgence.

A focus on artistic interests, fashion, decorating, music or entertainment activities can absorb and satisfy your emotional needs.

Jupiter square Venus: There are obstacles to your social and emotional satisfaction at this time. If your social life is wanting, you may have the frustration of longing for more peace and harmony, love and approval, but the right person is lacking or disinterested, and the ones who are available don't meet your needs.

You may feel restless and discontent, with an urge for a more exciting challenge in your social life. As your feelings are magnified, you are more responsive and profusely sentimental. You want more fun and romance, lavish entertainment, or indulgence in sensual pleasures.

These feelings may hamper your judgment and induce you to kick over the traces. A love affair could be based on rash impulse, tremulous with hope and great expectations, but it may promise more than it delivers. You'll be wiser to avoid excesses and temper your strong opinions and desires. The loyal, tried and true are more enduring than sensational dissipation.

If you are happy with your mate, a friend or relative may be putting emotional strain on your environment. Pompous or formal people who are socially pretentious, or who philosophize endlessly about life and love, are apt to be bores. But be patient with dear people and keep your love and faith with those who are sincere.

Entertainment functions tend to involve formality and show. You may go to a party, banquet or wedding where there are volatile feelings. Your aesthetic interests in art, fashion, decorating and music are handicapped just now by interference.

Jupiter trine Venus: This is a time of happy rewards in romance and relationships, as your loved ones are agreeable, honorable, fair and generous. In social affairs you are more tolerant, gracious, outgoing and effusive. It's an excellent time to have a big party, entertain, go to glamorous gatherings, plan a trip, vacation or marriage.

Your artistic endeavors can be profitable at this time and gain recognition and approval. You may have more interest in music, art, culture, religion and philosophy, and you can expand and beautify your environment.

Business and financial matters may be extravagant but are fruitful, indicating good investment or return. You could receive a gift or favor, hospitality and good will.

This tends to be a relaxed, settled, contented and peaceful time. Good friends give you approval and support; family and acquaintances are cheerful, busy and friendly.

Jupiter sextile Venus: This time is opportune to expand your social life with loyal, stable old acquaintances rather than with flamboyant attractions. Your social and romantic life offers good will, favors, and fun, as long as you don't overrate an indulgent possibility with great expectations.

You may make a social contact at this time that is helpful. An invitation to a formal occasion, a party, banquet or wedding can be elegant and hospitable.

Your aesthetic interests in art, fashion, decorating, music and entertainment are timely and receive approval and recognition that please you.

Jupiter semisquare Venus: Your social and romantic activities may fluctuate between outgoing, effusive optimism and passive, hopeful expectations. There can be profuse feelings about an unstable emotional situation and a longing for more fun and festivity, or sympathy and love.

You could attend a variety of functions, perhaps a concert or play, a party or wedding where you meet with people who are not part of your usual sphere.

Your decorating, artistic or fashion moves may be indecisive; you feel unsure of your own taste and decisions.

The formalities of entertaining can make you impatient and discontent; you may feel an impulse to kick over the traces. With moderation, tolerance and discretion you're better able to keep your serenity.

Jupiter sesquisquare Venus: A sudden change in your social and romantic interests can make you nervous and rebellious. You may feel like kicking over the traces with unconventional indulgence, to break up formal agreements and reach out for more fun and parties, or sympathy and love. Any great expectations are subject to inconsistent revisions.

You may have an unexpected invitation to a party or banquet, concert or wedding where you feel volatile and tremulous.

Your fashion, artistic and decorating tastes lean a little to the flamboyant just now.

Relationships tend to be unstable at this time, with profuse emotions or overrated promise; you are better able to reestablish serenity if you maintain moderation, tolerance and discretion.

Jupiter conjunct Mars: This is a busy and stimulating period of extra activities that challenge your poise, tolerance and expertise. You can put energy and constructive drive into objective problems of hard work, cleaning and repairs, as well as into professional projects.

In financial matters you tend to be impulsively extravagant, but you can make fortunate investments or purchases that improve your standard of living. Business expansion tends to be optimistic and productive. You could seek employment or take career training.

In your academic or religious community you can expand your philosophical program or enthusiastic studies.

With competitive zest you can enjoy games, exercise or sports, travel or an adventure with rowdy comrades. Your sex life tends to be lusty with rough play and vigorous indulgence.

Even if you encounter bad tempers, enmity or danger, fevers or trauma in your environment, the luck and protection you have now will keep you safe.

Jupiter opposite Mars: During this period there are demands on your time and energy; you must extend your capacities to the maximum to get everything done. With enthusiasm and zest you can plunge into vigorous activities that expand and improve your living conditions as well as your professional projects. You can attack obstacles of red tape and proprieties with a robust, cheerful tolerance.

There are some formal procedures that are restrictive to your optimistic impulse to get on with it. In your academic or religious life you may feel impatient with ritual and show. This is not the time to proselytize your philosophy, as there could be conflicts of disagreement or fanaticism around you.

In travels there can be some inexorable delays that are tedious or take extra effort. You may have to rough it or put out extra expense.

With zest you can enjoy games, exercise or sports, a trip or adventure; however, you may run into rowdy competition. Your sex life tends to be frustrated, as your lover is rough, lusty, or critical, and you tend to have expectations greater than realization.

You can make a financial gain at this time, or get a gift, bonus or favor. If so, hang onto it; an investment just now would end up being more costly than beneficial. Be careful of financial loss by theft or impulse buying.

If you should have restless, frustrated anger, expend that energy in objective problems of hard work, cleaning and repairs, extra professional hours, or career training. If there are bad tempers, enmity or danger, fevers or trauma in your environment, meet them with courageous buoyancy. You have protection.

Jupiter square Mars: This is a busy period of stress. With restless energy and impulsive optimism you tend to bite off a big chunk and make rash decisions without counting the cost. You may attack red tape and formal agreements with impatience to get on with it. As a result you hit barriers of criticism or hostility.

In your academic or religious life you may feel rebellious at the formal proprieties of the old guard; you could get involved in policy conflicts of procedure.

If you feel a willful, reckless temper you could be careless and plunge into activities for which you're not well prepared. There is risk of flamboyant fights, accidents, attacks, fever or trauma; or financial loss through theft, carelessness, or the indulgent extravagance of impulse buying.

Business or professional expansion could take a great deal of effort, with obstacles in timing and poor judgment. There could even be dishonesty or underhanded competition. Legal affairs are risky.

A trip can be an adventure but may be long, tiring and costly. Games or sports offer rowdy competition. Your sex life tends to have magnified passion, rough play and perhaps even lusty hostility, rash excess or infection.

If there is danger in your environment, you do have a measure of luck and protection as long as you observe some tolerance and discretion.

Jupiter trine Mars: With a buoyant, careless self-confidence you can take on extra activities that are invigorating. It's fun and exciting to be so busy with interesting people and affairs. Now is the time to expand with energy and enthusiasm.

Seek that job improvement, take career training, start constructive projects, attend to legal and business dealings. There can be a financial increase or a return on an investment.

Your academic or religious life can enlarge your tolerance with broader viewpoints from different people, who have faith in you. Exams seem to be easy, and the formal procedures are interesting.

In your personal life you can have a lusty romp of activity. With enthusiasm you can enjoy games, sports or exercise, a trip or adventure with robust companions. Your social life can increase with many functions and running around. Your sex life has a good-natured zest, and you may have a choice of partners who find you exciting and make complimentary offers.

If there is trauma or risk in your environment, you have the luck to be protected. Even if your impulsive judgment is not always wise, matters tend to work out to your advantage.

Jupiter sextile Mars: This is a time more favorable for expanding your energy and enthusiasm into constructive projects than for rash decisions or willful indulgence.

Put your restless energy into looking for new opportunities in your job and profession; examine the avenues that will improve your standard of living or increase your income. There can be a benefit or financial increase if you look for and work for it.

Activities in educational or religious fields tend to enlarge your tolerant viewpoint. You can have zest and fun in games or sports, a trip or adventure. In your social or sex life you may receive a new invitation or a complimentary offer.

Use discrimination lest your judgment be rash, but approach constructive improvements with confidence. You have luck and protection.

Jupiter semisquare Mars: Your energy and confidence may vacillate between optimism and restless indecision, as some of your areas of expansion seem a little shaky or subject to setback.

The job or business venture into which you put zest and effort can increase your income, but there can be an expense or loss due to carelessness, theft or extravagance.

Religious or educational ventures can be advanced, but there is the friction of disagreement in one area. An adventure or trip is stimulating but includes a slight obstacle of change of plans.

There could be a trauma, risk or flash of temper.

You do have luck and protection that will help you best when you hold a constructive line of honorable action.

Jupiter sesquisquare Mars: A sudden, unexpected breakup of present conditions may require your faith, confidence and courage to take a constructive step of growth.

Your job or profession may be unstable; by putting effort and zest into it you can gain a better position after the shake-up. Do be careful of financial loss from carelessness, theft or extravagance; you may have to detour on a legal or business matter.

With a surge of restless energy you could make an erratic decision and hit sparks of occasional criticism, risk or trauma.

Your religious, philosophical or educational activities could be in a period of flux, as you discard outworn concepts to reexamine your judgment.

Have faith in your luck and protection as you put your energy into areas of honorable expansion.

Jupiter conjunct Jupiter: This is a marked period of expansion in your life. Your ideas, your philosophy, your education and your experience can grow in leaps and bounds. Others will give you benefit and favors, recognition and good will, enduring faith and trust. Former differences can be reconciled, and now people regard you with respect.

You may find yourself deeply questioning your own moral, ethical and religious values and coming to meaningful conclusions on which to base your philosophy of life.

Business and economic matters can expand; new professional or educational goals set a standard of growth that leads to success and satisfaction. Sales and legal matters are well favored. Purchases tend to be expensive but are sound. Your financial position can be a matter of optimism and ease, and any investments should prove to be lucrative.

Travels at this time can be rich in a broadening of experience, with hospitality, enthusiasm and adventure. Foreign people and environments are friendly.

As your entire attitude is more generous and tolerant, you attract abundance, good luck and patronage.

Jupiter opposite Jupiter: In this period of expansion your tendency is to take on more than you can handle. You may feel so optimistic and sure of yourself that you overestimate your own capacities. In the effort to grow up to your goals and commitments you can make great strides in learning and experience, but take care not to promise more than you can deliver.

Financial, legal and business matters look exceptionally good, as long as you keep the wisdom and restraint to not overestimate or plunge into extravagance. You could lose money or possessions by misplaced trust. If you are less than ethical, your expansion can be costly. A delay on formal contracts, purchases or sales will be advantageous in the long run as it gives you time to reconsider.

Travels at this time can be adventurous but may be expensive.

This can be a period of growth in your religious and philosophical understanding, education and experience, but events do not establish a firm standard of enduring patterns, so keep some moderation.

Jupiter square Jupiter: There may be extremes in your affairs just now, as business, financial, legal, professional and personal matters promise so much but deliver so little. Your attitude tends to be overoptimistic, as you are expanding in growth areas of religion and philosophy, education, travel or experience. But the time as a whole indicates inner growth of wisdom from the experience rather than external benefit. Promises may be specious, and expectations are not always backed up by realization.

Financial and legal affairs may be nonproductive and should be regarded with restraint. People in your life can be costly, financially, and from a loss of faith.

Move carefully into this busy month, maintain your own sense of ethics and morality, and those persons with true loyalty will stand by you. However, there is less chance of disappointment if you don't exaggerate the possibilities.

Jupiter trine Jupiter: With personal ethics, faith, hope and optimism you can expand your experience and personal growth at this time. Good fortune and luck can come to you with the assistance and good will of others. New acquaintances will give you loyalty and acceptance; reconciliations of old differences can establish better relationships.

Business, financial, legal, professional, religious and educational matters are well favored for success. As you feel generous, tolerant and confident of the order and goodness of life, your expansive attitude attracts people and situations that will improve your entire environment.

Travels can be rich in a broadening of experience, with hospitality, enthusiasm and adventure. Foreign people and environments are friendly.

It is a period of growing mundane exhilaration or contentment in spiritual serenity; financial security and professional expansion. Matters you begin at this time can give what may be lifetime benefit.

Jupiter sextile Jupiter: The opportunities that come at this time can be highly productive to pursue as they can lead to greater expansion of your position and experience. You have the good will of others who are generous and loyal. New people accept you with trust, and old acquaintances are supportive of your goals.

Business, financial, legal, professional, religious and educational matters offer possibilities to improve your potential for success.

Jupiter semisquare Jupiter: You may vacillate between optimistic hopes in great expectations and misplaced confidence in poor judgment. Some of the matters that look so promising may not deliver, leading to a loss of trust.

It's time to question your own moral, ethical and religious values, as your philosophy may be unstable. Areas of personal indulgence tend to be nonproductive.

Try to hold a steady course with your financial, legal, professional, business and educational pursuits; it is not an opportune time to take extreme views or to initiate changes. Your present indecision in areas of expansion is realistic; wait for more data.

Jupiter sesquisquare Jupiter: There are sudden shifts and unexpected changes in your areas of expansion at this time that require you to reexamine your own ethical, moral and professional areas of growth. You may need to increase your education and understanding, modify your level of trust and tolerance, and reconsider your investments of time or expense.

This is an inconsistent period of growth that includes high hopes and misplaced confidence, detours and overoptimism.

Keep faith in your own capacity to adjust to expanding conditions, but avoid personal indulgences that may be costly or nonproductive.

Jupiter conjunct Saturn: You tend to generally take a more tolerant, optimistic viewpoint toward your responsibilities at this time. You can handle your work with cheerful efficiency and even expedite big jobs with relaxed management. You may feel liberated from past conditions of restriction with no clear-cut ambition for future plans. It's a good time to settle down with patient stability. You can put work into organizing your surroundings and bringing areas of profusion into order. There is contentment in self-discipline and satisfaction in completing your duties.

Business and financial matters should have less strain as income and expense are equitable. If you should strive for an increased position or income you're apt to make a lateral move rather than a gain. With an investment you could have big expectations but realize only more hard work or delays in return.

If there is a handicap in your life that monitors your freedom, there is someone there who will be supportive or come through when you have a need. In the observation of formalities you show poise and dignity.

If perhaps you should indulge yourself in irresponsible expansion, there can be a loss of security and honor, as the price will be equitable to the indulgence.

Jupiter opposite Saturn: Your freedom tends to be restricted at this time, as you are subject to routine and additional duties. Your obligations put you in such a position as to demand that you keep at your present jobs with patience and tolerance.

In work, business and financial ambitions, progress is slow, and money is tight. It's a poor time to invest, lend or borrow; hold the line. Professional and educated people are more demanding than generous; formal or legal contracts can put you in a bind. Your initial enthusiasm in a new job or move may be dulled; you find it requires order, patience, perseverance and poise as you gradually increase your education and experience.

If you are handicapped by extra expense, poverty or debt, worry or coldness, or stringent responsibilities, helpless or indulgent people who need your care, it may take the maximum of your cheerful serenity to keep your chin up and keep your faith that work and discipline will gradually improve your conditions. Under duress you can expand your own strength of character with honor and dignity. Your greatest satisfaction is in the patient maintenance of stability. You can't break out just now; serve your time. Someone there is loyal and supportive.

Jupiter square Saturn: With patient serenity you can take on more work and responsibility. You tend to be optimistic about pending changes; you feel confident you can handle the routine with discipline and efficiency. The work you pile into with enthusiasm can be highly productive. Big opportunities at this time require a great deal of planning, preparation and effort, but do advance your ambitions.

Business and financial matters tend to cause some strain, as areas of expansion take the limit of your capital. Your income may fall just short of expenses, as there is an extra bill or needy person. An investment tends to be beneficial in the long run but takes time and organization to develop.

Your freedom may be restricted by some specific handicap: fatigue, extra work or expense, a stringent duty or responsibility to another. With cheerful dignity you can persevere through obstacles. With tolerance and stability accept people and matters the way they are. Someone who is loyal will be supportive.

If there is a conflict between your need of security and your need of freedom, you are wiser to take the cautious, slow route of self-control. You could pay a heavy price for an indulgence.

Jupiter trine Saturn: This is a serene and secure period in which to gradually expand your personal responsibility toward your goals and ambitions. With a tolerant, optimistic calm you can handle routine, discipline and self-control. You have the enthusiasm and confidence necessary to take on a big job and you can plan and organize on a broad level with cheerful efficiency.

In business and financial affairs you tend to hold the line; your attitude leans wisely to economy. Your income is sufficient to be secure, and if there is extra money it can be doled out expeditiously in practical areas. If investments of time, effort or capital don't pay off immediately they are nonetheless laying a solid groundwork for future success.

You can handle formal affairs with poise and dignity. There is joy and satisfaction in your work and in the stability of routine.

Jupiter sextile Saturn: This is a time more opportune to plan gradual expansion than to take on big ambitions. As certain restrictions ease, you have more optimism, but other responsibilities are still pressing. The work you pile into with enthusiasm is productive, and you can handle routine with disciplined, calm efficiency. You may complete an old debt, finish a duty, free yourself of a problem, or gain the results of a prior effort. Business and financial matters tend to hold the line; income and expense are equitable, and you are observant of economy. Approach new opportunities conservatively; they need more time to mature.

Jupiter semisquare Saturn: This period can range from being mildly dull to being highly frustrating, as big expectations tend to fall through. Promises are not sound, and your restless urge for greater satisfaction is blocked by irritating changes. Rather than attempt expansion just now, hold the line in personal, professional, or financial matters. Little handicaps or expenses can come up, but your moral reserve or your income tends to balance them out if you keep steady on the job.

Draw on your serenity, faith and patience to accept people and things the way they are. Organize areas of scattered profusion and stay with a conservative program of responsibility.

Jupiter sesquisquare Saturn: Don't count too highly on promises at this time; the matters in which you hope to expand your experience, philosophy and viewpoint tend to be overrated. Something you begin with high hopes may be delayed or fall through.

Your business, professional, legal or financial affairs tend to be inconsistent and, for the most part, inconclusive. Investments of time, energy or capital meet with detours and minor handicaps. You may have a setback.

It's not a good time to lend money or overextend yourself. Stay with a conservative program just now and find your peace of mind in moral consideration of your own responsibilities. Take your steps of growth slowly into stable areas.

Jupiter conjunct Uranus: There is a matter of beneficial change in your life. Your present situation is educating you for another step of growth. As such it may mark a turning point. You are outgrowing the past in such a way as to never go back to a former condition with the same attitude.

With confidence in your own individuality you can make independent decisions. If your circumstances are such that you cannot yet have the freedom of expansion you're inclined toward, that urge is nonetheless gestating.

You may study occult religion or arcane philosophy if you are so inclined. Academic education tends to be more progressive or leads you into advanced fields of science or the humanities. You are certainly apt to gain new information or to learn unexpected facts that broaden your insight.

In business or finance, government or industry you can expand with innovative methods and sophisticated equipment. The purchase of an appliance or automobile at this time is an advantageous investment.

A sudden or unexpected benefit may come to you: a trip, a surprise party, a professional boost or favor, an unusual gift or exciting invitation. You may see an old friend or acquaintance, with whom you've had an unconventional relationship, who will give you supportive loyalty. Someone in your life is being contradictory, erratic or detached. A new person at this time could be a catalyst who points the way to the future.

New beginnings are fortunate. A venture started now can make a big change for the better with far-reaching consequences.

Jupiter Opposite Uranus: You are putting maximum effort into completing old patterns as you move into a new chapter in your life. This can be a turning point that is not yet stable; you must increase your education and experience before you can reap the reward you seek. You may have overrated expectations of the benefit that you'll accrue from your changing situation. You'll certainly learn a lot, but the final outcome will not be what you now anticipate.

If there is nervous tension or stress from an erratic situation, avoid precipitous or indulgent independence. Stick to the formal program on your job, school, with government or industry, and you'll gain more credit, confidence and self-satisfaction.

Purchase of an appliance or automobile at this time is an unwise extravagance, as sophisticated equipment tends to be elegant and temperamental rather than practical.

You could get a sudden or unexpected offer of a party, gift or trip, a professional boost or favor, or an unusual opportunity; however, the benefit has strings attached. The proposal could fall through, an employer may renege, or big ideas could be unsound. If you do carry through, you'll find that you've gotten into a lot more than you'd expected and, if you can change and grow up to it, the venture will have far-reaching consequences that include excellent benefits.

You may get caught up-to-date with an old friend at this time and perhaps even say good-bye, as you're expanding in different directions. Someone in your life is certainly unconventional, flamboyant or a little crazy. A new person you meet now, who is stimulating, magnetic, supportive, disruptive and unusual, could influence your life for as long as you know each other.

Jupiter square Uranus: Though changes are pending they are not in the area you expect nor at the time you anticipate. There are obstacles due to your erratic independence and the other person's unreliability. You could have overrated expectations at this time for big changes and unusual ventures.

If you can keep a measure of calm through the shifting variegations of experiences, you can gain insight and education that prepare you for another step of growth. Beneficial changes are pending, but the freedom of expansion you seek is not yet ready.

You could study occult religion, arcane philosophy or advanced academic subjects. Unexpected information and changes of schedule tend to be disruptive and a challenge to your confidence.

In business or finances, government or industry, innovative methods and unexpected obstacles tend to be overrated and unsound. Sophisticated equipment, a new appliance or automobile may be expensive and temperamental.

A trip can be exciting but is inclined to put you into unprecedented environments and situations that require all your poise.

You may see an old friend who is moving into crazy patterns and big ideas. Someone in your life may be magnetic and unconventional, stimulating and unstable. A new person you meet could have a flamboyant and disruptive effect.

During this period you could have the rebellious urge to break with traditional patterns. Do so for growth and experience but don't count on any promises for the future. It's a time of flux that may even be a turning point.

Jupiter trine Uranus: There is no better time to make a change than now. This can be a turning point that expands your life with joy, excitement and enthusiasm. Move, start that new job, go to school, take a trip or have an adventure. New doors can open with unprecedented good luck, attention and favors, greater affluence and expansion.

Don't sit back; get out and meet people. Extend yourself; make independent decisions with full confidence in your own individuality. You may have a high tension of exuberant anticipation, with which you feel free enough to soar.

Both studies and experience educate you with new courses and activities, and whatever you learn now will always be of benefit.

In business and finance, government and industry you can expand with unconventional methods and with sudden good fortune from unexpected sources. Sophisticated equipment, a new appliance or automobile is not only a pleasure but a good investment.

An old friend may be more interesting than before, and you can have a trip or adventure together or move into new patterns of change with shared insight. If new people are not enduring they are certainly magnetic and stimulating for as long as you associate. You could possibly meet someone now, or soon, who will always be a dynamic influence in your life.

New beginnings are fortunate. What you gain now you'll remember forever with gratitude. Reach for change and growth.

If you should sit back with contentment in placid independence, it can be a mellow month with modified good fortune.

Jupiter sextile Uranus: Changes that expand your position are more advantageous than are erratic moves of perverse independence. In one area you are outgrowing old conditions, and there can be a marked advantage in a certain move, job, trip or adventure that opens exciting new doors. However, the full freedom of expansion that you want is not yet ready; you may be over-optimistic about a premature change.

In your studies of occult religion, arcane philosophy, or academic subjects, one unusual course may catch your attention and turn out to be more stimulating than you'd anticipated.

In business and finance you can make opportune moves that are innovative as long as you don't suddenly start a crazy, big, new project.

An old friend can be more interesting than before with shared independence and insights, but someone in your life is acting nervous and exaggerative. A new person is stimulating but unstable.

It's a good time to start a new venture, as long as you maintain your poise and don't overrate your good luck. Matters are not apt to continue in the same tone as now, as there is a degree of flux.

Jupiter semisquare Uranus: You may vacillate between optimism and nervous strain just now. Certain changes in your life are unstable; though you have great expectations, matters seem to be unsound, crazy or untimely.

Sudden friction or unexpected restlessness disturbs the serenity of your environment; your confidence is shaky. If it's not yet time for the changes you want, neither is it time to break with traditional patterns.

Keep a steady course rather than one of erratic independence, with faith that the present experiences and education will add to your philosophy and understanding.

Jupiter sesquisquare Uranus: Sudden and unexpected changes may open up new possibilities for expansion and growth. You may be charged up with optimistic excitement or erratic independence, with a tendency to jump into a new job, move, trip or adventure that is unstable.

Don't go off half-cocked with indulgent and precipitous decisions, as matters are not yet ready for your next step of growth. Use your experience and education to expand your philosophy, to find an inner peace of insight and confidence.

Jupiter conjunct Neptune: You tend to be gentle and vague this month, with an urge to retire rather than pursue material goals. As your ideals and imagination are sensitive, you can care for others with consideration, hospitality and contentment.

A trip, vacation or outing can be ideal. A gift, favor or good will can nurture and protect you in your areas of vulnerability.

In creative expansion of aesthetic interests, you can interact with others on a community basis, where each person contributes his or her share voluntarily. Drama, music, poetry, mystical and religious matters, and philanthropy can catch your imagination and inspiration.

Though you tend to have faith and confidence in promotional schemes, sales, financial and legal matters, weigh other considerations before making a commitment. This is a time for growth of concept rather than mundane efforts.

Jupiter opposite Neptune: Matters in which you have great expectations may not be too realistic just now; you tend to be vulnerable to misplaced trust or vague optimism. Weigh carefully any promises, promotional schemes, financial and legal matters, as they may be exaggerated if not deceptive.

That trip, vacation, outing, or delightful occasion can be delayed or may not deliver all it promises. You have less interest in your work, as you'd rather retire or escape from mundane efforts. You may have a tendency to sleep more, daydream, or hunger for adventure and freedom.

You can interact democratically for the interest of a community where people contribute their share voluntarily. Drama, music, poetry, mystical and religious matters can catch your imagination and inspiration. You can make a gentle sacrifice to care for others with consideration and hospitality.

Look at what you have with grateful appreciation. Inspire and sustain others with humble service; have faith in your own ideals for a growth of spirit.

Jupiter square Neptune: You tend to have a vague restlessness just now with a hunger for more adventure and freedom but without the sense of direction to get it on.

As matters seem to be dissolving around you, nothing is firm or realistic. People you count on are not there or they're in a fog where you can't reach them. Something's going on that you can't get hold of or understand, and you may feel that you're in a miasma of confusion or muddle, if not actual deception.

Religious or mystical matters can be delusive, psychic advice is not right for you, or divine revelations may be an exaggerated drama.

In business, legal or financial affairs there is the possibility of total incompetence, so postpone important deals or decisions this month.

Your best course is to hang onto your faith in your own moral ideals, take care of those who need your trust and inspiration, and keep a gentle consideration for others. Avoid any and all promotional schemes that promise great rewards; keep your feet on the ground.

Jupiter trine Neptune: This tends to be a relaxed and optimistic period during which you are tolerant, hospitable, considerate, buoyant and content. You could have more freedom, take a trip or vacation, or have an ideal come true; at the least a gift, favor, pleasant outing, or adventure.

A financial, business or legal matter could bear fruit. You can promote, sell, or inspire trust and good will. Your income seems to be without strain, purchases are pleasurable or even elegant, and any expense is well worth the price. You could possibly win a luxury or indulgence, or make a favorable investment.

In your community life you find joy and peace in your consideration of dear ones, with sensitivity and democracy. Drama, music, poetry, mystical and religious matters stimulate your imagination and philosophical growth.

Jupiter sextile Neptune: There can be a delightful or lucrative opportunity this month that is advantageous to pursue with good will, tolerance and hospitality rather than with exaggerated indulgence.

It tends to be a relaxed period with less strain and an easy optimism. You could have more freedom, a little vacation or favorable outing, or a gift, favor or adventure.

If you should be vaguely restless, look for peace and joy in trust and consideration of dear ones. Drama, music, poetry, mystical and religious matters can inspire and sustain you.

74

Jupiter semisquare Neptune: You may have a restless sensitivity just now, a feeling of being unsure in your areas of growth and expansion. You could vacillate between buoyant optimism and vague anxiety.

A situation can be ideal with more freedom, ease or good will, a trip, vacation or outing, or a delightful adventure, but there is a note of confusion or muddle, mystery or deception that you can't seem to pin down.

Trust in your good luck but don't exaggerate big promises or promotional schemes that could be specious. There is a possibility of financial or legal incompetence.

Religious or mystical matters may be confused. Keep your own faith in moral values of consideration, democracy and hospitality.

Jupiter sesquisquare Neptune: Changing conditions at this time could give you inconsistent surges of vague restlessness. It seems hard to pin down your own feelings, and matters around you have a nebulous note of instability.

It's generally a more retiring period with greater freedom and ease. There could be an unexpected trip, vacation or outing, gift or favor.

Trust in your good luck but don't exaggerate a financial or promotional scheme, psychic advice, or legal proceedings, as they are inconclusive. Keep your own faith and trust in moral values of consideration, democracy and hospitality.

Jupiter conjunct Pluto: Your joy, contentment, and greatest expansion lie in cooperation with others for matters of mutual benefit. In group activities you elicit confidence and can sway others. Business matters require negotiation and compromise, and financial dealings with powerful corporations or individuals can be favorable to you.

Your experience and education can give you a broad step of growth as you evaluate the continuity and diversity of your past, present and future. With insight into your religion and philosophy in moments of serene solitude, you can bring out a greater awareness of your own potential.

Jupiter opposite Pluto: To gain trust, good will and confidence you must cooperate with others for matters of mutual benefit. Negotiations may not give you all you hope for, as powerful individuals are holding the reins, but with compromise you can expand your position.

In group activities you can make your presence known favorably by extending yourself to be cheerful, agreeable and optimistic.

It's a good time to evaluate the continuity and diversity of your past, present and future in regard to your growth and expansion. Areas of personal indulgence may show up. To have faith in your own potential you must trust in your own religion and philosophy. It's not the time to proselytize, but rather to set an example that will sway others.

Jupiter square Pluto: A coercive situation may present obstacles to your serenity and confidence. To keep good will you must compromise, and to grow you must increase your education and experience.

If negotiation does not elicit cooperation it may be time to make an ultimatum. You may eliminate a disturbing element for the good of the whole, with faith in your own moral judgment.

In job, business or finances, work optimistically with a team or group effort; you can handle more than you thought you could, as you bring out a greater potential.

In your religion or philosophy, there could be manipulation or dogma that strains your trust. It's not the time to proselytize, rather set an example of cheerful tolerance.

Jupiter trine Pluto: You gain contentment, peace, advantage and good luck by cooperating with dear ones in matters of mutual benefit. A powerful person will give you good will and trust, as you extend your hospitality with gracious compromise. Such a contact will pay off in the long run.

In group activities your cheerful generosity and optimism will elicit confidence, and you can sway others.

In business and financial matters, negotiations for a better price can be lucrative.

You can expand your religious, philosophical and educational programs with wisdom, tolerance and discrimination.

Jupiter sextile Pluto: In your areas of growth, you can expand your business and profession, education and experience, or religion and philosophy. The opportunities that come up can be advanced more smoothly with cooperation than with ultimatums. Others give you good will and trust, and your tolerance encourages generosity and confidence.

If a person or situation should be coercive or resistant, negotiate for better terms. Compromise is more advantageous in the long run.

Jupiter semisquare Pluto: You may vacillate between serene content and a restless urge to resist cooperation with others. It seems that you must compromise for the good of the whole, in business and finance, religion and philosophy, education and experience. Dear and pleasant people are agreeable, but someone is manipulative or coercive. Though your tendency is to make an ultimatum or to proselytize, this will not work as well as negotiation.

Matters are not conclusive; get more facts and information that will encourage your growth and confidence.

Jupiter sesquisquare Pluto: Present conditions of cooperation and good will may be unstable, as your faith and optimism are shaky. Sudden and unexpected changes in business and finances, religion and philosophy, education or experience can threaten loss, indulgence or coercion. To keep a level of trust, renegotiate, unless you are prepared to deliver that ultimatum that will eliminate the disturbance.

VII   TRANSIT SATURN

Saturn transits the horoscope in twenty-nine years five months seventeen days. Approximately every eight months Saturn has an apparent retrograde motion that lasts four to five months. In its thirty-year cycle Saturn will conjunct and oppose each planet once; square, trine, sextile, semisquare and sesquisquare every planet twice. An aspect it makes near the change of station may repeat three times.

At mean motion of two minutes a day, Saturn has a two-month influence of one degree applying and one degree separating to partile, going through one sign in two-and-a-half years. When Saturn moves at its maximum daily motion of eight minutes, it makes an aspect orb in fifteen days, with a modified influence. When slowing to retrograde, Saturn holds an aspect for sixty-eight days, little over its mean motion period of two months; however, Saturn may engage a planet at change of station three times in an eight- to nine-month time span. In this case it certainly holds its influence from the first contact through the last, and marks that year intensely. The effect is discernible within a two-degree orb.

As Saturn is the significator of work and responsibility, by following its indications we gain security and the satisfaction of a job well done. As we advance our ambitions we gain more control; the greater the capacity, the greater the responsibility. The obligation of Saturn is insistent; if we do not choose self-discipline, duty is imposed upon us.

Saturn's touch is never light. At its heaviest, Saturn gives a cruel cross to bear that can lead to depression, discouragement, and despair. As a monitor, it inhibits pleasure and gaiety with limitations and frustration.

We learn with Saturn that we have to work for what we get—and that we get what we work for. There is little advancement and achievement without the industrious resolution of Saturn. The order, sanity, and stability of our lives come from the methodical patience of Saturn, and from its lesson we learn to have the enduring calm that comes from inner strength.

Indeed Saturn, as Chronos, marks a register of events in the great order of time.

Saturn conjunct Sun: This represents a critical period in the development of your career and reputation. Progress seems slow, and your self-expression is checked. Your work is heavy or tedious, or presents stringent problems. It is time to take on ambitious goals, as you have self-discipline, resolution, and patience. The duties and responsibilities you accept will mature and stabilize your character, and will lay firm foundations that advance your position in life.

This is not the time to pursue pleasure or romance, as you feel poor and ungracious. Even if you are bored or lonely there is less interest in frivolity or games. Your energy level can be depleted if you overwork, but generally your sense of self-survival is strong. It can be a good time to get new glasses or go to the dentist, or diet or put yourself on a healthful regimen. Do be careful to avoid falls, breaks or bruises.

Men in your life are poor, frugal, cheap, or troublesome. Old friends or stable persons are a rock of stability, but you may worry about an older person, or a specific man who is selfish, ambitious, or upstaging you.

It's a good time to discharge old debts or obligations. Get yourself and your affairs in order. Get the job done.

Saturn opposite Sun: During these next weeks you are likely to find yourself frustrated and blocked by those in authority, especially by your employers or by the government. You may find yourself involved in a struggle to achieve ambitions or status. If you have not put in the work preparatory to your present goals you may find that your ambitions are greater than your capacities.

By keeping your nose to the grindstone you can maintain a safe harbor. You can get recognition and respect for your discipline and the work you put into facing your responsibilities, but there is little that does not have a price tag at this time. If you attempt to force issues, impose your regime on others, or demand a position of authority, you will meet heavy obstacles.

You're apt to feel serious, poor, bored, lonely, and overworked, but have little interest in frivolity. Your energy could be depleted, with a loss of weight, or a need for new glasses or to see the dentist.

The men in your life are lacking in supportive warmth, or they are poor, cheap, or selfish. Stay with your own sense of duty and obligation, and do the jobs you must with faithful maturity. Get enough rest and take care of yourself. The work that life demands of you just now will give you the experience and character with which to meet the future.

Saturn square Sun: Your work load may be heavy during this period, or dull, tedious, and seemingly unproductive. Your security could be threatened by inappreciation or criticism from superiors that brings out any fear of failure you may have. Your energy and confidence can be easily depleted, and your shortcomings are obvious. You could start an austerity program as you feel poor, worried about your future, and oppressed by your responsibilities.

A man in your life could be a bore, lacking in supportive warmth, or be disappointing, depressing, deceptive, or in trouble. Take a serious view of your future, regard your responsibilities with mature stability, keep your nose to the grindstone and work it out. It's not the time to invest money or extend your credit. In business or personal commitments avoid conflicts of egotism or authority by quietly doing your own job and minding your own business.

Protect yourself from colds, falls, or bruises, or undue loss of weight. Attend to dental work if necessary. Get your rest, and keep busy with matters that are your duty.

Saturn trine Sun: With confidence, take on mature responsibilities, as you are efficient, calm, patient, and disciplined. If there are tedious duties that you've neglected, now is the time to sort, clean, discard, and organize. You are quite capable of handling work projects, administrative authority, ambitious goals, and getting your affairs in order.

Though money may not be too plentiful, you can discharge old debts and obligations. Investments in the future—whether in business matters or in time, effort, and planning—will lay the foundations of security.

Older persons and those in authority tend to approve your reliable capabilities. A steady man can be a rock of comfort, and your stable environment is a safe harbor.

Saturn sextile Sun: You have the calm, patience, and serenity to handle your responsibilities with maturity and efficiency. Sort, clean, discard, and organize, in order to be ready and prepared for a new opportunity to take on a job, assignment, or administrative goals. Your work could have some useful and interesting facets at this time. Any extra effort can impress superiors, as older persons and those in authority tend to give you approval.

If there are financial restrictions, tedious duties, or delays, you can keep a safe harbor in steady, efficient control, and quiet self-discipline.

Saturn semisquare Sun: Your work may vacillate in time and tempo just now, as you tend to vary between ambitious efficiency and bored discontent in the routine. There can be changes in procedure and planning and a need for more information or training. Your goals tend to be blocked by annoying obstacles and delays, detours, and restrictions.

Older persons, superiors, and those in authority, are none too helpful, and may cause you worry by their criticism. A man in your life could be dull or indifferent, as he's busy with his own work.

Be patient and keep a steady self-discipline. Matters will stabilize again into their secure patterns.

Saturn sesquisquare Sun: Unstable conditions in your work can challenge your security and cause you worry just now. You may feel restricted, hampered, poor, and discontent. Sudden changes in procedure and planning throw an extra load of responsibility on you, with a need to organize.

Your energy can be erratic; others may make unexpected demands on you and be inappreciative of your efforts.

Be patient. Work toward discarding inefficient methods and paying off old debts and obligations, in order to gain greater control of more stable satisfactions.

Saturn conjunct Moon: Routine domestic affairs take more of your time, discipline, and responsibility. With efficient work you can make a safe harbor of your home. Clean, organize, and make major maintenance improvements of a practical nature, such as fixtures, glass or cement work, fences, gardening or landscaping.

It's not a cheerful time for a move, as neighbors, kin and dependents tend to be worrisome just now and not too supportive of your domestic or personal goals. A woman in your life may have poor health or financial worries that concern you, and she may require your assistance.

Your own energy at this time could be somewhat depleted; take care of dental work if needed and be careful of colds or of getting overtired.

Past debts, bad checks, or necessary expenses can make demands on you; even if your income is good you tend to feel poor, frugal, and gloomy. Therefore it is a good time to pinch pennies and to put money in the bank. It's not the time to invest or make luxury purchases.

With a stable and responsible attitude you insure sound domestic relationships and security. Make mature plans for your future as your character develops in strength of purpose.

Saturn opposite Moon: Domestic matters at this time demand maximum organization, planning, work, and self-discipline. Your home may seem dirty, poor, and shabby, but changes are delayed or take time, effort, and expense. If decorating you may find it hard to get the right pattern, the paint is wrong and has to be exchanged, or you simply must scrub the kitchen clean. If you face up to these routine responsibilities, maintain or replace fixtures, you can gain the good satisfaction of getting tedious jobs done for a more comfortable future. However it's not a good time to move, as you could feel lonely, gloomy, overworked, overtired, and depleted.

Women, children, or kin could be worrisome or disappointing at this time. Just when you need some supportive assistance, it's necessary that you take on an additional responsibility for another. Your attitude may drag from the present limitations and insufficient funds. Avoid any unnecessary purchasing, expending, investing, or lending money just now. Be frugal, economical, stable, and responsible, and work hard to improve your environment.

Saturn square Moon: Domestic matters tend to be tedious just now, if not actually depressing. Your home seems poor, shabby, or dirty; your time and energy are insufficient to get in and clean or fix it up, and you lack money for repairs. As your energy and enthusiasm are low, your attitude could be gloomy, cynical, and suspicious; the future looks bleak.

Matters will improve, but more easily if you draw on your inner strength of character and conviction to be patient and enduring. Try to keep up on routine jobs with some semblance of cheerful stability.

Women, children, and kin may be a worry to you and require more effort and responsibility; a specific woman in your life could be cold to you, or in poor health or spirits. With a steady, patient maturity you can be a rock of inner strength for others, who will remember later with enduring gratitude that you were firm in a time of need.

Saturn trine Moon: In your domestic and family affairs, you tend to be efficient, practical and well-organized. With stability, you can make a safe harbor of your home. It's a good time for long-term investments or maintenance improvements of a practical nature, such as fixtures, glass or cement work, fences, gardening or landscaping.

You can be the mature, supportive person to whom others turn in their time of need; you care for women, children, and dependents with dignity and patience. You can work diligently to solve problems and plan worthwhile goals for the future.

Older and stable persons regard you with respect as you deepen your sense of responsibility and reliability.

Saturn sextile Moon: There are opportunities at this time to improve your domestic and family relationships. If someone in your environment is weak, troubled, or in need, you can take a responsible and supportive attitude. Encounter problem areas with efficient expediency to find practical solutions. You can organize your home and make maintenance improvements with self-discipline and dignity.

Saturn semisquare Moon: Domestic matters tend to be unsatisfactory just now, as your home seems less attractive or comfortable. Maintenance, cleaning, and upkeep are dull or tedious, and your time and energy are scattered and depleted.

Women, children, or kin can be annoying to you if not worrisome, as they need care and attention that you're reluctant to give. A woman in your life may be intermittently cold or distant, or have some health or economic problem that you'd rather avoid.

Meet these little irritating problems with self-discipline; finish up odd jobs and keep your finances in order, so you can hold a stable environment together.

Saturn sesquisquare Moon: Domestic problems can be hectic as sudden repair needs, cleaning, or maintenance requirements drag on your time and energy. Women, children, or kin may alter their plans and programs, requiring you to cope with sudden setbacks and changes.

Your own functional system is inconsistent in vitality; you may feel the need of some nesting solitude. Cope with your work by wading through the details; be patient with those for whom you do care, and keep a stable environment.

Saturn conjunct Mercury: This is an excellent time to plan and organize your future, and to put those plans into practical application by starting a methodical program of self-discipline. In personal areas where you wish self-improvement, put yourself on a routine schedule.

Catch up all your old correspondence, revise or complete notebooks and diaries, sort and organize your files and paperwork. Make lists of what you wish to accomplish, and complete one thing at a time in its order of importance.

Settle into a routine of study and patient effort to learn a tedious subject that will be of lasting value to you.

It's not the time to take exams or look for immediate results, as this is the foundation period. What you learn or work on now can be fruitful later. Contracts or business deals tend to delay just now.

If your thoughts tend to be pessimistic and discouraged, you may express criticism and sarcasm that make you unpopular. This is not the best time for sociable exchanges, but is well suited for responsible, intellectual ambitions.

Saturn opposite Mercury: Circumstances may demand maximum effort on your part to write, study, or communicate with others in a methodical and industrious manner. Though it seems difficult to get your ideas across, if you organize your thinking and take the time to write out your plans, revise and correct them, and to discipline yourself, you can formulate the ideas and data to reach a better understanding.

The routine may be depressing just now; you could feel dull, inert, and convinced that life is a drag that won't change. You may tend to be cynical or sarcastic, and to express discouragement at every turn. Don't get caught in these blues, but keep busy. Use self-discipline to organize your life and surroundings. Clean up old correspondence, sort your files, organize your business and personal affairs. Travels or contracts just now could be a worry and take a lot of work. You'll be more secure in keeping a steady conservative routine.

Saturn square Mercury: You may feel your limitations keenly at this time as there are obstacles, stumbling blocks, and restrictions in your path. If your education or understanding is insufficient, start a methodical program of study to learn the subject you need to improve yourself. Put yourself on a routine schedule to organize your work, your surroundings, and yourself.

Avoid depression blues by keeping busy; sarcasm or cynical pessimism is negative and not only drags you down but hampers your progress and popularity. Dig into all the tedious tasks that need to be done; the foundations you build now will enhance your future security.

Saturn trine Mercury: This is a favorable time to pursue serious study of efficient methods to improve your work, surroundings, and yourself. You can advance your career and areas of self-improvement with practical planning. Sort, clean, and organize, catch up on letters, bills, correspondence and duty calls.

Mail, news, and communications are favorable. Moves or travels for business reasons require work but are expeditious. Contracts, writing or teaching, and accounts may be put in methodical working order. A conservative routine gives you satisfaction and security.

Saturn sextile Mercury: Take advantage of work opportunities, as they can lead to more ambitious advancements that improve the security of your economic position. Keep busy. Handle all the routine tasks that may have been neglected, or study that serious matter that will benefit you in the long run.

If you should feel pessimistic or discouraged by limitations and routine, pull yourself together and start a program of self-improvement. Dig into all the tedious tasks that need to be done; the foundations you build now will lead to more stable ambitions.

Saturn semisquare Mercury: Your work may be hectic just now, with vacillating responsibilities and nagging restrictions and obstacles. Some of your calls, letters or communications may be postponed, delayed or cancelled. You could tend to feel depleted and ungracious.

Your education may be lacking or insufficient to handle certain jobs, and you'll need to study carefully to organize new plans or data. Be prepared to cover extra details or routine to keep up your efficiency.

Saturn sesquisquare Mercury: Sudden breakups in the routine of your job could cause you agitation. If your education or understanding is insufficient to handle present data, you may need a crash course of study in order to keep up your efficiency. If you feel impatient and restricted by the limitation of routine, you could tend to an ungracious independence. You'll do better to reorganize the duties at hand and to consider a conservative program of self-improvement.

Saturn conjunct Venus: Your social and emotional lives are hampered at this time. Even if you feel lonely and in need of a secure love, you are not giving out any easy warmth. As you are sensitive to slights, your friends and loved ones seem to be indifferent, unfaithful or cold to you; consider whether your own attitude is causing this. There could be a sorrow in your life with the loss of a dear friendship.

People may be leaning on you; try to respond to their needs and take on the responsibility of being supportive with a loyal and mature attitude. This is not the time to start a new romance; be tolerant of your present mate who may seem faithful but dull just now. Even if you feel low, cold, or mean, draw on your reserves of stable serenity to hold your emotional world together.

An excellent way to avoid negative feelings is to keep busy—get in and work to beautify your surroundings and to create more comfort. Clean your house or office, reorganize, paint, be creative in artistic work, surround yourself with music, color and forms that are pleasing.

Saturn opposite Venus: You could feel bored and cut off from others, with a sense of loneliness, loss, or social discontent. Your love life is drab, as your mate is a worry or responsibility, or is dull, disinteresting, or undemonstrative. It's not a good time for a new romance. Even your dearest friends are leaning on you with demands or problems.

Face up to your social or emotional responsibilities, be supportive to those who need you, and stand by your commitments with stability. If there is a sorrow in your life take a mature attitude, but don't cut off your own feelings; accept the lesson and the growth.

Dig in and keep busy. Work to beautify your surroundings and create more comfort. Clean your house or office, reorganize, paint, be creative in artistic work, surround yourself with music, color and forms that are pleasing.

Saturn square Venus: You could feel emotionally discontent at this time, lonely, shy, or longing for a secure love. Your present mate may be a worry or responsibility, or seem dull and discouraging, but it is not the time to start a new romance. The people you may be attracted to are either unavailable or disinterested in you. There are obstacles with lovers and friends, as the timing is poor just now for warm, easy camaraderie.

It's a better time to work out existing difficulties with old friends and loved ones, to take a mature, responsible attitude of stability. Keep busy by putting your efforts into beautifying your surroundings and creating more comfort. Clean your house or office, reorganize, paint, be creative in artistic work, surround yourself with music, color and forms that are pleasing.

Saturn trine Venus: This is a good time to stabilize your surroundings. Organize your home or office, paint, get new decorations or furnishings, to create more beauty, serenity and pleasing form. Fix yourself up with new clothes of a style that is conservative, trim, and attractive.

Extend yourself socially to old friends and loved ones. Your emotional relationships can be secure and supportive. You tend to be more discreet, calm, serene, and poised. Organization and efficiency are improved and give pleasant results.

Saturn sextile Venus: This is a time to hold a stable emotional life rather than to seek new social exchanges. Though your friends and loved ones may not seem too exciting, they do tend to be safe and reliable. If they are leaning on you with some needs, you can be supportive and gain their appreciation.

You can find security and serenity in beautifying your surroundings and creating more comfort. Paint, clean, reorganize, or plan decorating goals. Old-fashioned virtues and traditional social exchanges with family and dear ones can be a comfort.

Saturn semisquare Venus: There can be minor changes in your work and responsibilities that cause some emotional upset just now—sudden jobs, cancellations, or delays that interfere with your social life, or that cause you to question your ability to cope. Keep a practical attitude and handle each detail to create a serene working order.

If you feel neglected or rejected you may get the lonely blues. It's better to keep busy and put your time and effort into improving yourself and your own surroundings.

Saturn sesquisquare Venus: Your feelings may have ups and downs now, as your social or emotional life is inconsistent. Your mate may seem unstable, or friends are here today and gone tomorrow. A sudden romantic attraction may not work out, and you feel neglected or lonely. Keep busy and organize yourself into a more attractive package; beautify your surroundings, and work for harmony and pleasing form.

Saturn conjunct Mars: You can discipline your energy with an unemotional, cold, hard core of purpose at this time. If you feel restriction, limitation, or delay to your personal desires that stimulates brooding or resentment, you can direct that energy into finishing up tedious repairs and constructions. There is satisfaction in work that is methodical, industrious and responsible, as you have the capacity to handle long hours, overtime, difficult problems, or harsh conditions. You're less apt to change conditions just now than to complete the routine and necessary efforts of present-time duties.

If there is pain, trauma, or hardship in your life, you can endure patiently with quiet courage. You have a sense of caution and expediency. Your sex energy is disciplined and controlled and may be sublimated into work ambitions.

Saturn opposite Mars: You can put maximum energy into organizing your efforts at this time, to gain a more efficient approach to your work and ambitions. It may be necessary to put in overtime, long hours, and tedious routine to handle the demands made on you. Difficult problems, harsh conditions, and stringent challenges are a responsibility. Though you want to do things your own way, or have your own way, control by others may limit you. Your tendency could be to a rash disregard to caution if you feel bitter and mean about being abused. If there is hardship, pain, or trauma in your life it may be strictly necessary for you to endure a trying time with patient courage. You may encounter feelings of loss, grief, frustration, and resentment.

Your best course just now is to direct all your self-discipline into constructive purpose. Use a hard core of cold caution to attack all the obstacles and to assert your positive courage. Use this driving energy constructively toward a specific goal.

Saturn square Mars. This can be a trying time that requires your patience, self-discipline, and courage. The matters you desire are blocked and delayed; other people are restrictive or cold to you in a way that could cause you to feel bitter, mean, abused, and resentful. Your tendency is to push things through or to strike out against the obstacles.

Be careful of burning your bridges behind you or disregarding your sense of caution in order to have your own way. You may possibly be at your most disagreeable just now. Beware of falls, weapons, instruments, or trouble with the law. If you must fight with someone, coldly assess your own position first, not only for jeopardy, but for the price you'll pay.

The best course just now is to tackle the problems that will have a constructive result; direct your cold, harsh energy into areas that can improve your environment.

Saturn trine Mars: You have a controlled vigor that cries out for constructive application. You want to get to work to accomplish something; your endurance and energy are such that difficult problems are an exciting challenge, and even your sex energy is subordinated to the construction of a specific goal. You may feel impatient at restrictions, and may push or drive to do things your own way. Use that self-discipline and drive to a good purpose so as not to antagonize others.

Saturn sextile Mars: As you have a cold, clear, driving energy, use it to constructive purpose to accomplish specific goals. Efficiently organize your time and efforts to cover all the routine and tedious duties and not scatter your force. Meet challenges directly, using your sense of caution to not be rash, and you can find more opportunities to advance the matters that you desire.

Saturn semisquare Mars: You want to organize and direct your energies constructively, but the matters you attack won't stay still and fight. Plans are changed or cancelled, or the routine matters that you commence turn into blunt encounters. During this time your ingenuity and effort are required to counter trying and irritating affairs.

Saturn sesquisquare Mars: Your energy may be acattered just now, as a variety of inconsistent responsibilities and jobs demand your time and effort. You may feel some hostile resentment at being used or abused, and may jump from methodical caution to rash impulse. Restrictions hamper you, and your desires beckon. Try to hold a consistent routine to work out trying problems, and direct your energy toward a constructive goal.

Saturn conjunct Jupiter: New doors are opening up to you; don't be afraid to step through! It's a serious matter to expand your profession or your public standing; have faith in your own ambitions, and grow. You can meet new people, some of whom may be important, wealthy, or notable. With organization, caution, and planning, with fortitude and maturity, with work and responsibility, you can move ahead. It's a slow, steady, uphill period of growth.

Older or stable people will help you, and your needs will be met. The work you've done in the past will pay off. Your stability will help your judgment. By putting yourself in a responsible position you can gain credit and importance.

Legal and financial matters gradually improve. Your education, speaking, or public appearances are well worth the work they require. Business travel is favorable. Purchases and expenditures are not rash but well thought out for maximum value.

Saturn opposite Jupiter: The work that seems like dull, tedious routine at this time is actually laying a foundation for further education and growth in the future. As much as you may want freedom, adventure, or more abundance of benefits, it's requisite just now that you put in a maximum of steady, serious, responsible work. In this way you gradually expand to better conditions. Your philosophy can grow and sustain you. Church, school, or professional work, or public appearances require a firm foundation of methodical study and preparation.

Your needs are modest, as you are wisely cautious about expenses at this time.

Saturn square Jupiter: Work hard for that advancement or that goal of greater abundance. It's there, waiting for you to keep looking and keep trying. Put in extra hours, volunteer, persevere, and work through the obstacles and delays. New vistas can open up for you if you take the responsibility and don't limit yourself.

In legal and financial matters your natural caution and prudence are wise at this time. Small expenses may be restrictive.

If you feel a conflict between your need of security and your need of freedom, look for the wisest area of growth that will not be at the expense of others. You do find serenity and satisfaction in steady, responsible work that develops your future.

Saturn trine Jupiter: This is a good period in which to take on the responsibilities that will enlarge your education and experience, and advance your life style to a more expansive, optimistic view.

Business, professional, and economic moves tend to be made with good judgment and luck. Important older or stable people help you. There is pleasure and satisfaction in the work and responsibility that give you greater control of your own freedom. In church or school work, and in public appearances, you are recognized for your dignity and maturity.

Influences are favorable for real estate and long-term investments, legal and financial organization, publication, and business travels.

Saturn sextile Jupiter: New doors can open for you; with a mature and responsible attitude, take a deep breath and move ahead. Enlarge your philosophy, your education, and your experience. If there is conflict between your urge of freedom and your need of security, your growth is more opportune with slow, steady, cautious steps.

Business and economic moves are favored, as your judgment is sound and money sufficient to enhance your life style. Influences are favorable for management and organization of real estate and long-term investments, as well as legal and financial planning, church and school matters, publications, and travel.

Saturn semisquare Jupiter: Your present restlessness and urge to leave dull, tedious restrictions are premature—it's not quite time to take that step of growth. Make careful plans, consider your moral, legal, and financial responsibilities, and take the preliminary steps slowly. With preparation you'll soon be ready to take the next step of expansion in your profession, legal, or financial affairs, in your school or church work, or in your personal experience. Weigh your decisions carefully and lay a secure groundwork—it's not time to bust out just yet.

Saturn sesquisquare Jupiter: You may be looking forward to steps of expansion to break up your present conditions of lack or restriction. Keep working at it with perseverance, planning, and holding a conservative program. The new situation of growth is pending and can suddenly fall into place in the near future. New doors can open in your career or profession, in financial and legal affairs, church or school work, and in expansion of your personal freedom and experience.

Saturn conjunct Saturn: You tend to take on more hard, tedious, methodical, industrious work at this time. Your conditions can be highly restrictive, as your money is tight or tied up; your job or career is demanding of your time and effort; and your personal environment limits you to less freedom of motion or choice.

You have a debt or duty to others. If you are taking on more responsibility for constructive ambitions there can be great security, stability, and satisfaction of accomplishment. There is someone who is supportive and stands by you.

But if your ambitions are for ego-centered selfishness you may find yourself used, abused, in debt, or in trouble with your career or reputation. There is a condition in your life that is a payoff for prior character commitments; either in achievement and results, or in a hard lesson to learn.

With patience, perseverance, discipline, and steadfast effort you can pay off old obligations and establish long-range goals for the future.

Saturn opposite Saturn: Conditions at this time are highly restrictive and demand tedious, methodical, industrious work, or patience and discipline. Money may be tight or debts pressing; your job or career takes steadfast effort, and your personal environment is limiting your freedom of choice or control.

If you have unpaid financial or moral debts, you could find yourself used, abused, or alone, with a loss of credit and with trouble in your career and reputation. In your ambition the obstacles seem to drag on interminably. The results are not commensurate with the work you've put in and you just can't seem to break through or get ahead. With maximum responsibility and perseverance you *can* establish an ambition that is constructive and enduring in long-range goals, but it will not happen unless you keep after it with steadfast effort.

You may feel a sense of loneliness, loss, and insecurity; life seems tedious and routine without much fun. A person close to you may be cold, disappointing, or a heavy burden, or self-involved with overwork and problems. To keep the security of a safe harbor in your personal environment, be supportive of those who need you, but be aware that your own dependency needs cannot be met if you close yourself off.

Saturn square Saturn: Your work may seem tedious, dull, boring, and restrictive at this time. Your freedom of choice is limited; money can be tight or tied up; your job or career demands time and effort; and you may feel that life has settled into an endless rut.

A person who is close may be cold, disappointing, troubled, depressed, or overworked, or a heavy burden or loss.

Old obligations must be met, and perhaps hard lessons learned. With patience and perseverance, work hard with calculating ambition for the long-term goals you wish to establish. Gain your satisfaction of accomplishment for doing your duty. Though your responsibilities are a drag that you may resent, they must be met. Organize your life to keep a secure order.

Saturn trine Saturn: The methodical, steadfast, persevering effort you put into matters will pay off in enduring structure and form. You can meet and finish old debts and obligations, complete hard lessons, plan and organize better patterns for a more secure future. Patience, dignity, industry, and responsible ambitions can give you a great satisfaction of accomplishment.

If someone in your life is worried, depressed, or a burden, you can be supportive and stand by them with strength of character and endurance. If your personal conditions are restrictive, your traditional values and established habits will give you stability of purpose and an inner security.

Work hard for long-range goals and you can achieve something of permanent and lasting value.

Saturn sextile Saturn: You can establish patterns of stability at this time by taking the opportunities to advance your ambitions in orderly, conservative steps. With patience and perseverance, work with methodical industry toward long-range goals that give you the satisfaction of accomplishment.

If you feel tired, that money is tight, your job is tedious, or your personal conditions are restrictive, you can gain a greater sense of security by organizing your affairs into a stable order. Be supportive and conscientious with dependents, and pay off old debts and obligations.

Saturn semisquare Saturn: There can be some intermittent responsibilities at this time that are dull or tedious. A restriction or lack in your work or goals is worrisome, and you may feel impatient at limitations and delays. Stick to it! Problems and obligations require patience and perseverance to turn them to organized and regulated stable patterns. With steadfast effort you can pay off old debts and achieve ambitions of enduring accomplishment.

Saturn sesquisquare Saturn: There may be a breakup of conditions in your work and responsibility at this time as you finish past obligations and pay off debts. Your own stability can be inconsistent as your organization is erratic. There can be a sudden restriction or criticism that is agitating, and your tendency may be to rebel at the limitations and delays.

Keep to your duty with enough flexibility to finish old jobs and be ready for new ones. For your own security, reestablish your work on a more methodical basis. Stick to that constructive ambition.

Saturn conjunct Uranus: Give form to your original ideas. With a sense of duty and responsibility, plan and organize the areas in your life that you can change to gain greater control and independence. Put your creative and innovative ambitions to practical use.

Your work may be unusual at this time, with sudden changes and unexpected responsibilities. Unstable conditions may require that you juggle and regulate your time to finish old patterns while laying a secure groundwork for a new step. If you feel that your duties limit your independence, or that ties from the past delay your new beginnings, restrain that urge to force change. Keep at your work; this is a preparatory period to a new chapter in your life.

A person you've known for a long time could leave your life, or else have a deeply serious, sudden concern for which you must be supportive. You could meet a new person at this time who is a catalyst to your own unconventional ambitions.

Saturn opposite Uranus: New conditions take a lot of work, and matters that you want to change tend to delay. Maximum responsibility and discipline are required to handle sudden or unusual circumstances, or matters that are not customary to you. Your independence is restricted, and though you may wish to rebel, you must conform to the limitation of stringent necessity.

There is tension between traditional establishment and your own urge to be creative, original, and innovative. Your own conservative attitudes are challenged by conditions that demand ingenuity and efficiency to give form to new concepts.

Sudden and unexpected responsibilities take work and effort. Even if you feel that duties are tedious, you must complete the obligations before you can start the next chapter in your life.

Other people could be undergoing disturbing changes that require your time and effort to be supportive. A new person you meet at this time could be a catalyst to your own future directions.

Saturn square Uranus: You may feel a great loss of security at this time as new and unexpected matters suddenly bring changes to the secure order of your life. With a deeper sense of duty and responsibility you have to cope with high nervous tension, fear, rebellion, or erratic patterns in yourself or in those around you. Your independence is limited, and you may have extra work that is restrictive.

Those in control may be critical to your career or job, and certain people are being unconventional or unstable in your personal affairs. A person may leave your life, or have a sudden stringent problem for which you must be supportive. A new person you meet at this time could be a catalyst that stimulates your ambitions to independence or changes.

Saturn trine Uranus: There are sudden, challenging, and exciting changes in your work and responsibilities. You may take on a position of greater control or of independent effort to further your ambitions. Your work can be unusual or innovative, and your shrewd calculations and planning are effective in developing an original approach to traditional situations. This is an excellent time to start a new job or go into a new environment, as you feel secure, efficient, and capable. You could get a new appliance or a car.

People in your life for whom you have responsibility are becoming more independent, and new people you meet at this time can be interesting to work with. You could meet a long-term, dynamic acquaintance with whom there would always be a measure of tension and excitement.

Saturn sextile Uranus: There can be a sudden change or an unusual opportunity in your work and career. By taking on more responsible patterns, you can organize your affairs with originality and ingenuity in a way that improves the secure order of your life. Sudden encounters may challenge your independence and freedom of choice; with shrewd planning and calculation, try new and original ways to put innovative ideas into practical form.

People in your life for whom you have responsibility are being more independent, giving you greater control of your own unconventional interests. New people you meet at this time can be interesting to work with, or may even open a new door of novel experience.

Saturn semisquare Uranus: Your work and responsibility are subject to erratic changes at this time. You could feel sudden brief losses of security as the stable order of your life is thrown off balance with others' unexpected criticism or independence. There may be restlessness or high tension in yourself and in those around you. Meet new conditions with a sense of duty, and calculate how to make original solutions practical.

Persons you've known for a long time could leave your life, or be vacillating about their responsibilities and changes. Don't count on new people you meet, as they are unstable and could be a worry.

Saturn sesquisquare Uranus: Your work and responsibility are subject to erratic, inconsistent changes at this time. It will require your ingenuity, shrewd calculation, organization and planning to cope with sudden and unexpected situations that tend to break up and reform. Though you may feel a high tension of independence, stay with your duty.

As new people you meet at this time are for the most part unstable, don't count on them; but there can be one person who acts as a catalyst for a new chapter in your ambitions.

Saturn conjunct Neptune: Your specific duties may be a little vague just now. Though you are trying to form order out of chaos, or to hold a nebulous condition together, you're not able to grasp all the complexities. Certain other people seem incompetent, unreliable or lazy, late or disorganized.

You may be working to attain an ideal but, like Don Quixote, find yourself tilting at windmills. Though your work inspires you, and you believe in its practical value, there can be some worry, anxiety, and frustration; you'd like to be done with it.

Community activities with music, drama, charity or social work, or promotional concepts can take form gradually with stable results; perhaps not all you'd envisioned, but with some specific conclusion.

The practical effort you put into consideration for others will certainly be acknowledged. There will be at least one person supportive of your sensitivity.

Saturn Opposite Neptune: The secure order of your life could be subject to chaos at this time, as a strange and nebulous condition would require practical effort to correct.

Your imagination can be stimulated to unrealistic ambition. You could be inspired, as was Don Quixote, to charge at windmills, or to abandon your duties and follow a dream. Take only what is real and true for you. That fascinating person with the promotional idea could indeed touch your ideals, but if the promise is for a great return on very little investment, you could be fooled.

Schemes, romantic glamour, drugs, deceptions, fraud, or mystical divine intercession are vague and potentially scandalous.

If that promise is for a better condition that is practical, useful, and that takes perseverance and discipline, it can have an ideal outcome.

Take what you want and pay for it.

Saturn square Neptune: You could feel a vague anxiety or worry at this time as the secure order of your life seems to be dissolving. A person or matter you were sure of is unstable just now, or in a strange shifting pattern that leaves you confused. There are obstacles to your control, you're not sure of what your responsibilities are in this present nebulous condition, and you may exaggerate your sensitivity.

If there are deceptions, drugs, schemes or hidden matters in your life that could cause scandal, you have cause for fear or guilt. Business or financial promotions require a great deal of caution as they may be unrealistic or incompetent.

Hold onto a secure serenity in your own ideals; work for a better community effort that will improve your surroundings; take responsibility for those who need your consideration; beware of lies or tricky deals, and this period can stabilize into better conditions.

Saturn trine Neptune: The responsibility that you put into the work in which you believe can bring you an ideal condition at this time. With stability, you can hold safely and securely to a matter that may appear to be vague and unstable. If other people are being strange or unrealistic, you can be the considerate, supportive, practical idealist.

Your community service and involvement can have concrete results in form. Aesthetic, musical, dramatic, mystical, charitable or social work activities may be presented as a polished product, to inspire people and catch their imagination. You can promote your ambitions and have some reward for your hard work.

Stable conditions that seem to be dissolving are actually opening up new possibilities for a dream to come true. If you put the work behind it, you can achieve an ideal.

Saturn sextile Neptune: There are opportunities now to reach out for that ideal condition of which you've dreamed, and to put it into practical form. With planning, organization, and imagination you can work for that vision and make it real.

If someone is being elusive or unrealistic, you can gain more stability with practical idealism than with exaggerated anxiety. As a certain stable condition seems to be dissolving, there could be some chaos, but you can easily organize this into a secure result.

Community involvements in aesthetics, music, drama, charitable or social work can promote your ambitions. Business matters respond well to practical, shrewd, calculating schemes and imaginative efforts.

Saturn semisquare Neptune: In your work and responsibilities there can be vague disappointments, strange restlessness, worry or anxiety at this time. The secure order of your life is subject to loss of control, or some matter seems to be dissolving, and you're not sure how to handle yourself or what to do in this situation. Your specific duties are a little vague, and your efficiency may tend to be a bit muddled.

Sit tight, face up to the jobs you must do, and try not to exaggerate your worries; it will straighten out as you keep a steady hold on your own practical beliefs.

Saturn sesquisquare Neptune: There can be a breakup of conditions in your work and responsibilities just now that gives you worry and anxiety. Your jobs are inconsistent, and your specific duties are nebulous. Someone in your environment may be unrealiable or elusive, and it's difficult to organize an unstable matter.

Though you may wish to be done with the whole affair, mundane demands insist that you cope with day-to-day adjustments in your community involvements.

Work hard, stay with it, hang onto your own ideals, and the efforts you make will create better conditions in your long-term ambitions.

Saturn conjunct Pluto: You have a responsibility for the welfare of your group, team, party affiliation, or organization. With serious ambition, you can work with determination, concentration, compulsive drive, efficiency, and purpose. Your contribution can strengthen the force of the whole program; you do your best by cooperating with your coworkers and those in positions of power.

If you're starting a new job, it can be quite a project. There can be a massive amount of work that involves the organization of various units to complete a total. You could be attracted to a situation that involves mass production or syndication, but where you are the only one who can do this particular job.

In your private life you may well be concluding a cycle. Though you may feel restricted by compelling circumstances and frustrated by your limitations, you must complete your present activities and manage old responsibilities and debts. Profound changes in your long-range plans may be imminent; they will be in full force within a year or less. You can lay firm foundations at this time for your own greater security and more powerful control.

Saturn opposite Pluto: To advance the welfare of all those in your group, party affiliation, or organization, you must keep at your work with drive, efficiency, and purpose. Even if you feel restricted by compulsive circumstances or coercive people, the best long-range result will come from your efforts to cooperate with your coworkers and with those in power.

Some collusion or insubordination could challenge your control and force you into taking greater responsibility. A massive amount of work is required to coordinate an efficient, well-organized situation; it seems that you are the only one of the team who can do your particular job.

Keep your nose to the grindstone, as you are completing a cycle. Profound changes in your life can come out of your present determination, concentration, and focus of purpose, that will be apparent within a year or less.

Saturn square Pluto: In your team, party affiliation, or organization, there are obstacles of insubordination, resistance, and uncooperative attitudes. Some persons may be in collusion to your disadvantage in trying to manipulate or undermine you, and those who wish to be helpful don't have the power to do the job for you. Keep at your own work and ambitions with determination, concentration, drive, efficiency, and purpose. Though you may be restricted by compulsive circumstances or coercive people, your best long-range results will come from your efforts to cooperate with your coworkers and those in positions of power. If negotiation and compromise do not keep order, it may be necessary for you to deliver an ultimatum, in order to keep control.

The responsibilities you carry can affect the welfare of your entire group. Apply serious, intense effort to your present demanding activities, and it will lay firm foundations for a secure future.

Saturn trine Pluto: You can work with your group, team, party affiliation, or organization as a key figure. As you cooperate with others for the good of the whole, your own position will gain in stature. Older persons and those in power recognize your potential force and will work with you to full capacity. If there are hidden factors, secret collusion, or manipulation in your life, it will come to the surface where you can gain control.

Your work can involve the organization of various units to complete a total, in a situation of mass production where you are the only one on the team who can do a particular job. Keep at it with determination, concentration, drive, efficiency, and purpose.

A period of restriction in your life may be reaching completion, to pave the way for a new cycle. Lay firm foundations in long-range goals to take on a greater level of responsibility.

Saturn sextile Pluto: In your work, you can easily elicit the cooperation of others by keeping alert for the opportunity to take on more responsibility. In your group, team, party, or organization, older persons or those in power will acknowledge your potential and give you that chance to prove yourself. You gain control through pleasant negotiations and agreeable efficiency rather than by manipulation or collusion with a faction.

You can work out the restrictive factors or get around coercive people by your own quiet determination. Constructive responsibilities will lay certain foundations that are enduring to the benefit of a future cycle.

Saturn semisquare Pluto: You may vacillate between cooperative responsibility and inflexible resistance in your work. If you feel manipulated by a coercive person, or by underground collusion, you may be undecided about the extent of compromise you can make without losing control.

This wavering weakens your position. Determine your responsibility in this matter, and be fully cooperative to that degree. Beyond that, make a firm resolution that sets a precedent. By making your own position clear you can sway others to the course of greater good for all concerned.

Saturn sesquisquare Pluto: Your work and responsibility may be inconsistent at this time, with sudden compelling circumstances that demand your efficiency and cooperation. Your own control may be weakened by unexpected resistance, collusion, or insubordination. Reversals and detours bring nervous tension and frustration, and your urge may be to break out of restrictive circumstances with independent force.

As this period is unstable, compromise with those in positions of power for the welfare of all who are involved. Complete your present activities to pave the way for a pending change of cycle.

94

Uranus transits the horoscope in eighty-three years nine months three days. Approximately every seven months Uranus has an apparent retrograde motion that lasts close to five months. In its eighty-four-year cycle, Uranus will conjunct and oppose each planet once; square, trine, sextile, semisquare, and sesquisquare every planet twice. An aspect it makes near the change of station will repeat three times.

The mean motion of forty-two seconds a day is the average daily motion of Uranus between its stationary position and the maximum of four minutes daily. When moving at maximum, Uranus has a one-month influence of one degree applying and one degree separating to partile. When slowing to change of station, the aspect orb time is three to four months. However over the change of station period, Uranus may engage a planet three times in a nine-month period. During these times the influence is valid from the first contact through the last, and marks that year intensely.

Uranus goes through one sign in seven years.

Though transit planets are impressionable to the natal chart and seldom influence the major progressed planets, in the case of Uranus, Neptune, and Pluto, their major progressed position is only one to three degrees more or less than the natal; aspects made by transit planets *to* Uranus, Neptune, and Pluto obviously affect the natal and progressed position. Therefore *any transit to Uranus, Neptune, and Pluto will have a larger orb range.*

The aspects *of* transit Uranus, Neptune, and Pluto have striking dynamics in effect.

Uranus is the significator of change; its value in our lives is to bring us abruptly to the end of one chapter and the beginning of another. The matters we have outgrown are suddenly, often unexpectedly, passe, and we are thrown into a period of chaos out of which we must formulate new insights and realities. It is the process that Descartes described as thesis, antithesis, synthesis.

Interestingly, the Moons of Uranus move in a direction opposite from most solar bodies, and the effect of a Uranus aspect is often that of eccentricity, of going against the ordinary, usual, and customary. Independence as self-reliance is admirable but as perversity and separation it can be disturbing. We tend to disassociate with a Uranus aspect, to walk with one foot in the past and one in the future. There can be a high-tension nervous estrangement with the Uranus-crazies.

We are none too subtle as we make this change from past to future. Our whole environment seems to be unstable and erratic; our interaction with other people is markedly affected. People we have known in the past return to our lives, perhaps as brief reminders. We meet new people who are for the most part a transitory influence, but who may act as the catalyst for our unconventional patterns of growth toward greater independence.

The very nature of Uranus is unusual and exceptional. From the beginning to the end of the aspect there is an insistent urge for change, but the timing is unpredictable. If that change is made at the beginning of the aspect it will be subject to reversals and detours. If made at the end of the aspect it can indeed close a chapter of life, to start another.

No matter what we anticipate, Uranus always throws us a curve, brings us something unpredictable.

Uranus conjunct Sun: This can be quite a period of change for you, going into places and situations where you've never been before and meeting new people who are interesting and dynamic. An entire new area of experience can open up for you.

As you feel restless and dissatisfied with customary matters and people, you may act with volatile rebellion toward tradition. An old relationship may disintegrate or shift to a different basis. A man in your life may be detached or separative; willful or perverse, or may make assertive changes. A sudden infatuation tends to be disruptive, exciting, and tempestuous.

If you are a shy or quiet person you may disassociate in periods of withdrawal. If you are a high-tension person you could be extremely nervous and erratic, with a tendency to kick over the traces and take off in five directions at once. If you are set in your ways this time may be disturbing due to unexpected events and sudden changes.

Vital interests can develop in astrology, occult sciences, inventions or discoveries, electronics, and fields of private enterprise. You are stimulated to work alone or in areas where you have a greater control of your own independent expression of authority.

Uranus opposite Sun: You may feel a volatile urge to change your situation at this time, to break old patterns and assert your individuality. You're apt to be more erratic and willful than usual, restless, dissatisfied, and rebellious toward convention.

If you make a move or change your position, it can turn your life upside down and require maximum ingenuity to readjust under conditions that are in total contrast to your customary life style. This is exciting and stimulating, but also causes high tension.

If circumstances block your independent moves, new experiences nonetheless do open up to you vital interests in unconventional subjects. New people you meet are interesting and dynamic, unusual or crazy, disruptive, and magnetic. A sudden infatuation could key you up to a peak of excitement and drop you in equally sudden detachment.

There can be demands that you stand on your own feet under unstable conditions of change. Your tendency may be to disassociate in independent withdrawal, or to kick over the traces to get away from it all, but circumstances are such that you must use your insight and originality to be yourself.

Uranus square Sun: You can be feeling independent and rebellious at this time, with the urge to break old patterns and assert your individuality. Routine and tradition are boring; you may want to move, change jobs, or break off old relationships.

Certain matters can be in an unstable period of turmoil that makes it difficult to set firm plans. Though new conditions are exciting they may need a little more time to mature before you can relax that nervous tension. It's not the best time to take off in all directions at once or to kick over the traces. Your patterns are apt to be too erratic; a sudden decision may be premature. Carefully weed out the areas you have outgrown, make ingenious inventive plans to the extent of your insights and conscious understanding, and toward the end of this period you'll be better prepared to make the changes you want.

Express your individuality in fields of occult studies, discoveries, unusual hobbies, or private enterprises.

Uranus trine Sun: Interesting and exciting changes can occur in your life during this period. You can go into new and novel situations and meet with people who are dynamic and stimulating. Though new people who come into your life just now are not indicated to be enduring, they nonetheless open doors of insight and experience that will always be of help to you.

In the sciences, astrology, and occult studies you are intuitive, inventive, and original. In your fields of private enterprise you have more ambition to make your own mark in a step of independent growth. On the whole you're more inclined to leadership and individuality; a sudden activity can possibly give you unexpected authority or acclaim.

Uranus sextile Sun: There are opportunities in your life to make interesting and exciting changes. New and novel situations present interesting and dynamic people who open new doors of experience, insight, and personal change. It's a good time to advance your independent activities of private enterprise. With a nervous verve, you can assert your individuality and take a step forward.

Interests in astrology, the occult, or the sciences open up areas of intuition, and unusual hobbies can unexpectedly catch your attention.

Uranus semisquare Sun: There can be vacillating periods of nervous restlessness; sudden changes and upsets are disturbing. Your individuality may be blocked; you may tend to unstable detachment or to erratic independence.

Moves or changes are not timely, but stable conditions cause tension. To handle this dilemma, put that volatile tension into original hobbies, occult interests, or independent enterprises. Breaking old patterns and relationships is premature; weed out the areas you've outgrown and make ingenious plans for changes toward the end of this period.

Uranus sesquisquare Sun: Changes may be erratic and unsteady at this time; you tend to feel nervous, restless and dissatisfied. You may be detached, jumpy, and may feel the urge to kick over the traces and break old patterns.

Work it out from day to day; if you jump into major changes, they are unstable. Carefully weed out the areas you've outgrown and make ingenious, inventive plans to the extent of your insight. Toward the end of this period you'll be better prepared to make the independent changes you want.

Uranus conjunct Moon: During this time there can be changes in your domestic life that range from moving the furniture to moving your life around. Your day-to-day activities fluctuate in unusual ways; you may not always know how many people, or who, will be at the dinner table—or whether you will be! You can have unexpected company, visiting relatives, or have a family member move in or out.

Though you tend to nervous moodiness or erratic disposition you also have a magnetic sparkle. As your creative imagination and unconscious intuition are increased you have a greater feel for music, mood, sudden empathy, and a feel for the public pulse. You could easily be accumulating more possessions, trading or dealing with commodities or real estate.

Women tend to be unstable, erratic, or independent at this time, with the greater sense of individuality that comes from new experiences and insights.

Uranus opposite Moon: Changes in your domestic life may cause you some nervous moodiness or erratic disposition at this time. It may be necessary for you to be more sympathetic and adaptable to unstable conditions in your home and private life. There could be a need to move the furniture or your personal possessions around, as you have unexpected company, visiting relatives, or a family member move in or out.

Your day-to-day activities fluctuate in unexpected ways; even on the job you're expected to respond to sudden changes on a minute's notice. In trading, commodities, or real estate, unusual conditions can force purchasing decisions that are not timely to your advantage.

Women tend to be emotionally unstable at this time, with nervous health problems, or erratic and independent eccentricities. Handle others with a maximum of tenderness and intuitive understanding in order to make changes for the better in your daily habits and in your domestic relationships.

Uranus square Moon: As you have a strong tendency to make drastic changes in your domestic and private life at this time, you may break with old patterns or traditional values and act in a sudden, unpredictable way.

Relationships can be lost, strained, or unstable. New people, moves, home or job changes now are not indicated to be enduring; your better course is to postpone important decisions until you are less erratic and willful.

Trading, commodities, or real estate can fluctuate wildly, and marketing is highly variable.

Women tend to be emotionally unstable at this time, with sudden or nervous health problems, or eccentric independence. You may be called upon to show tenderness and intuitive understanding in caring for others in need.

You can put your independent or nervous, moody restlessness into moving the furniture, visiting relatives you've not seen in a long time, or taking up unusual hobbies.

Uranus trine Moon: Domestic changes can be exciting during this period; they give you greater feelings of independence and creative imagination. If you are nervous or moody, someone will come along to stimulate your interest. A flow of unexpected company, sudden events, and new situations keeps you on your toes.

The fluctuation of your day-to-day activities brings interesting people and situations to which you respond with a magnetic sparkle. You can move easily into new hobbies and activities.

Trading, commodities, or real estate can present sudden marketing advantages that are highly favorable.

Women are emotionally dynamic at this time, independent and willful. New relationships may not be enduring, but they certainly have impact.

Uranus sextile Moon: Follow up those opportunities to make changes in your domestic and private life during this period. Whether it's moving the furniture, visiting relatives, or handling commodities, trading, and real estate, new situations can suddenly give you a greater range of independence and advantage.

New people may not be enduring in your life, but they certainly have impact; they can open unexpected doors of new insight and experience.

Women are emotionally dynamic at this time, with more independence and originality.

Uranus semisquare Moon: Vacillating changes in your domestic and private life can leave you nervous and erratic. You may have a restless, willful tendency to break with old patterns and traditional values, but either you can't make up your mind or you can't stabilize conditions to make the changes you want. You may have to adapt to visiting relatives or to a family member moving in or out at unexpected times.

Women tend to sudden eccentric independence at this time, or shifting nervous or health problems, to which you must respond with sympathy.

Handle your changes from day to day with intuitive understanding, adapt to those around you with empathy, and your domestic relationships will settle down again.

Uranus sesquisquare Moon: Sudden changes in your domestic life may be inconsistently agitating and unstable at this time. An unexpected setback or detour in your private life requires your ingenuity to cope.

Women can be perversely independent at odd times, with emotional instability or sudden nervous and health problems. If a relationship is broken off, it would have to be reestablished on a different and better basis than before, as the mood, timing and tempo have changed.

Unexpected company, visiting relatives, and unusual domestic conditions could keep you in nervous knots. Be adaptable from day to day.

Uranus conjunct Mercury: This tends to be a stimulating, interesting period in your life, as you are receptive to new ideas and experiences. You may be restless, nervous, curious, and alert, with a high tension of independent thought and radical attitudes.

Your work is apt to be more varied, with changes in schedule and unexpected opportunities for job advancement. Innovative techniques or sophisticated equipment may be employed, or you may get new appliances or a car. If you write or teach, your subject matter will be more original, as you tend to be more progressive, inventive and ingenious in all areas of problem solving. You may take an interest in astrology or metaphysical subjects, science or humanities, or take up an unusual hobby.

Travels or a move at this time would change your life style to give you a more interesting environment and greater independence. There can be sudden news, unusual studies, unexpected communications, and contract revisions. You can meet new people, gain publicity, break old habits and routines, reverse prior beliefs, and open new doors of intuition and action.

Uranus opposite Mercury: This is indicated to be a period of high nervous tension where it may be difficult to relax or sleep. New and unusual ideas are brewing in your mind, and your thoughts are of restless independence. As you're reaching out for original solutions and radical changes, avoid impulsive decisions based on perversity or rebellion. Other people may be unstable, erratic, or disruptive to you. Your routine can change from one day to the next.

Sudden news, contract revisions, or unexpected communications require maximum ingenuity and alertness, as they can bring dynamic changes. If you write or teach, your subject matter can take a more original turn, and you may champion unusual causes or take a contrary stand. In metaphysical subjects, humanities, science or electronics, new information or sophisticated equipment will require that you increase your education.

Sudden publicity, travels, or a move could be unexpected or have an unprecedented effect on your life. Though eccentric, this can be an electrifying time that is stimulated by new experiences and attitudes.

Uranus square Mercury: During this time you may have a high nervous tension that makes sleep or relaxation difficult. New and unusual ideas are brewing in your mind, and your thoughts are of restless independence. You're reaching out for new ideas, original solutions, and radical changes.

A sudden trip or move could drastically change your schedule. You tend to be distracted, excitable, erratic, detached, and rebellious; avoid impulsive and impractical decisions. This is not the time to buy new appliances or a car.

It's a poor time for contracts and publicity, as they may be unstable. Your studies or routine work may be erratic; changing conditions could keep you jumpy. Sudden news or unexpected communications will require that you be ingenious and alert. If you write or teach, your subject matter may take a more original turn; you could take on perverse or unpopular causes.

This period of flux can bring new ideas, people, experiences, and attitudes. You may well weed out and discard deadwood you've outgrown.

Uranus trine Mercury: This is indicated to be a fortunate period of change; your mind is open to new ideas, and you're reaching out with a nervous, curious, alert tension for new attitudes and experience.

There tends to be a shift of emphasis in your work to a different approach or environment. There is less routine and more innovation, new people, variety and sudden progress or publicity. Your contract agreements and communications can include sudden good news. Unusual studies increase your education to advantage. You may take an interest in astrology, humanities, or metaphysics.

A sudden trip or move at this time could be exciting; old habits and beliefs drop away in the presence of new ideas or a different environment.

On the whole, you're moving into a period of greater independence that is stimulating and interesting.

Uranus sextile Mercury: There are opportunities for change at this time. You're feeling restless, nervous, curious and alert for new ideas and experience; it's a good time to keep your eyes open for original people and innovative thought. Accept invitations that take you into a different environment, as someone there may open a new door for you.

Your work tends to be more varied, with sudden shifts in routine or a turnover in the people around you. Unexpected news or publicity, or contract revisions may seem unstable but can be turned to your advantage with progressive attitudes that are open to suggestion.

An unexpected trip or move, a new car or appliance can give you greater independence.

Uranus semisquare Mercury: New and unusual ideas may be brewing in your mind; your thoughts are of change or restless independence. On some days, when your sleep or relaxation has been difficult, high nervous tension can make you irritable.

You're reaching for original solutions to solve problems or improve your condition, but you can't seem to get your scattered information or decisions together. Contracts could be unstable, studies and routine work may be erratic, and sudden news or unexpected communications could make you jumpy.

Take it a day at a time; avoid impulsive and impractical decisions, but keep alert for the new data or education that can unexpedly improve your position.

Uranus sesquisquare Mercury: Changes at this time could be inconsistent and unstable; you are prone to impulsive and impractical decisions. New and unusual ideas may be brewing in your mind, and your thoughts are of restless independence. At odd times, high nervous tension can make you irritable; sleep or relaxation is difficult.

Matters seem to break up and reform with erratic or rebellious communications or sudden news that makes you jumpy. Contracts could be unstable just now, and studies or routine work could have shifting patterns.

Take it a day at a time, and keep alert for new data or information that can unexpectedly improve your position.

Uranus conjunct Venus: Changes in your social life can be exciting and interesting as you meet new people who are dynamic or magnetic. Someone may come into your life who is unusual or independent and who has a marked effect on your feelings; or someone you have loved in the past may return to your life.

Relationships may not be entirely stable at this time; they are subject to sudden changes or unusual circumstances. You have a high emotional tension that is restless and volatile; you may be attracted to unconventional or rebellious social conduct.

There can be sudden changes in your financial position that give you more ease or comfort in your surroundings, and you may spend money for luxury items that are pleasurable. Entertainment, artistic or musical interests will have more creative originality. Decorating or fashion activities will be striking.

This can be a sparkling, magnetic, and happy period, if you don't take off on erratic emotional tangents of indiscretion.

Uranus opposite Venus: Changes in your social life can be unstable and volatile at this time, causing you emotional nervous tension.

Someone may come into your life who is unusual or independent and who could have a marked effect on your feelings, or a person whom you have loved in the past may return to your life. You have a strong tendency to break up old relationships, or someone you love may suddenly have new ideas and erratic behavior.

New relationships or unconventional love affairs are totally unstable and could turn your life upside down. Indiscreet or rebellious social conduct could leave you drained or detached.

Artistic or musical interests, decorating or fashion activities can be pursued with originality and striking taste, but public acceptance of your efforts will not come easily at this time. These matters are too advanced or innovative for conventional recognition.

You may feel it necessary to spend more money on clothes, home or family comforts, or entertainment, and may find your finances suffer erratically.

Enlarge your social circle with interesting people, but try to keep away from emotional tangents and crazy extravagance.

Uranus square Venus: Changes in your social, emotional, or family life during this time can be unstable and unsatisfactory. You may feel restless, nervous and volatile, with a strong urge to break up old relationships and indulge in indiscreet or rebellious behavior.

There are obstacles to your social satisfactions; the people you want to see are independent, unconventional, unstable, or unavailable; and the ones you are in contact with don't seem to fit your interests. You could feel a sudden attraction to a magnetic new friend or lover; this person will leave your life as suddenly as he or she entered, or, if you establish a relationship, at some future time your life will turn upside down with unexpected changes.

You can re-meet people you've loved in the past who are now different; your paths have diverged too widely to resume that same old relationship.

Artistic or musical interests, decorating or fashion activities can be pursued with originality and striking taste, but public acceptance of your efforts will not come easily at this time. These matters are too advanced or innovative for conventional recognition.

Your finances seem to be unstable, to be preventing you from enjoying the comforts and luxuries you'd like.

Enlarge your social circle with interesting people, but try to keep away from emotional tangents and crazy extravagance.

Uranus trine Venus: Changes in your social life can be interesting and exciting as you can meet new people who are dynamic or magnetic. Someone may come into your life who is unusual or independent and who has a marked effect on your feelings. A new friend or lover at this time tends to be unstable, but acts as a catalyst or doorway to a different attitude that changes your life either now or in the future.

Your relationships with persons you have known in the past shift to a new level. If you cannot share your changing attitudes and feelings with them you may go your separate ways; they too are having original experiences and insights. Persons who are solid in your life will accept your originality and respect your individuality.

It's a good time to be independent. Enlarge your social circle with new and interesting people. Others are generous and helpful to you; you may find yourself the center of attention. You're more sparkling, magnetic and vital, with a nervous verve.

There can be sudden changes in your financial position that give you more ease or comfort in your surroundings. If you don't have the cash to spend on luxury items, you will nonetheless receive the help and favors to improve your looks or environment. Artistic or musical interests, entertainment, decorating or fashion activities can show striking taste.

Uranus sextile Venus: There are opportunities for changes in your social life that are exciting and interesting, as you can meet people who are dynamic or magnetic. A new acquaintance who is independent and unconventional could open doors of insight and action to you that will have a marked effect on your attitudes, now and in the future. Relationships that are not entirely stable can be shifted to a new basis.

People are more inclined to be generous and helpful; you may find yourself the center of attention. You may receive a gift, some financial benefit, or sudden approval and good will.

Your artistic or musical interests, entertainment, decorating or fashion

103

activities can be striking and fun, if you're not too unconventional.

Enlarge your social life with interesting people, but try to keep away from nervous, emotional tangents or crazy extravagance.

Uranus semisquare Venus: You may vacillate with erratic indecision in your social life, and detach from an emotional situation. Unexpected behavior with a loved one, or sudden attractions tend to change tempo from day to day. Direct your nervous verve into artistic, fashion or decorating endeavors rather than through unstable relationships that will settle down when you regain your serenity.

Uranus sesquisquare Venus: Inconsistent changes in your social life are unstable and volatile, with varied activities and unusual people around. You may consider breaking off old relationships, or a loved one may be erratic and unstable. Unconventional affairs are exciting but temporary. Enlarge your life with interesting people and striking artistic endeavors, but watch out for emotional tangents or crazy extravagance.

Uranus conjunct Mars: There can be sudden changes in your objective environment—business problems, impulsive, critical, or hostile people, or unexpected reversals of activity. You may detach yourself from competition and change the thrust of your own action as you reevaluate your desires. Some experience can begin and end abruptly that leaves you with an impersonal determination to cut off certain people.

A new sexual relationship at this time can be exciting, but is apt to be socially unconventional and not end as you'd anticipated; your involvement is apt to shift to other interests in the development of your own individuality.

If you have a driving, dynamic nervous energy, you could tend to rash decisions, challenge, and excitement that expose you to risk or danger, but generally your reflexes and coordination are quick and incisive. On the whole, you're most inclined to cold war and detachment. The shift in direction of your energy drive can set a new force into motion that leads to greater independence.

Uranus opposite Mars: There can be abrupt changes in your objective environment—business reversals, job stress, restlessness, or sudden problems, competition, or criticism. Though your tendency is to detach, the stress of circumstances may demand that you make decisions and take action. By meeting challenges directly with courage and honesty you can cut off people or matters that are destructive, or you can eliminate situations that frustrate your aims.

There can be a trauma in your life, as you or another person could be in danger from a sudden accident or surgery. If you feel a nervous, reckless disregard for convention you could run wild or make rash decisions. But on the whole, you tend more to a cold determination of your own independence.

Sexual attention at this time could be unwelcome; it's from the wrong person or is too unconventional in social context. A sudden affair would have little stability and could be under unusual and disturbing conditions. Your steady mate may be absorbed in other matters that are foreign to you.

Uranus square Mars: There can be disturbing changes in your objective environment—sudden trauma or injury, restlessness, or rebellion, explosive nervous tension, competition, or criticism. Job decisions, moves, or business reversals are untimely; they tend to be unstable, perhaps impulsive, and require more effort than you'd considered.

New relationships that are started at this time will always have some note of hostility, strife, or trauma, or else a continual pressure from which you tend to detach. A new sexual affair has little chance of enduring, and your steady partner is either uncooperative, radical, or involved in separate interests.

Unexpected problems can come as a shock, and you may feel isolated and frustrated by abrupt situations. Rather than resorting to independent detachment, make an effort now to combat your problems with a new approach; plan an original course of constructive action.

Uranus trine Mars: At this time you can make constructive changes in your environment by starting a new program of practical action. You can handle competition, criticism, or objective problems with zest; unexpected challenges are stimulating. As you have the energy and determination, you can advance your independence.

If there is a shock, trauma, or radical change in your life, you can handle it with impersonal detachment and resourcefulness. Situations that frustrate your aims tend to drop away or ease off; it's a good time to start new jobs, relationships, hobbies, or decisions of independent enterprise.

Uranus sextile Mars: There are opportunities at this time to get into different activities; changes are stimulating. Where you may have been a detached observer, you can now take action to develop more of your own independent initiative. Competition, criticism, or objective problems can be handled with ingenuity, courage, and skill.

If there is a shock, trauma, or radical change in your life, you're more receptive to a different and constructive approach. There can be a way out of certain old problems to start new areas of challenge.

Uranus semisquare Mars: There may be vacillating changes in your life, now or pending, that cause you to feel restless, nervous, and detached. Job problems or sudden reversals of decision or activity can be irritating and disturbing. The safe order of your life becomes unstable, and you don't seem to care.

There can be sudden friction, erratic competition, strife, or trauma, from which you simply wish to detach and follow your own independent activities.

It is necessary that you make some decision, so be constructive and practical rather than rash.

Uranus sesquisquare Mars: In spite of your urge for change it may seem difficult to take decisive action at this time; objective problems in your environment are unstable. Job decisions, moves, and personal relationships are subject to sudden reversals and inconsistent changes of direction. Your impatience and restlessness are frustrating; you may detach yourself from the situation, to pursue areas of independent initiative.

It's possible to have a sudden trauma, criticism, or explosive strife that's unprecedented. If so, you'd feel rebellious and resentful, with a tendency to cut off that person or matter. Better face it with courage and ingenuity to reach an original solution.

Matters will stabilize more constructively if you keep alert and vigorous in looking for the detour around obstacles.

Uranus conjunct Jupiter: There can be an unexpected change of fortune at this time; sudden situations and events tend to reverse prior attitudes. With independence and great expectations you can expand your philosophy and education. Formal studies of advanced and specialized subjects give you new insights that are broader, more tolerant, and humanitarian. A trip or move gives you more freedom and opens new doors of beneficial experience unprecedented in your life.

In legal, business, or financial affairs you attract good will and assistance in unexpected ways or from unusual sources. An investment at this time may be remarkably lucky; it can pay off at a later date with more increase than you'd anticipated.

You have protection in unconventional aspirations; others are supportive with favors and approval. You may gain recognition or publicity for a rare situation or exceptional quality.

People come into your life who are wealthy or important—professional people, or those in the clergy, academic or advertising fields; foreigners, salesmen, publishers, or lawyers. Someone who is flamboyant, unique, magnetic, and individualistic may influence you to greater independence.

Uranus opposite Jupiter: Unexpected changes or unusual situations at this time demand maximum faith and trust in your own moral judgment not to make erratic decisions. In reaching for more freedom, joy, or affluence you could go overboard with great expectations in an unconventional aspiration. A sudden situation or unusual opportunity may appear to offer the greatest good fortune, so your tendency is to overrate the possibilities, to put your faith in the wrong person, or to bet on the wrong horse. Put your trust only in formal contracts and honorable dealings.

As you tend to be optimistic about a change of fortune you are receptive to crazy, big ideas. In business, financial, and legal affairs, sudden gains can be promising, but they are unstable and, in the long run, promise more than they deliver.

Your experience, philosophy, and education can increase in radical or innovative views, broader insights, and expansion of an independent philosophy. You could gain recognition or publicity for an unusual situation, or for a unique or exceptional quality that you have.

Uranus square Jupiter: New direction, or a change of fortune at this time can meet unexpected setbacks, obstacles, and delays. As matters initially look so promising, your tendency can be to overrate the possibilities, to put your faith in the wrong person, or to bet on the wrong horse.

Someone's crazy, big ideas could be costly in business, financial, or legal

106

affairs. Guard against sudden losses from careless trust or from taking your protection for granted. Matters could promise more than they deliver.

Your religion, philosophy, and education can increase in radical or innovative views, and you can gain recognition or publicity for an unusual situation or for your originality. However your best course of growth and protection lies in maintaining an independent expansion. Put your trust only in formal contracts with honorable people.

Uranus trine Jupiter: This is an excellent time to make fortunate changes; to expand your philosopby, education, and standard of living. Good luck can come in unusual ways or from unexpected sources. As new doors open, people or matters that have hampered your growth tend to drop away to give you more freedom and independence.

You can gain attention, good will, recognition, or publicity for your individuality. As you tend to be more generous, buoyant, optimistic, and humanitarian, honorable people will extend to you their loyalty and support. You could meet more people who are educated, wealthy, or important—people in the professions, academic or advertising fields; salesmen, publishers, laywers, or the clergy. Your business and legal affairs could take a sudden advantageous turn.

Sudden insights into religious or philosophical concepts can make your spirit soar; a new study or unconventional hobby can expose you to a stimulating, different world of ideas and experience. Travels or moves at this time can expand your fortune.

Uranus sextile Jupiter: Be alert for opportunities that can lead to sudden advancement. Good luck can come from unexpected sources, as you come in touch with educated, wealthy, or important people in the professions, the clery, academic or advertising fields; salesmen, publishers, or lawyers.

If you should feel the urge to unconventional self-indulgence, your tendency would be to overrate the possibilities and to put your faith in the wrong person. You have the chance for more freedom and independence that will give you joy and protection in a formal and honorable situation.

Religious or philosophical concepts can expand, and new hobbies or business ventures are favorable to your interests. Travels or moves are stimulating and interesting.

Uranus semisquare Jupiter: Areas of expanding change may vacillate between optimistic stimulation and worrisome instability. A professional, business, financial, or legal matter could be indecisive. Your growth seems to go in fits and starts, as certain matters that you count on may be overrated or have sudden setbacks; other matters that are unprecedented suddenly open new opportunities.

Your religious or philosophical concepts are subject to new data and information that cause you to question your level of trust.

You can grow in independent ventures, hobbies, and attitudes; there can be unexpected good luck, but don't count on big ideas that are crazy; keep a steady level, and trust only formal and honorable contracts.

Uranus sesquisquare Jupiter: Any sudden or pending changes in your life at this time can break up old conditions to give you more freedom and independence. This may cause some agitation; present matters are unstable, and the future seems indefinite. New directions have unprecedented implications, and you're unsure of where to place your trust.

Sudden insights in your religion and philosophy can be disturbing as your faith is shaken.

You're in a period of growth, but it can be erratic and uncomfortable at times. Keep your eyes open for one area of sudden good luck from an unexpected source.

Uranus conjunct Saturn: There are changes brewing in your attitudes and environment that shake up the routine order of your life. People you meet at this time can open unexpected doors that stimulate you to greater personal ambition. By working with an unconventional program, using inventive methods and radical calculations, you lay firm foundations that lead to greater control of your independence in private enterprise.

You may be presented suddenly with unusual responsibilities, or have a change in the authority structure of your job. Though you tend to feel rebellious at restrictions and delays, your perseverance and resolution will pay off by keeping you secure through an unstable period.

A person who is cold, gloomy, a worry, or a handicap may leave your environment. New people, a new job, or a move just now can be a gradual step of improvement that you approach with caution. The changes you want will come as you work for them.

Uranus opposite Saturn: There can be sudden, unexpected, even radical changes in your life that demand maximum calculation, efficiency, planning, and organization on your part. Old or outworn concepts and methods are no longer practical; new and inventive solutions must be found to further your ambitions.

Changes in the authority structure of your profession can thrust you into a position of greater responsibility. There may be electrical or sophisticated equipment, or unusual conditions with your job. You work best with a measure of independence at this time, or in the jobs where you can work alone with your own original approach.

Uranus square Saturn: The secure structure of your life is subject to erratic changes at this time. It may seem that the steady, tried and true is disintegrating into unstable patterns. Nothing is sure or safe; you may tend to disassociate in nervous worry, or to strike out with unexpected actions that are not like you. Sudden or radical changes may give you unusual responsibilities or may demand your planning, organization, and efficiency to cope.

Keep a calculating drive going in yourself; look for insights and original solutions. Though it may be a time of tension and concern it can open a whole new life for you by removing old or outworn matters to give you a greater view of how to grasp your long-term independent ambitions.

Uranus trine Saturn: There may be sudden or unstable changes brewing in your life just now that are cutting off the old, tried and true, secure order of your life. Let go of that which you've outgrown; it's time to move on, move ahead, take the next step. Even if these changes cause you to feel nervous or worried, be assured that they will open new doors that lead to greater independence.

Changes in the authority structure of your job can give you more responsibility. Electrical or sophisticated equipment, or unusual and inventive interests can take form as you advance your ambitious achievements. You can devise original and even brilliant solutions in your work, with greater efficiency, organization, planning, and calculation.

Uranus sextile Saturn: A variety of changes in your work and responsibilities just now open up new opportunities. Pursue the ones that offer greater increase to your capabilities of management and organization. Use inventive and original methods to handle problems and reach practical solutions. If unexpected or sudden opportunities arise that seem to threaten the secure order of your life, calculate how they may advance your ambitions and move ahead accordingly.

Uranus semisquare Saturn: The security of your life may seem unstable just now as there is a variety of erratic changes. The old order of things may be disintegrating, causing you nervous worry. Let go of outworn or impractical concepts, and reach out for the work and responsibility that will advance your long-range goals. Avoid precipitous or radical action but use inventive and original methods to reach solutions.

Uranus sesquisquare Saturn: The secure order of your life is subject to inconsistent changes at this time. You may tend to nervous worry or to radical and impractical actions. Keep a cool, calculating control of your management and organization; new doors are opening that will advance your long-range ambitions. Use original and innovative methods to overcome delays, negotiate detours, and reach solutions.

Uranus conjunct Uranus: (Approximately age 83-85) You're in a time of change that includes vivid insights, eccentric behavior, marked individuality, and periods of disassociation. You are unique as much of your past is not familiar to those around you, and your environment is subject to the influence of new people and unprecedented experiences. People you have known in the past are not the same as you've once known them, and many have left your life. With an alert and progressive attitude, every day can be new to you.

Uranus opposite Uranus: (Age 41-43) You're in a transition period between the past and the future. Matters you've outgrown drop away to be replaced by new conditions and people. You may feel disoriented and detached at times, as familiar situations seem strangely different, and new situations have a disturbing exhilaration. You may swing from indifferent or abstract disassociation to a high tension of nervous independence.

On some days the world may move too fast; sudden and unexpected changes are thrust upon you. With a progressive attitude you find this an exciting period, but it requries maximum ingenuity and originality to adjust.

Your life could be impacted by a new person who is a vital, challenging, and unconventional catalyst. Relationships tend to be unstable; your tendency is to break old ties and form new ones that seldom endure. Familiar people around you are also making changes in patterns and attitudes; at times there can be direct clashes of independence.

A move or job change puts you in a state of flux that will not stabilize until the aspect is completed. Any situation started at this time will not continue as you plan, but will take unexpected turns, reversals, detours, and modifications before it is resolved.

Make your changes. Reach out for unprecedented concepts and new activities. Eliminate the matters that hamper your growth, but don't throw out anything of value.

Uranus square Uranus: (Age 20-21, age 61-63) You may feel that your freedom of choice and action is blocked by continual obstacles; your urge is to break out with a high tension of nervous independence. Your affairs can be erratic and unstable; sudden and unexpected changes further trigger your rebellion. You may be struggling to achieve your individuality with unconventional hobbies and interests.

You could feel disoriented by a move or job change. The effort you put into it would establish a greater level of independence in the long run, but it is not indicated to be enduring or stable at this time.

Relationships tend to be unstable; old ties are strained or possibly broken. Familiar people around you are also making unprecedented changes in patterns and attitudes. A new, magnetic person can enter your life with impact, and can leave as quickly. Any situation started at this time meets with continual reversals, turns, detours, and modifications that require your ingenuity and originality to handle.

If you are unable to make progressive changes you may detach in an abstract disassociation. It is a period of flux; you need to reach out for new concepts and independent activities.

Uranus trine Uranus: (Age 26-28, age 55-57) This can be a most progressive period in your life; you can make a fortunate transition between the past and the future. Matters you've outgrown drop away to give you a greater choice of independent action. Sudden changes, turns, detours, and reversals all work to your advantage.

In a move or job change you can be more original, inventive, and ingenious, with a greater capacity for private enterprise and innovation. An experience or situation started at this time can give you a lifetime benefit.

Your life could be impacted by a new person who will always be an interesting and vital influence. Old relationships that have held a note of tension tend to improve; familiar people are also making changes in patterns and attitudes to match yours.

Though it is a period of flux that can cause some nervous tension, you can be assured that the new doors that are opening lead to more exciting or interesting satisfactions.

Uranus sextile Uranus: (Age 13-14, age 68-70) There are opportunities to make this a progressive period of change. Certain matters you've outgrown will drop away and will be replaced by new conditions and people. You have a choice of independent action; you can detach in independent rebellion or you can reach out to open new doors of original hobbies and unconventional interests.

If you feel that your freedom is blocked, keep your eyes open for turns and detours; a new experience or situation will be available that is beneficial.

New people in your life may not be entirely stable, but they do offer a new outlook or attitude for you to examine. Familiar people around you are also making changes; many relationships seem to be in a state of flux.

You could take on a short-term job or extra activity. A move may shake up your life but does add to your experience in a way that aids your independent future enterprises.

Uranus semisquare Uranus: (Age 10, age 72-74) There may be some unstable changes during this period that hamper your freedom of choice and action. Your affairs could suffer sudden setbacks and disruptions that cause you to feel nervous and tense. Certain matters or people in your life seem to be different; new people or conditions are erratic.

You may feel disoriented or strangely detached at times; at other times you could be excitable and independent. The world may be moving too fast for you. Keep a progressive attitude.

Uranus sesquisquare Uranus: (Age 31-32, age 50-52) There can be some inconsistent and unstable changes during this period; some matters may leave your life to be replaced by new conditions and people. You may feel rebellious at times if your freedom of choice and action is hampered. At other times you may be tense with nervous excitability.

Make your changes in the areas where you can without discarding anything of value. Reach out for new concepts and independent interests. Keep a progressive attitude and readjust your goals to match the pace of the times.

Uranus conjunct Neptune: This period tends to begin with a vague discontent and desire for a change. A matter in your life may be strange and nebulous, with unexpected disappointments and frustrations to your dreams. In moments of detachment you can feel rebellious, with the urge to escape by unconventional conduct.

If you should take drugs you can experience some far-out crazies; and if you should follow perverse or evasive courses, unstable situations will plague you with anxiety and insecurity.

Unexpected events in your community life will bring the changes you want. A new door will suddenly open, and a dream can come true. If you have been striving for independent aspirations based on your individuality and integrity, a new chapter can begin that answers your ideals.

Your community involvement may be unusual at this time. You could easily be attracted to the metaphysical or theatrical, art, music, social work, or visionary concepts. Areas of public service can be highly satisfactory.

New people who come into your life tend to be interesting, fascinating, magnetic, and unstable. If other indications concur, you could take an unexpected trip or vacation that is idyllic.

Uranus opposite Neptune: Changes are nebulously strange and disturbing. Unstable situations bring anxiety and feelings of loss of control and you may detach from your customary community involvements. Alcohol, drugs or medications tend to cause unexpected reactions.

Uranus sesquisquare Neptune: Changes which may look ideal tend to be unstable at this time and you, or someone in your environment, is shifting into different patterns that are elusive and disturbing. Alcohol or other drug habits cause sudden situations or erratic drama. Avoid sudden decisions that are unrealistic.

Uranus square Neptune: This can be a rather strange period of sensitive detachment, with a tendency to retire or escape. You may exaggerate your vague discontent and nebulous anxiety over matters that are suddenly evasive, or unusually competent. You could make impulsive moves and decisions that are out of context with your usual patterns.

Excessive liquor or drugs could lead to delirium tremens, disassociation, or unexpected consequences; at the least, strange illusions. Perverse independence in unconventional behavior, started as a lark, could lead to unstable and potentially scandalous experiences. If not you directly, someone in your environment is practicing deception, concealment, or escape.

A business deal, move, or job transfer at this time could meet unexpected obstacles. If changes are pressing, strive for independent aspirations based on your individuality and integrity. Stringently avoid promotional schemes and the various business and social forms of cheating; you may be the one who has the rug pulled out from under you.

Uranus trine Neptune: Though changes may seem vaguely disturbing at this time, they are indicated to have a favorable outcome. An area of anxiety can be removed from your life; you tend to enjoy more leisure and independence.

Tension areas can be relieved by drugs or liquor, or more naturally by meditation. You may dream of the past, and picture idyllic conditions of the future. Your imagination is vivid and original; creative concepts can show insight and brilliance. Unexpected events can put you in a stimulating communal situation. Reunions with family or old friends are vivid with remembrance and appreciation of the changes that time has wrought.

Retirement, either permanent or temporary, can give you a different level of community involvement in leisure interests. Vacations can take you to historic sites, to your own heritage of the past, or to unprecedented places that you'd never anticipated. You could meet someone during this time who has a marked effect on your own idealistic dreams and visions. You tend to have a sensitive insight into aesthetic concepts, drama, art, or music. Your independent aspirations, ideals, and areas of voluntary public service are acknowledged.

Uranus sextile Neptune: During this period there can be some opportunities to make changes to a more idyllic condition. If these changes are for original independent aspirations, they can take you into a new level of community involvement. But if you feel a vague discontent and sensitive anxiety, it can be a rather strange period of evasive detachment.

There seem to be mixed blessings at this time that require your discrimination in order to avoid perverse and unstable rebellion, but be alert for a business or social opportunity that can open new doors to an idyllic experience. Use your imagination to promote your private enterprise rather than exaggerating any areas of insecurity. Reach out with insight and intuition to explore untouched areas of your own creative vision.

Vacations can be enchanting. You can experience a comraderie with unusual people. You could meet someone who would stimulate your idealism or open up new interests.

Uranus semisquare Neptune: This can be a period of elusive changes; you vacillate between independence and insecurity, between perversity and compliance. Sudden and unusual opportunities can appear fascinating and stir your imagination to explore independent areas of new experience. However you'll have to keep both feet on the ground and hold onto your own insight and intuition in order to not be confused, deceived, or incompetent. Crazy promotional ideas could be as solid as fog.

Avoid drink, drugs, pills, or psychic trips, or you may see little green men from another planet.

New people can be unusual, interesting, and fascinating — but unreal. Cope a day at a time with your areas of service and don't exaggerate. Use independent judgment, and stay in this world!

Uranus conjunct Pluto: In work or play areas involving groups, you can start some new activities, hobbies, or interests. It is necessary that you cooperate with the gang or with your team for the good of all concerned. There may well be an area where you must compromise your independence to the group standard.

If your group is working for a common goal or unified result, you can nonetheless add your own distinctive contribution. Your innovative methods or inventive approach can contribute to the general benefit.

If you should be isolated from group contact at this time, there can be some deep psychological changes as you examine your own areas of repression and rebellion, compulsion and manipulation, segregation and integration. There is a need to belong, to be part of the gestalt, concurrent with a need to individualize; if these areas are not resolved they can create conflicts out of which you form a determination either to be independent or to integrate.

If you attempt to ally yourself with a peer, that one 'best friend' or lover, you may find that you are not on a basis of equitable reciprocity; your cultural and psychological foundations preclude the deep unity you seek.

Changes are not immediately apparent, but either the events or the forces set into motion at this time lead to the elimination and conversion, in the years ahead, of some condition or attitude that had its roots in this period of experience.

Uranus opposite Pluto: The changing times suggest that you cooperate with others for the good of all concerned and let go of compulsively held old patterns that are no longer viable. Develop new interests to keep up with this powerful time of transition. A person who is not appropriate to your present life may have a profound influence; enjoy whatever depth is there and be prepared to release your attachment at any time.

Uranus square Pluto: In work or play areas involving groups, you may find unexpected obstacles to cooperative unity. There may be factions in your gang, team, or collective, led by strong individualists who use coercive or manipulative tactics in their attempt to push through a progressive program. Even if you disassociate from direct involvement in any power struggles, you are nonetheless implicated by association and may be forced into a vote or made to take a stand.

If you try to change your condition at this time, you can meet a high tension of uncooperative resistance. You may feel that certain people or circumstances are closing in on you with a subtle force that robs you of your right of choice; your tendency could be to act with unconventional rebellion or with secretive detachment.

An intensely close relationship may put pressures on you to conform. As you do want that agreement, you may compromise to keep unity, or you may even acquiesce; but there is a tendency to build up an explosive independence.

If you have to go along with the group or the program, try to cooperate for the welfare of others, but meet obstacles with ingenuity rather than compulsive perversity.

Be careful of people who wield an iron hand in a velvet glove. If you have reservations about a situation, better keep your involvement impersonal. Intense commitments just now could turn your life inside out.

Purge yourself of your own destructive habits and patterns; if ruthless changes are inevitable, make them to your advantage and not to your disgrace.

Uranus trine Pluto: In work and play areas involving groups, the gang or team can cooperate for the common good. The stimulating force of a collective goal can regenerate your progressive ideas; with the strength of unity you can make reforms that recognize the rights of the individual within the body of the union. If you have a powerful strength of conviction you will have a sweeping, compelling force that magnetically impels others along with you. Dissenting or uncooperative factions tend to detach themselves or resign from the group - leaving a tight core with a concordant aim.

In personal areas you can have an unusually close bond, an integration or intense commitment with a friend, teacher or peer. This bond can span age, language, and cultural barriers, or even time and distance. In your general contacts with people, there is an unconscious mutual recognition of affinity with those persons with whom you share an equitable reciprocity; a give-and-take on a level of mutual respect that may even be nonverbal.

If you should feel independent, detached, or apart form your present situation, changes can be brewing in you for a new condition that brings out your greater capacity for personal involvement. Though the changes may not be immediately apparent, some activity or attitude that you set into motion now will continue to grow and flourish for your benefit and for the good of others.

Uranus sextile Pluto: In work or play areas involving groups, there can be sudden opportunities that are advantageous for you to pursue. Where the gang or team is cooperating for a common goal, there is a strength of unity that gives benefits to the individual as well as to the whole.

You may be aware of some dissenting factions that try to pressure you into voting or making a commitment, but with your strength of conviction you can take a politic stand of agreement while maintaining your own independence.

In personal areas you may feel a certain detachment from your present situation as this is a period of flux. Strong directions are gradually forming out of your need to be part of an integrated collective, versus your need for individuation. You can cooperate with those persons with whom you share an affinity of common goals, and even form a close lifetime bond at this time with a peer. Toward persons who have a subtle coercive manner of manipulation, you'll feel uncooperative rebellion, and may disassociate from such a relationship.

Though changes may not be immediately apparent, some activity or attitude that you set into motion now will continue to open new doors in the future.

Uranus semisquare Pluto: In work or play areas involving groups, you may vacillate between a close affinity of cooperation and a detached independence. Where your gang or team has a common goal your strength of unity can advance the cause in a way that aids the individual as well as the collective. However, there will be some opposing reactions that cause irritation, as their program tends to be indecisive. Though there are strong individualists, their effectiveness is depleted by unstable agreements.

In personal areas you seem to be in a period of flux. Your need for peer validation varies with a restless rebellion. Even in your close give-and-take relationships you may feel a certain detachment.

Though strong directions for the future are gestating they have not yet taken form. You may feel pressured by circumstances and your own indecision. You can't force a change now; weed out the nonessentials, keep your reservations to yourself, and your determination will take shape for more progressive individuation.

Uranus sesquisquare Pluto: Changes in your gang or team tend to be highly disruptive. Strong-willed persons are making independent moves which are agitating and not what you expected. Don't panic, but step slowly into new situations as you test the level of give-and-take.

IX   TRANSIT NEPTUNE

Neptune transits the horoscope in one hundred sixty-seven years five months seventeen days. Approximately every seven months, Neptune has an apparent retrograde motion of close to five months. In half a cycle of eighty-four years, Neptune will conjunct the planets once in the dexter half of the horoscope, and will oppose the planets once in the sinister half. It may or may not square, trine, sextile, semisquare, and sesquisquare each planet once or twice, depending on the position of Neptune relative to the other planets at the time of birth. An aspect it makes near the change of station will repeat three times, or even five times.

The mean motion of twenty-two seconds a day is the average daily motion of Neptune between its stationary position and the maximum of two minutes (or, rarely, three minutes) daily. When moving at maximum, Neptune has a two-month influence of one degree applying and one degree separating to partile. When slowing to change of station, the aspect orb time is a little over four months. However, over the change of station period, Neptune may engage a planet three times in a year, and possibly five times in two years. During these times the influence is valid from the first contact through the last, and marks that period intensely.

Neptune goes through one sign in fourteen years.

As Neptune is the significator of idealism, its value in our lives is to bring us to a poignant awareness of our personal Utopias. The effect is highly individual; to the aesthetic person, Neptune brings a sensitive, imaginative hunger to believe in and belong to the virtues of purity and service. To the pragmatist, Neptune brings an exaggerated longing for more mundane rewards, perhaps through promotional schemes or complex webs.

Neptune is elusive and subtle; the external effect is extremely hard to pin down and define. Largely, it seems to mark periods of retirement and obscurity, seclusion, and subordination. There is often a note of mystery or confusion, deception and anxiety in the life from some vague source. We are vulnerable with a Neptune aspect, as it touches a hidden secret core.

The measure of the outcome is the measure of our own iniquity, incompetence, eroticism, sensationalism; our own philanthropy, consideration, and voluntary service; our own dream of a better life and a more ideal community. Our phobias are exposed, our illusions are painful, but out of Neptune we bring the dream, the vision of the perfect ethic, the better product, the creative inspiration, and the selfless aspiration.

Neptune conjunct Sun: You have a greatly increased sensitivity during this period; you may feel that the world is brutal or unfair, or that people are crass and materialistic. You are more prone to retire, take a subordinate or compliant role, or seek a seclusive environment. Beware of the extremes of escape, running away, evasion, drugs, alcohol or fantasy. You could be more dreamy, lazy, inattentive, impractical, and imaginative than you've been earlier in your life.

Goals that benefit the community are well favored, such as charity or social work, public service, music, art, drama, poetry, or fields of creative imagination.

Relationships with men can be ideal if based on mutual respect and consideration, but you must be realistic; a man pursuing a private dream of glory or sensation may not be practically beneficial to your life's purpose.

You can find peace and inspiration in meditation or religious mysticism, remembering that spiritual awareness should be applied to daily life for best results. In all matters, keep your integrity, honor, and pride in your own identity.

Neptune opposite Sun: With increased sensitivity at this time, you may feel that present conditions are harsh, unfair, or unsatisfactory. You've dreamed of so much more or so much better than this! Your goals and efforts are unappreciated, and you'd like to escape with drugs, alcohol, negative cynicism, or running away to a desert island with the company funds and your dream-mate. Alas, it would only lead to scandal, muddle, and confusion. Your public service activities are necessary, and it seems you must sacrifice personal ideals to your community position.

During this period relationships may be unrealistic, with exaggerated romanticism or illusions. Your beloved may be unattainable, incompetent, deceptive, or simply absorbed in a private dream world that excludes you. Take care that you're not deceiving yourself—or anyone else. A secret affair could be more disappointing than ecstatic; your lover could be promiscuous, impotent, married to another, or a potential handicap to you. You're better off to stay with the mate and friends you trust and believe in, even though your imagination hungers for something more grand. Relationships you base on mutual respect and consideration can inspire and sustain you.

Keep your feet on the ground. In your private and public dealings conduct yourself with honor, integrity, and pride in your own identity; you *can* achieve the ideal goal for which you've worked and dreamed. In your meditation or contemplation, search for a purity of vision on which to base your deepest goals of significance and maturity.

Neptune square Sun: You may find yourself dissatisfied with your life at this time and reaching out for goals that are bigger, better, grandiose, or ideal. Present conditions seem harsh, unfair, and unsatisfactory; you may dream of schemes with big returns, a perfect romance, or divine intercession.

Be careful! Life is full of pitfalls and deception now as never before nor again. There is actual danger in drugs, alcohol, water, gas, oil, or other liquids. Business or community affairs, especially those that promise big returns, promotional concepts, dealings with aircraft, theatre, aesthetic arts, or incorporation structure deceive you with an unreal fantasy.

A secret romantic affair could be more disappointing than ecstatic; your lover could be married to another, impotent, homosexual, unfaithful, or in some way a potential handicap to you. Take care that you're not deceiving yourself—or anyone else. Strive for relationships based on mutual respect and consideration.

You tend to be more of a pacifist at this time, and may feel that running away or retiring is a solution.

In religious matters you could be attracted to the mystical, cults, or to psychic revelations. Remember that spiritual awareness should be applied to daily life for best results.

In all, your best protection is your own pure motive. Yes, of course, reach for something better in life; you *can* attain your ideals if you work with honor, integrity, and pride in your own identity.

Neptune trine Sun: This can be one of the ideal periods in your life, with increased sensitivity and inspiration. Creative work will flow with an acclaimed brilliance. Community involvement is favorable with business incorporation or promotional concepts, theater or the arts, church, metaphysics, or psychic awareness. Philosophical insight can be applied to daily life with serenity, consideration of others, and a modest sacrifice. You may be awakened to deeper spiritual values by some messenger.

A matter you've dreamed of can come true at this time: an ideal move, trip or vacation, a romance based on mutual respect and consideration, an inheritance or financial return, or a career advantage.

If you feel lazy, dreamy, or retiring, you may relax easily; someone will nurture your seclusion. There is gentle solicitude for your well-being.

Neptune sextile Sun: There is an increased imagination and sense of drama; you could exaggerate your joys or your worries with poignant sensitivity. If you are lazy, dreamy, and retiring, you could be anxious about your goals.

An ideal opportunity may come up for a trip or vacation, an inheritance or financial benefit, a career or avocational advantage, or a change for greater ease and relief from strain. Relationships with your dear ones can offer more consideration and gentle regard.

Involvement in community charity or social work, public service, music, art, drama, or poetry may catch your interest, and may be pursued with creative imagination. Your metaphysical or psychic awareness can be applied to daily life with serenity.

Neptune semisquare Sun: You may feel a vague discontent, worry, and anxiety during this time. Moves or changes you make in your home or career are not working out quite the way you'd envisioned them. Community involvements are not receiving the acclaim you want, and some matter may fall through. Regard all promises with caution, avoid investments or promotional schemes just now, and keep all your affairs on the up-and-up with honor and integrity.

A secret affair would be most unwise; it could be disturbing and could result in a loss to you. Be careful not to deceive yourself—or anyone else. Avoid drugs, be temperate with alcohol, and keep your feet on the ground.

Keep striving for that ideal condition, with serenity and with consideration for others.

Neptune sesquisquare Sun: A certain matter in your life comes up suddenly that may cause you feelings of loss or anxiety. Other people may be highly unstable, or there could be confusion, distress or disappointment. Beware of incompetence, exaggerated promises, or vague commitments, whether in business schemes or personal involvements.

Continue to strive for your community, public service, or aesthetic goals in spite of the disruptions, in order to achieve that ideal result. Put your trust in relationships of mutual respect and consideration. Look for peace and inspiration in meditation or contemplation, remembering that spiritual awareness should be applied to daily life for best results.

Neptune conjunct Moon: Sensitivity of your mood is increased, giving you a greater understanding of women and children. Your feelings probably will be more tender, sympathetic, considerate, submissive, and compliant. As you care for those who need you, you attract warmer empathy from others.

Family vacations, outings, and reunions are indicated. All domestic relationships tend to greater ease and less effort, even though there may be anxiety or concern over one of the family members. Your home life can give you something ideal of which you've dreamed, or you can envision plans for the perfect home that you want.

You have a feel for the public pulse; your creative imagination can bear fruit, with music, drama, or the arts, or in business matters relating to commodities or promotional schemes of benefit to the masses.

Avoid reminiscences or negative impressions, lazy inactivity, or psychic daydreaming, but draw on your meditative sensitivity to make a better private life.

Neptune opposite Moon: Solutions may be needed for family and domestic problems that are vague, complex, or tied into confusion and muddle. Your feelings tend to be hypersensitive and moody; you may feel rejected, anxious, and overemotional. You may dream of running away, or you may imagine escape in drugs, liquor, strange and erotic or psychic fantasies. If these fantasies are extreme, have your functional health and glandular balance checked.

Women or children tend to be deceptive at this time; they unintentionally lack the feelings of sympathy and consideration you are looking for. One family member may be the cause for concern, and it seems you must respond with care and empathy.

Try not to exaggerate negative impressions or to dwell on moody reminiscences. Lazy inactivity, or a mystical daydreaming, will not manifest solutions for you; draw on a meditative serenity to make a better private life.

Your imagination is keen; creative pursuits in music, drama, or the arts, can be an outlet, and you can be involved in areas of public service. Regard with caution any business matters relating to commodities or promotional schemes; they may be exaggerated.

Neptune square Moon: Family and domestic matters can present certain obstacles to your serenity; your home can seem unstable or vaguely disappointing. A family member or some woman in your life can cause you concern and anxiety and may require special care and solicitude.

Your own feelings tend to be compliant and submissive or hypersensitive, impressionable, and moody. You may dream of running away, or may imagine escape in drugs, liquor, psychism, or strange erotic fantasies of romantic situations. If you should feel rejected, anxious, and overemotional, you may need to have your functional health and glandular balance checked.

Draw on a meditative serenity to assure a better private life; put some effort into sympathetic consideration for others. Pursue your creative imagination in music, drama, or the arts; work with foods, commodities, or in public service, but regard promotional or incorporation schemes with caution.

Neptune trine Moon: This can be an ideal domestic period for you; your home will seem more comfortable, or you may even find your dream home. Family and domestic relationships are serene, with tenderness, sympathy, consideration, and fun. A woman in your life can be empathetic and compliant to your wishes. Family vacations, outings, and reunions can be easy, if not idyllic.

You could have a dream come true at this time—at the least, receive a provision, or enjoy more leisure or enchanting satisfactions. A strain or pressure area tends to smooth out, so you can relax with relief and appreciation.

In your feel for the public pulse, your creative imagination can bear fruit in music, drama, or the arts, in business matters relating to commodities or the masses, or in promotional schemes for the public welfare.

Neptune sextile Moon: There are opportunities to improve your domestic life with greater ease, comfort, or even luxury. Family relationships are harmonious as you cultivate more understanding, tenderness, and consideration.

If you're lazy, daydreaming, woolgathering, or taking drugs or alcohol, you'll miss out on some of these chances; use this time wisely to gain the benefit.

In your feel of the public pulse, your creative imagination can bear fruit in music, drama, or the arts. You can advance business matters relating to commodities for the public needs, or promotional schemes of service to the masses.

Neptune semisquare Moon: The serenity of your domestic life may vacillate with some intermittent family problems that cause irritation and anxiety. Your home may seem unstable or disappointing, and you're finding it difficult to make decisions or to reach solutions.

You may consider running away or may imagine escape in drugs, alcohol, or strange fantasies. There could be confusion or muddle. Keep a clear head by avoiding moody hypersensitivity; draw on your own meditative instinct, and be considerate and understanding of those who need you. You can have a happy home again as things straighten out.

Avoid all promotional schemes; they may be overrated. But do put your creative imagination into music, theatre, or the arts, or in working with public service.

Neptune sesquisquare Moon: You can have some highly erratic days of domestic confusion, muddle, deception, or drama. You may have vague forebodings and strange moods. A woman or some family member can be a source of anxiety, and may require special care or solicitude.

You may dream of running away, or may imagine escape in drugs or drink, or may entertain fantasies of erotic or romantic scenes.

Better keep a clear head by avoiding moody hypersensitivity; draw on your own meditative instinct to be understanding and considerate of those who need you.

Avoid all promotional or grandiose schemes, but do put your creative imagination into music, theatre, or the arts, or work with public service.

Neptune conjunct Mercury: During this period in your life you're not particularly logical or well-organized. Your thinking may tend to woolgathering, and your conversation to rambling. On some days your mind is filled with no more than used Kleenex and empty bubble gum wrappers. On other days you clear your head and soar with imaginative plans, promotional schemes, and grand ideas.

Even if your own thinking is basically rational, there is someone around you, or a communication situation in your life that is vague, mildly confusing, illogical, mystical, or deceptive. News may be unusual or dramatic. Try to wade through whatever miasmic information is available; sort through gossip, exaggeration, and fantasy to find the facts.

You can do very well in areas where you need to inspire others, to sell them an idea, a product, or a service that you represent. Creative writing, music, drama, or the arts, will flourish if you can get it past the stage of imagination into creative action.

There can be travel: a vacation trip or work that involves transportation. However, a move would be apt to put you in a more seclusive, retiring, or subordinate position.

Neptune opposite Mercury: During this period it may require your maximum logic and reason to keep from exaggeration or woolgathering, or from being lazy, confused, and muddled. Impractical schemes and complex promotional concepts may give you a miasma of misinformation to wade through.

News may be strange or unusual; it's difficult to sort the fact out of gossip, confusion, and fantasy. Communications are difficult and, in some cases, impossible, due to vagueness, mystery, or deception.

If you're not escaping in drugs or drink, or actually running away, consider whether you may be evading a direct encounter with a problem you should talk out.

This may be a seclusive, retiring, or subordinate period in your life; your creative ideas and imagination are blocked by a multitude of nebulous details.

Work it out and hang on to your dream. If you can't get into creative action, at least take notes of the writing, music, drama, artistic or business ideas that come in brilliant flashes, so that you can pursue them later.

Neptune square Mercury: Are you tilting at windmills? You could be caught in the inspirational fascination of reaching for an impossible dream, or longing for more and greater than you have. It may be a seclusive, retiring, or subordinate period in your life; your greatest tendency is to exaggerate and woolgather, or to be lazy, confused, and muddled. Even if your own thinking seems clear, there is someone around you, or a communication situation in your life that is vague, confusing, complex, illogical, mystical, or even fraudulent.

If you're not escaping in drugs or drink, or actually running away, consider whether you may be evading a direct encounter with a problem you should talk out.

Sort it out, and hang on to your dream. If you can't get into creative action, at least take notes of the writing, music, drama, artistic or business ideas that come in brilliant flashes, so that you can pursue them later.

Neptune trine Mercury: This may be a seclusive or retiring period; your activities tend to subordinate response and introspection. You are certainly more sensitive to your environment, and to music, art, drama, poetry, and mystical concepts. Your imagination can flourish in writing, metaphysics, or the occult, but more ambition and organization are needed to carry it into creative form.

Promotional schemes can flourish, along with activities where you need to inspire others, to sell them an idea, a product, or a service you represent.

Travel or a vacation could be ideal, and may even come as a gift. A situation, or people around you, could be a little vague, strange, nebulous, but enchanting. You have a gentle insulation that protects you from harshness.

Neptune sextile Mercury: Opportunities come up that offer imaginative concepts to advance your community position. In promotional schemes or public service areas you can inspire others to use an idea, service, or product that you represent.

Though your tendency is to be seclusive and retiring, you can express your creative ideas to a responsive ear. With a gentle insulation from harshness, you have a more sensitive awareness of music, art, poetry, and metaphysics.

Travel or a vacation could be a little strange, but would give you some enchanting experiences.

Neptune semisquare Mercury: Discontent with your present situation brings periods of restless clarity that vacillate with lethargy, seclusion, or subordinate retirement.

You can do well representing a service or product, but promotional schemes may be exaggerated or illusory. You can develop artistically in music, drama, creative writing, or the arts, but putting your ideas into action may result in only frustrating intermittent disappointments.

Even if your own thinking is rational, there is someone around you, or a communication situation in your life, that is vague, mildly confusing, illogical, mystical, or deceptive.

Try to keep a cool head and not be caught in dramatics or persuasion. Matters will work out.

Neptune sesquisquare Mercury: There are intermittent disruptions and upsets in the seclusive serenity of your life that will shake you up and stimulate you to action. If you have a tendency to daydreaming, vagueness, laziness, or fantasy, you'll have to pull your thinking together in order to cope with changes now. News can be unexpected; strange or odd communications can be dramatic and confusing. There could be a sudden trip or unusual outing.

Even if your own thinking is rational, there is someone in your life, or a situation around you, that is illogical, mystical, or even deceptive. Sort out the facts, and if you can't get into creative action right now, at least make sensible plans. Don't rely on someone else's promises.

Neptune conjunct Venus: There may be an emphasis on your community social life during this period where you are more courteous, considerate, and well-mannered. This is an excellent time to pursue cultural matters of art, music, drama, fashion, decorating and beauty, as they touch your imagination and sensitivity.

In your emotional life you tend to be highly romantic and idealistic, perhaps unrealistically so. You may be emotionally dependent upon someone who is not entirely 'there'; your beloved is self-absorbed, abstract, vague, or impractical. As you are impressionable to the harshness of life, you are not inclined to make decisions or to assert yourself; you take a compliant, acquiescent role, with the illusion that everything will somehow work out perfectly.

There can indeed be some ideal emotional, home, or familial situation of greater ease or comfort, beauty and serenity in your private environment. Platonic and gay relationships are warm and delightful; you are more gentle, passive, shy, impractical, lazy, imaginative, and aesthetic.

Neptune opposite Venus: Though your tendency is to be passive, your social and community activities can make maximum demands on your courtesy, manners, adaptability, and consideration during this period. In the world of fashion, art, music, drama, decorating and beauty, or of social work, you must extend yourself to grasp imaginative concepts and to be creative.

You may be unrealistically romantic and idealistic, and could be drawn into a fasinating but unstable situation or affair. An emotional dependency could leave you drained and feeling anxious, lost, or rejected. This dependency is potentially scandalous if your choice is based on illusion or deception. Your beloved is not really 'there' due to being self-absorbed, abstract, vague, or mysterious. Your tendency is to take the path of least resistance, with the illusion that somehow everything will work out like a movie script with a happy ending.

Some idyllic situation may come into your life—a boon such as a luxury, gift, or vacation, a poignant romance, dramatic or cultural events. It's an excellent time to pursue painting or decorating, music or aesthetic interests. Avoid drugs, promotional schemes, and elusive promises.

Neptune square Venus: Though you may sense a restless discontent and lonely longing, your tendency is to be vague, unrealistic, or disinclined to make decisions or to assert yourself. The matters you attempt to promote have elusive obstacles or imperfect results. If you assume a compliant, acquiescent role of least resistance you can get involved in the sensation and possible scandal of drugs or drink, erotic indulgences, or exaggerated schemes and vulnerable fantasies.

A romance may seem ideal and fascinating at this time, but your lover could be married to another, be impotent, unstable, or not really 'there.' You could bog down in confusion, muddle or mystery if you base a relationship on illusion or deception.

You can make some beautiful steps of growth if you hold to aesthetic ideals of consideration and purity. Platonic and gay friends can be helpful, even if not entirely down-to-earth; and you can work for community service or in fields of drama, art, music, fashion, and decoration with imaginative creativity.

Avoid temptations to invest in luxuries or in a get-rich-quick scheme; all promises are suspect just now.

Neptune trine Venus: Involvement in your community's cultural and artistic pursuits can flourish: music, drama, art, fashion, decorating, all fields of beauty, or of social and service work.

You are more gentle, courteous and considerate, compliant and acquiescent; people are inclined to find you fascinating and charming. There can be an ideal home or familial situation in your private life, of greater ease and comfort, beauty or serenity. Areas of stress will ease; there will be someone to nurture and care for you.

A romance can seem like a dream come true with the sensitive, emotional feeling of belonging. If that love is based on true consideration and unity, and not on deception or fantasy, it can indeed be ideal.

You can tap your own wellspring of creative inspiration to make your dreams real.

Neptune sextile Venus: There will be opportunities to broaden your cultural, artistic, and social involvement in your community. Music, art, drama, fashion or decorating, and all fields of beauty and social or service work can bring you more popularity.

There is greater ease or comfort, beauty or serenity in your environment, if you are not too lazy to reach out for it. Certain social situations are ideal; there is the possibility of a friendship or romance that can be delightful, if not entirely solid.

Neptune semisquare Venus: You may vacillate between a restless lonely hunger and a passive relaxation. Some decisions may be difficult to assess; facts may be clouded, and your feelings indecisive.

A sudden romance, or a loved one in your life, can cause anxiety by being elusive, vague, or actually deceptive. Avoid temptations of a love affair that could be scandalous or painful. By holding steadily to your own ideals, you can gain in your social and aesthetic values.

Your service to others, given with consideration and courtesy, will enhance your serenity. There is comfort in social work, or activities in music, art, drama, fashion, decorating and fields of beauty.

Neptune sesquisquare Venus: There is indicated a breakup in the conditions of your social or familial life, or in your community standing. This disruption could cause you emotional agitation. Matters for which you long with a lonely hunger seem to be elusive, and you may feel anxiety.

Avoid situations that are potentially scandalous; your protection is in your own pure motive. In striving toward your ideals with serenity, matters will gradually turn, and a sudden new opportunity can resolve the inconsistencies.

If a matter does not work out in your cultural, artistic and social life, keep alert for detours. It may not yet be time for that perfect answer, but an alternative can be attractive.

Neptune conjunct Mars: During this time, your imagination can be stimulated by high ideals to constructively better your position. You can promote your public service aspirations of incorporation, social work, art, music, or drama with constructive results. With the integrity of your own vision strive to attain creative action; you can inspire others to follow your imagination and example.

To the young or unsophisticated, your drive may seem muted and mellow; you have energy enough but seem to be content to go along with more forceful people. You have a gentle and quiet magnetism that attracts others, and you could acquire popularity or a following.

Some doors can open to fascinating adventures, interesting and imaginative people, or a colorful and highly enjoyable vacation or move. There is a sense of camaraderie and stimulation in communal activities; you tend to be more democratic and considerate of those persons in lesser circumstances than yourself—even the downtrodden or decadent.

However, if you have secret desires for self-gratification, this can be a tricky or dangerous time, as hidden passions come to the surface. You could get involved in dope, seduction, abortion, molestation, entrapment, or homosexuality, with possible scandal or trouble with the police.

In either case, the ordinary and humdrum are touched by some occasion of excitement, drama, and challenge. Some note of confusion, exaggeration, or mystery may stir you.

Business schemes can have Machiavellian intricacies that are complex and devious. In all, exaggerated speculations or sensational aspirations are highly suspect, whether in your business or personal life.

Though clean-living yourself, certain of these matters can touch your environment or those close to you. Your own purity of motive is your protection.

Neptune opposite Mars: At this time your imagination is stimulated to discontent with the status quo. With a strange, restless, dreamy hunger you long for more and better from life.

With high idealism and creative aspirations you can strive to constructively improve your community position. Though complex and intricate obstacles block your efforts, your pragmatic efforts can be advanced in civic or public service areas of social work, art, music or drama. If you maintain the highest integrity you can avoid the possibility of iniquity that is now present.

However, it is not the time to achieve that ultimate vision. In either your business or personal life there is a level of evasion, confusion, or incompetence. A person or a situation can be a bitter disappointment or, at least, not be up to expectations.

Your own level of duplicity will be the measure of the circumstances and results. If you have within yourself secret phobias or sensational desires of hidden passion you can be attracted to deception, eroticism, or incompetence. You could get involved in dope, seduction, molestation, or homosexuality, abortion, entrapment, scandal, or trouble with the police. Business schemes can have Machiavellian intricacies that are devious or fraudulent, with unsavory connections and tactics.

Religious mysticism could be fanatical, dealing with black magic or eroticism or, at the least, could be illusory.

Even if your powerful passions are controlled and you are clean-living yourself, these matters may touch your life. Your protection is in your own pure motive. Keep your own idealistic vision and strive to attain creative action.

Neptune square Mars: This is potentially a tricky or dangerous time that can be subject to trauma, anxiety, deception, or iniquity.

At the worst, there can be rape, assault, seduction, abortion, sexual perversion, scandal, or trouble with the police; business duplicity or fraud; drug overdose or miscalculation; or heavy alcoholism. Exaggerated promotional schemes could be built on quicksand.

In lesser instances there is anxiety from the pressure of other people's forceful desires, confusion and discontent, evasion and incompetence, with complex and intricate obstacles that block your efforts. There can be loneliness, loss, or disappointment.

Your protection lies in your own pure motive. When you are clean-living yourself, these matters may touch your environment without harming you. If there are conditions of deception around you, or unsavory people, put your practical ideals to work by cleaning up your life.

If you are restless or bored by humdrum ordinary affairs, take decisive actions that are constructive for better conditions in your community service and standing. Your own passions can be discharged in social work, art, music, or drama.

As your imagination is stimulated to a strange, brooding hunger, any phobias or duplicity that you have could surface. However, with integrity, you can move through this period safely, out of the shadows into a clearer vision. Put your highest ideals into creative action and maintain strict self-control.

Neptune trine Mars: A matter of which you've dreamed can come true if you have invested your energy, imagination, and action in the struggle for a creative result. The way can now smooth out, and the doors open to its demonstration.

There can be a vacation or move that is idyllic, stimulating, and colorful, or that gives you conditions of greater ease in a pleasurable environment.

There is camaraderie with others who are interesting, fascinating, and imaginative. You yourself have an attractive zest and magnetism.

Public service areas—social work, art, music, or drama—can be promoted successfully. You could gain a role or position that is not only an outcome of past efforts, but an affirmation of future directions. Though it may not be the ultimate success, this step has great practical benefit. Business and corporate investments can pay off, and your civic standing may improve.

Someone in your environment is lazy, evasive, or having some strange trauma that may vaguely trouble you. As your own attitude tends to a practical, matter-of-fact, robust content, you can be helpful with a consideration that cuts through the confusion.

Neptune sextile Mars: There are opportunities to advance your public service at this time, in social work, art, music, or drama. In business or promotional matters there can be practical, constructive advantages. If you invest your energy, imagination, and action in improving your position, certain doors can open with idyllic results.

There could be a colorful vacation or outing; communal activities give you a camaraderie with interesting people; and you yourself have an attractive magnetic energy.

If there is someone in your life who is lazy, evasive, or having some strange trauma, you can handle this with practical matter-of-fact assurance.

Neptune semisquare Mars: You may feel a restless indecision about your community standing, as ordinary humdrum conditions are a bore; in your imagination you desire something more and better out of life. There could be a competitive undercurrent, or you could feel a vague anxiety about complex or intricate obstacles that occasionally surface. Strange fantasies or exaggerated promotional schemes catch your imaginaton; you are potentially susceptible to duplicity or miscalculation, intrigue, or trauma.

Keep a cool head and a clear mind; with your own pure motive you can see through any tricky or dangerous persuasions. You may even realize some ideal satisfaction in creative results from your striving to better your idealistic visions.

Neptune sesquisquare Mars: You may feel a restless indecision about your community standing at this time; ordinary humdrum conditions are breaking up into new patterns that are exciting and stimulating, but potentially tricky and dangerous.

Strange fantasies or hidden passions can surface intermittently, and you're susceptible to exaggerated schemes, or exposed to strange trauma, drugs, liquor, or erotic situations.

Keep a cool head and a clear mind with self-control; avoid fraud, persuasion, or scandalous trouble with the police. Put your highest ideals into energetic action in order to constructively better your conditions.

Neptune conjunct Jupiter: This is the time to expand your visions and dreams of a better, richer, and fuller life. You can promote your community standing with important people who are inspired to give you patronage. Your ideals can be advanced in such a way as to benefit yourself and those around you for better conditions.

Though promotional and incorporation schemes may be exaggerated and highly complex, they are timely to catch the imagination and good will of others, and can prove with time to be highly lucrative. Business expansion in professional or private enterprise, drama or the arts, public or community service will flourish when based on moral values, honor, and hard work.

If you are in a retiring period, you have protection and welfare. A vacation could be a dream come true, with ease, camaraderie, and even luxury. Your own optimism inspires trust in others who are eager to give you favors and following.

An interest in religious mysticism or psychic awareness may increase, taking you either into illusive cults and phenomena or into a sense of reverence and spiritual destiny.

Neptune opposite Jupiter: It's time to take a giant step of growth. Believe in yourself and in what you're striving to attain. Put maximum moral value, honor, and professional ethics into promotional matters. Increase your education and experience, and keep your trust in your own ideals.

However you must discriminate; some of your affairs are overrated or exaggerated. In business expansion or private enterprise, in drama or the arts, public or community service, complex persuasions can collapse with muddle, confusion, and expense. One person in your life may be an unsuitable vehicle for your future, if that person makes pretentious promises of dramatic grandeur.

Religious mysticism can put you in touch with strange cults and peculiar people, false prophets, or psychic phenomena. Protect yourself from deception by expressing your highest ideals of reverence and a realistic code of faith that will improve yourself and your community.

Neptune square Jupiter: Though you have a vision of expanding your career, or of a better, richer and more peaceful life, there are vague, illusory, or even deceptive obstacles to your dreams. Your professional aims, your community service and standing, or business expansion in private enterprise corporations could be overrated or unrealistic. Be careful of confusion and muddle in financial and legal matters. You must develop your discrimination and increase your education in order to take your next step of growth.

You could be attracted to strange religious or mystical cults and to peculiar people, false prophets, or psychic phenomena. Protect yourself from deception by expressing your highest ideals of reverence, and live by a code of faith that will make your struggle one that leads to growth.

Neptune trine Jupiter: This tends to be a mellow, relaxed period when opportunities or advantages come to you with little effort on your part. A step of growth may be offered with good will from important patronage.

Your work is not hard or demanding, but rather may ease up, or phase into a period more stimulating to your creative imagination. In business or professional expansion, drama or the arts, public or community service affairs, you have a gentle charisma that attracts a following. You can sway or inspire others to trust your optimistic views. Though promotional and incorporation schemes tend to be complex, you have the protection and discrimination to make the moves that can be fruitful or lucrative.

A vacation, trip or move could be ideal with camaraderie, good accommodations, and hospitality. Your education and experience can grow as you trust and believe in the basic virtue and goodness of life.

An interest in imaginative concepts may increase; fantasy, daydreams, psychic awareness, or religious mysticism, give you a deep contentment and serene joy.

Neptune sextile Jupiter: This tends to be a fairly mellow, relaxed time. Your work is easier, or phasing into a more retiring period, as you have protection, welfare, or favors given to you. In business or professional expansion, drama or the arts, public or community service affairs, you can expand your position, but you must discriminate. Certain people may offer exaggerated and overrated promises, or you could touch on financial and legal matters that have some confusion or muddle.

You'll do better to increase your education and experience in order to prepare yourself for that next step of growth, rather than to be swayed by fantastic persuasion.

Base your religious mysticism on your highest ideals of reverence and a realistic code of faith that will improve yourself and your community.

Neptune semisquare Jupiter: Blessings may be mixed at this time: certain matters bring ideal results, other matters contain anxiety or confusion. You may vacillate from optimistic joy to vague exaggerations. Your visions and dreams of a better, richer, more creative life may be in a formative period; you need more education and experience to bring them into realization.

Business or professional expansion, drama or the arts, public or community service can be expanded fruitfully if you use discrimination. Be careful of complex persuasions or pretentious promises.

Base your religious mysticism on your highest ideals of reverence and a realistic code of faith that will improve yourself and your community, not on strange cults or psychic phenomena.

Neptune sesquisquare Jupiter: Your community standing or financial status is in a period of flux, showing areas in your life that you're outgrowing. Let go of vague, illusive, or deceptive matters, and take that next step in the development of discrimination and increasing education.

Certain matters of business or professional expansion, drama or the arts, or community service, could collapse with confusion, muddle and expense if they are overrated or exaggerated. You must put maximum moral value, honor, and ethics into promotional efforts.

Neptune conjunct Saturn: With work, responsibility, and organization you can now bring an ideal into concrete form. Creative and aesthetic pursuits that require long hours of disciplined practice may be pursued with deep satisfaction.

Business or promotional affairs may be founded on complex schemes of interwoven structure that require efficiency and imagination to manage. If there are strange events or peculiar people in your job environment, they are nonetheless interesting. A person who appears to be a solid conventional citizen may actually be a visionary who inspires you to practical ideas.

However, strange fears and forebodings could bring a sense of lonely solitude that cuts you off from the established order of those around you. You may attempt to work alone or in retreat, but reality interferes with your dreams. A vague discontent pulls you back into community interests of responsible involvement with others. Lack, or fear for your material security, will inspire greater ambition.

Security may be found in religious or mystical interests that you approach with serious reverence.

Neptune opposite Saturn: It will require maximum work, responsibility, and organization to bring your ideals into concrete form at this time.

Long hours of practice and discipline are required, over and over, to perfect your skill in and control of creative and aesthetic pursuits.

Business and promotional affairs that are built on complex schemes of interwoven structure are potentially deceptive. It will take tricky maneuvering of strategy and finesse to keep efficient management. Fear for your material security could push you into overweening ambitions.

If there is any deception or fraud in your affairs or in your environment it can come out, bringing muddle and guilt. Your own part may be exaggerated, or the whole matter become a morass of confusion. Strict honesty in your own integrity, and idealism based on personal responsibility, will carry you safely through to a greater vision.

You may look for security in religious or mystical interests that are founded on an hierarchical order of control, and on service.

130

Neptune square Saturn: You may wish to work privately or in retreat at this time for a secret ambition or goal, but reality interferes with your dreams. A vague discontent pulls you back into community involvements.

Business and promotional affairs that are formed around complex infrastructures are potentially deceptive. It will take tricky maneuvering of strategy and finesse to keep efficient management. Be careful of deception or fraud in your business or personal affairs at this time; there could be muddle, guilt and exaggerated confusion.

You could feel a lonely foreboding from a loss in your life, or a strange solitude from a certain lack of the personal satisfactions for which you hunger.

Creative or aesthetic pursuits take long hours of practice and discipline to perfect your competence.

In order to gain security, you must take a greater responsibility for your religious or mystical life.

Work through the present obstacles with strict integrity, and with idealism based on responsibility and consideration in order to strive for ideal conditions of security and comfort.

Neptune trine Saturn: You can bring into concrete form certain matters of which you've dreamed, to the extent of the work and effort you put into their preparation. Though business and promotional affairs may be structured on complex schemes, you have the strategy and finesse needed to solve tricky problems.

Creative and aesthetic pursuits can be acknowledged as a polished product of your imagination and discipline. You may take on a position of greater responsibility in community affairs. In your church, religious or mystical interests you can find security and reverence.

A disappointing or even fraudulent situation, or a person in your life with a weakening dependency, will drop by the wayside, leaving your time clear to build more ideal patterns of integrity based on personal responsibility and consideration.

Neptune sextile Saturn: Opportunities will be presented now for you to bring certain ideals into concrete form. People or matters that have held you back will drop by the wayside, leaving you free to build more ideal patterns. If there is deception, fraud, or tricky dishonesty in your life it will be exposed, and you can handle complex problems with strategy and finesse.

Cultural and creative pursuits can be acknowledged as a polished product of your imagination and skill. You may take on a greater level of responsibility in your community. In your religious or mystical interests you can find security and reverence.

Neptune semisquare Saturn: You may vacillate between an anxious foreboding and an isolated sense of calm during intermittent periods or situations of dissolving security. A vague, complex scheme or problem can nag at you, or there can be a single incident that shakes your stability. If there is deception or fraud in your life, it can be exposed in an uncomfortable way.

Business or promotional matters must be regarded with caution; they may be based on schemes that require maneuvering and strategy to keep control of efficient management.

You can find safety within your own sense of responsibility and integrity. Disappointing or weakening matters will fall away as you work to bring your ideals into concrete form.

Neptune sesquisquare Saturn: Certain tricky or complex problems that arise during this period require your stamina or endurance, work or effort, or an increase in responsibility.

An ideal may be shattered. If there is any deception or fraud in your life it can suddenly break open, bringing anxiety, guilt or forebodings.

Business or promotional matters must be regarded with caution; they may be based on schemes that require strategic maneuvering to maintain control of efficient management. Work with strict integrity and idealism based on responsibility and consideration of others in order to strive for ideal security conditions in your long-range goals.

Neptune conjunct, sextile, and semisquare Uranus are aspects not applicable to persons born in the twentieth century.

Neptune opposite Uranus: Generally this is a vague period of unstable transition. Circumstances in your search for personal identity and direction impose unexpected blocks to your aspirations. You need to draw on your ingenuity and imagination in order to relate to conditions that are not what you'd expected.

There can be days or weeks of detached anxiety, feelings of disassociation or confused independence; and days or weeks of high tension, sudden dramatic excitement, and feelings of mystical inspiration and insight. In giving philanthropic service, or in following an aesthetic vision of a unique dream, you gain an inner satisfaction; but your outer life tends to follow a path of least resistance. You're in a rare period of flux, when you are neither fish nor fowl. Matters you reach for now are not indicated to be enduring patterns, as you make a gradual shift to a different attitude. These experiences are necessary in the search for the reality of who you are and what you want.

Your position in the community or in your environment may be unique; your interests and activities are certainly different from those of others. Whatever potential of creative or inventive intuition you have is apt to flash out in brilliant decisions or actions when needed. Keep your high ideals and be your own crazy, wonderful self!

Neptune square Uranus: This is an unusual period of flux during which matters that seem ideal turn out to be unstable and subject to sudden changes. Your high aspirations and hopes for a new condition may be unrealistic; be careful of being promoted against your independent judgment.

A matter that's been gestating in your imagination could make you hungry for a different life style. A dramatic, unexpected door that looks ideal may open—and then slam in your face. It will take your highest idealism and insight to steer through this rare time without making some crazy moves.

Your position in the community could change or be unique. Your interests are certainly apt to be unusual; you may feel that you are neither fish nor fowl in a world that doesn't fit.

There can be deep satisfaction in driving through obstacles to express service and philanthropy, and in following an aesthetic vision of a unique dream.

Neptune trine Uranus: If ever a dream can come true, this is the time. A sudden change of condition, an unexpected opportunity, or a unique offer can open a door to a better future.

You can establish an interesting or even unique community involvement. Any inventive or creative work that you do can tap your sources of inspiration and can be promoted in an unusual way that catches the imagination of your society. Persons who come into your life, or matters that you begin at this time can set better patterns of personal identity and self-determination that benefit you for years to come.

If there are days or weeks of isolated anxiety, feelings of disassociation or confusion, they can only precede a greater vision of change and insights into your own intuitive independence.

Neptune sesquisquare Uranus: Sudden and unexpected changes in your environment, or in people close to you, trigger unstable reactions. Your tendency is to break up and reform relationships, as well as your community position. Strange feelings of anxiety or isolated confusion are brewing in your imagination; it's not the best time to make firm plans. With erratic independence you find yourself in an inconsistent period of flux. Be careful of persuasion that sways your independent judgment.

It will take your highest idealism and deepest insight to steer through this rare time without making some sudden crazy moves.

Neptune conjuct Neptune: One hundred sixty-four years. Not applicable.

Neptune opposite Neptune: (Approximately age 82-84) There is a withdrawal from mundane involvements, a retirement into fantasy and memory, to prepare for the aesthetic experience of transition.

Neptune square Neptune: (Age 40-42) This can be a strange, unstable period, as you have a vague discontent with what you have and an unformed or unrealistic idea of what you want.

Certain matters may slip from your hands; the children are growing up, you wonder who this person is that you've married, or if your job really satisfies you; and you yearn for something more.

There can be a resurgence of religious, mystical or metaphysical interest. A withdrawal into solitude or retreat can give you the meditative insights into your own creative imagination.

If your temperament is more active and pragmatic you may search to satisfy this hunger in community involvement in the church, art, music and drama, or charity and social work that require your service and sacrifice.

Business or promotional schemes may present some complex problems; it is important to keep all matters straight and in the open. It's not difficult at this time to slip into confusion, muddle or incompetence. Your motives may be suspect, as you do not tend to take a clear, sharply defined position.

If you feel unsure of your sexual potency, you may tend to indulge in erotic or romantic fantasy, or in secret affairs that are largely disappointing. Love relationships, built on trust and belief, service and consideration, can be idyllic.

You'd best look well into yourself at this time: to ask, "In what do I believe? What are my ideals? What is real and sustaining? Am I considerate of the values and welfare of others?"

Neptune trine Neptune: (Age 54-56) Certain matters you've dreamed of as ideal can be realized. Community involvements in the church, in art, music, drama, charity, social work or service can be inspirational. Meditation, mystical or metaphysical interests can sustain and uplift you. In solitude or retreat you can find insights of creative imagination.

Less pressure is indicated in your mundane affairs; business or promotional schemes can pay off, and there is more leisure to enjoy contemplative pursuits. There could be a vacation or trip that you've always wanted, or you can have short frequent outings that permit you to relax and enjoy yourself.

Neptune sextile Neptune: (Age 26-28) Certain ideals can be realized in the way of a gift, bonus, vacation, or an inspiration. Opportunities for community involvement in the church, in art, music, drama, charity, social work or service, or in creative pursuits, can be pursued now.

There is less pressure in your mundane affairs and more leisure to enjoy contemplative pursuits. In solitude, meditation or retreat you can touch on your own mystical or metaphysical insights.

Business or promotional schemes can open new avenues of possibility that catch your imagination.

Neptune semisquare Neptune: (Age 19-21) Certain ideals can be realized now, if you hold steady to that in which you believe. However there is some measure of confusion, exaggeration, and vague indecision that may plague you. Your youth and inexperience have not yet equipped you to deal with complex, deceptive, or potentially scandalous situations. Be careful of community involvement with drugs, drink, or sensational dramatics. Keep a clear mind for meditation and pure inspiration, and give service and consideration to others.

Neptune sesquisquare Neptune: (Age 61-63) There could be a measure of confusion or deceptive conditions around you at this time that cause you anxiety and discontent. If you are, or another is, drinking, taking drugs or heavy medication, if into psychic, mystical or illusory fantasies, you are in a potentially scandalous position.

Business or promotional schemes are tricky; be careful to keep all matters clear and on the straight and narrow; as they could make you suspect of incompetence if not actual foolishness. Community involvement with the church, art, music, drama, charity and social work can be inconsistent at this time.

Some people, or certain matters, may be slipping away from your life, giving you a sense of loss. Make realistic plans for your retirement or for the vacation you've dreamed of.

Neptune conjunct, sextile and semisquare Pluto are aspects not applicable to persons born in the twentieth century.

Neptune opposite Pluto: You are vaguely disturbed by the feeling that a transformation or transition is pending, in which your power to control the situation is elusive or diminished. Stay where you are until a decision improves your community position, then cooperate with those who share your dreams.

Neptune square Pluto: Deep gradual changes are indicated in your community position. Under the circumstances, for your own good, you must learn to cooperate with the group, the team, the collective commune, even if you feel a vague isolation from these people - feel that you don't entirely "belong." You could meet people from different backgrounds or cultures whose ways are strange to you and you need to draw on your instincts of consideration to find those with whom you can share common goals and understanding.

Though your power to control your situation may be blocked, actually more of your potential is being developed through your service and acquiescence to the welfare of others.

You are in a transition period of your life; there is a culmination of certain dreams. Learn well your lessons; whatever efforts you put into sympathetic cooperation with others will better your community standing, and also prepare you for greater control of your own vision and destiny later.

Neptune trine Pluto: During this period the changes you make in your community position can give you greater power to control your own destiny and vision. You can cooperate with the group or team effort to promote a common goal in a way that contributes service to the community and improves your standing.

People you meet from different backgrounds and cultures may stimulate your imagination and sympathies, and there may be someone with whom there is a deep mystical sense of unity.

You are in a transition period of your life; any deception, manipulation, or weakening influences are exposed or outgrown in order that you may develop your greater potential.

Neptune sesquisquare Pluto: This is a subtle transition period marked by unexpected cooperation breakdowns, disillusionment, and compulsive rebellion. Your power to control is weakened by the manipulation or fascination that others hold over you, and at times you may feel vaguely anxious and coerced.

You are touching on some patterns that are foreign to you, or venturing into a circumstance where you don't belong. Cooperate with consideration and service for the welfare of all concerned, but for your own position, renegotiate until you are ready to let go and move on.

X   TRANSIT PLUTO

Pluto transits the horoscope in two hundred forty-five years four months. Approximately every seven months Pluto has an apparent retrograde motion that lasts close to five months. Pluto will never aspect all the planets in a given horoscope in one lifetime; in eighty years it will go through only three to six signs. When Pluto engages a planet with a conjunction, opposition, square, or trine, it will not make that aspect again in the lifetime; it can possibly semi-square and sesquisquare a planet twice in a lifetime.

However, with the change of station, Pluto will always make that one aspect three times in two years, or five times in three years. As the influence is fully valid during that entire time span, it not only marks the period intensely, but can have a dynamic effect when it is three or four degrees away from the partile aspect, in between the first one-degree applying to partile and the last one-degree separating to partile.

The mean motion of fourteen seconds a day is the average daily motion of Pluto between its station and the maximum of two minutes a day.

Pluto goes through the signs in the following time span:

Aries	30 years	Libra	14 years
Taurus	31 years	Scorpio	12 years
Gemini	30 years	Sagittarius	13 years
Cancer	25 years	Capricorn	13 years
Leo	19 years	Aquarius	19 years
Virgo	14 years	Pisces	25 years

As Pluto is the significator of culmination and regeneration, its value in our lives is to mark a subtle transition. We come to the end of a phase, and gradually, with a change in our deep-rooted attitudes we go through a meta-morphosis. Though there is often a peak experience—a dramatic incident or a situation of great pressure—the end effect of Pluto is slow and thorough. The final perspective seldom reaches our awareness until the aspect has fully completed its last engagement with a planet.

As Pluto is one cell within the body of the collective, we often have a sense of isolation, of singularity. We are all alone in time and space on our own path of development.

At the same time Pluto brings us into contact with groups: the family, the tribe, the nation. The common denominator within Pluto groups is unity of a band of people with a common goal that is of benefit to its members. The members ascribe their allegiance to the code and bylaws of the collective in a desire to participate in both the common good and the individual benefits. If members do not follow the program, doctrine, dogma, or rules of the group, they are subject to fine, coventry, anathema, ostracism, or exclusion. In simplistic terms, Pluto says, "Do it my way or else," as it makes us an offer we can't refuse.

These various groups may be political parties, labor unions, clubs (Elks, Masons, etc.) Scouts, the Church, the Mafia, Scientology, Alcoholics Anonymous, the Bar Association, the Accounting Society, sports teams, PTA, Mensa, the Neighborhood Committee, etc., etc. There is strength and benefit in unity for the cultural welfare of the whole and for the good of mankind. But if the group gains absolute power, it becomes corrupt. Therefore, the nature of Pluto provides a system of checks and balances, in counter-factions that become insubordinate to coercion.

Pluto aspects mark memorable periods that transform our lives: the conjunction, opposition, square, and trine aspects seldom go by without a personal renaissance. The three lesser aspects—sextile, semisquare, and sesquisquare—(as in all cases) are apt to influence only one segment of our environment or experience, and may or may not demonstrate a discernible effect.

Even when Pluto brings massive repression, it influences us so deeply that out of the cocoon we form a resolution that shapes the future.

In a refining process, Pluto brings up the hidden material in our psychology. We may be reluctant to deal with covert attitudes and compulsions that we find uncomfortable, but we must purge or eliminate our wastes in order to survive on a healthy level. Our potential and our power unfold by our choice of either segregation or integration of disparate factors within our character.

Pluto conjunct Sun: This is a transition period in life when you move to a new phase from former goals, awareness and self-expression. You are not changing your basic character, but rather bringing out another dimension of your potential through purposeful action.

Certain situations and attitudes of the past are to be resolved and completed in order to root out and discard the matters that are nonessential to your further progress, just as a refining process brings up the slag. Look at your passions and attachments, your goals and personal realities, your own integrity of direction, in order that you may leave behind the unnecessary baggage as you move ahead.

You have the power to sway others in your group, whether this be the PTA, church, business, club, or service group; you can influence political action or public opinion. You could initiate reforms for the general welfare of your sociological environment. There will be some counter-group or powerful individual with whom you must cooperate for the good of the whole, and there could be insubordination or power plays in a possible attempt to undermine your authority. You may be pulled into manipulative politics that require resourcefulness and compromise. A powerful man can influence your decisions.

Stand behind what you believe; your strength and power stem from the integration of your own character. You will pull through this period with greater capacity, discrimination, perspective, and conviction than you've ever had before.

Pluto opposite Sun: During this transition period in your life you may be forced by circumstances to bring out your maximum potential for purposeful action. You may feel frustrated by inexorable environmental repression of your creative self-expression; as much as you put into your work, business, or personal life, you can't seem to move that mountain of necessity with which you're confronted. If not sociological pressure, your own compulsion to see it through can keep you at the foot of that mountain until you resolve and complete the present situation and attitudes.

Your own authoritative, dictatorial methods meet resistance, insubordination, or a battle of wills. You could act with headstrong impulsiveness that causes you to make false starts and serious mistakes. If your attitude is "my way or else . . . ," you could be pushed to the wall, where you must not only com- -promise but knuckle under to a more powerful authority.

This period requires maximum self-evaluation of your passions and attachments, your goals and personal realities, and your own integrity of direction, in order to segregate and eliminate the nonessentials that are handicapping to your future development. It is a time of purge; as you complete this era, you may conduct a refining process that brings up the slag for you to discard.

Your group activities, whether in PTA, church, business, clubs or service groups, politics, or public opinion, impel you to cooperate for the good of the whole, but there is an implied counter-force, with power plays and manipulative politics. You could be swayed, against your will and better judgment, to an obsessive involvement that challenges your pride and self-control. A specific man could have a powerful influence on your decisions.

Assimilate the changes in your consciousness, learn to discriminate and you'll pull through with a different value perspective of your own integrity and goal capacity.

Pluto square Sun: This is a transition period in your life as you work through obstacles to complete a matter in preparation for your next step of progress. Your strength of character, maturity, and integrity may be challenged by conditions that repress your creative self-expression. Though you may be unwilling to compromise any further, you must cooperate for the general good of all concerned in order to see it through, and to resolve situations and attitudes of the past.

In your group activities, whether in PTA, church, business, clubs or service groups, politics or public opinion, you may encounter insubordination, power struggles, segregation, or manipulative politics. A specific man could have a subtle but powerful influence on your decisions, and you yourself are inclined to covert compulsion or hidden motives. Examine your own goals and convictions in order to compromise without a loss of integrity.

An ultimatum that forces an issue could be drastic, as it may not work to your advantage.

Eliminate the nonessentials in order to purge yourself of handicaps. Your integration of personal character with decisive goals can overcome the obstacles and carry you through to a different value perspective that will lead to potentially greater achievements.

Pluto trine Sun: This may be one of the most important transition periods in your life; your goals, awareness, and self-expression are gradually and subtly moving to a new dimension. A refining process in your psychology could bring up old material for you to recognize and deal with. Situations and attitudes from the past are to be resolved and completed; root out and discard matters that are nonessential to your further progress. A specific man may have a powerful influence on your decisions. Matters that you begin during this time set forces into motion for years to come—forces that bring deep satisfaction and significance to your life. It's a period of regeneration.

You could easily take a role of leadership in group activities, whether in PTA, church, business, clubs or service groups, politics or public opinion. You have the power to sway others and to elicit cooperation in any negotiations or arbitration.

Your strength comes from your own integrated character; you are gaining greater capacity, discrimination, perspective, and conviction than you've ever had before.

Pluto sextile Sun: During this time there are opportunities to make certain transitions in your goals, awareness, and self-expression. One area of your past is coming to a conclusion; you must resolve and complete a prior attitude—leave it behind as you develop a deeper dimension.

It is an advantageous period for activities with groups. If there are counterfactions or power plays, you can be an arbitrator in negotiations. One man may have a powerful influence on your decisions. Cooperate with others for the general good; if compromise is required you can gain respect for taking a stand for what you believe in.

Pluto semisquare Sun: You may vacillate between authoritative self-expression that sways others to cooperate, and being swayed by the manipulation of another. A certain man could have a powerful influence on your decisions, and you tend to be indecisive about how to resolve a past attitude or situation. Though reluctant to compromise, you are not ready to deliver an ultimatum.

Your goals tend to be in a state of flux. It's a transition period that requires more time, information, and experience to shape into purposeful action.

In your group activities you may lean one way then another in policy, as counter-factions are pulling at you. You must find a perspective in your own reality of integrity in order to discriminate and stand up for your convictions.

Pluto sesquisquare Sun: This is an inconsistent period of transition; certain obstacles of the past reach a point of completion, then return for further resolution. Some man could have a powerful influence on your decisions. Though reluctant to cooperate, you may find that compromise will be more effective in the long run. As your goals are in a state of flux, you need the experience of this time to shape, discard, and integrate varied conditions into a new dimension of perspective.

There is such a variety of counter-factions and policies in your group activities that you tend to detach yourself from involvement. Work with the team for the good of the whole, but make your own decisions.

Pluto conjunct Moon: There can be a fluctuating variety of activities during this time that bring you into more contact with the general public. You feel a more acute responsiveness to the public pulse: to commodities, foods or marketing, matters of mass production, music, interracial persons, groups, teams or committees.

Intense relationships with your parents and dependents are indicated. Women tend to use subtle tactics—passive resistance or manipulation—and to exert a potent force on their environment. A specific woman may be a powerful influence in your life.

Emotional upheavals can occur in your domestic or family sphere with the removal of one of your kin, or a revision of the family structure. You have a deepened sensitivity; matters in your private life have a profound effect on your psychological growth. Deep-seated experiences from your past, coupled with your own childhood conditioning, may lead to focused emotional insights.

You may attempt to go underground in some of your affairs, either with secret activities that invite collusion, or in psychological or metaphysical groups. There can be a conversion or transformation of many of your mental and emotional attitudes by the time the experiences of this period are assimilated.

Pluto opposite Moon: You are impelled into a fluctuating variety of activities that bring you into closer contact with the general public. As you have a compulsive responsiveness, it seems impossible to say no; you could find yourself on committees, on teams, in music groups, in interracial or inter-cultural affairs, or in matters dealing with mass production, commodities, foods, or marketing.

Unconscious tendencies, based on unhappy past experiences, may surface during this time and bring emotional upheavals to your domestic and family life. There could be intense conflicts and encounters with your parents and dependents. Women tend to use subtle tactics of passive resistance or manipulation to exert a potent force on their environment. In extreme cases, a woman may seem driven to her own destruction. One of your kin may be removed, or your family structure may be revised in some other way.

You may attempt to go underground in some of your affairs, either with secret activities that invite collusion, or in psychological or metaphysical groups. The very force of your heightened sensitivity, and the intensity of your mental and emotional urges, can convert or transmute the motives that drive you. As you embody the lessons of this period, you emerge a tempered, stronger and wiser person.

Pluto square Moon: A variety of activities give you more contact with the general public on a fluctuating basis. You could be more involved with committees, teams, music groups, interracial or intercultural affairs, or with matters of mass production, commodities, foods, or marketing.

You must be more responsive to the needs and demands of people, in both your private and public life. You may feel keenly the dependency of others who pull at you with a coercive force. Women tend to exhibit compulsive emotional needs and drives, and may use subtle tactics that exert a potent force. A specific woman could be a powerful influence in your life. You could be subjected to heavy emotional pressures and upsets, mostly connected with family relationships and domestic affairs. One of your relatives may depart, or your family structure may be revised in some other way. A move, or activities that take you away from home, could markedly alter your life style.

The events of this time will bring up some of your own covert material and unresolved conflicts of emotional conditioning from the past. If you can effect a conversion or transmutation of your sensitivity into a more cooperative attitude for the benefit of others, you will complete this period with more unity in your relationships and a more potent force for your own psychological growth. If you evade the demands of experience by going underground, or if you use passive resistance and manipulation to your own ends, you could lose that important female contact, or the supportive familial nourishment that is vital.

Pluto trine Moon: You can easily set better and happier patterns of unity and cooperation in your domestic and family relationships at this time. You can experience intuitive insights into those automatic emotional responses that have been shaped by past family and social conditioning. Giving up self-destructive habits and relationships, and correcting past mistakes, can lead to a conversion or transmutation of your attitudes in order to allow a flow of natural response. Whatever stress you have weathered in your process of mental and emotional assimilation has left you tempered, wiser, and ready to use your potential to capacity.

You can reconcile differences with your parents, dependents, or kin, with sympathy and compromise. Women exert a potent force and easily gain cooperation and attention. A specific woman could be a powerful influence in your development. A move, or activities that take you away from home, could not only change your life style markedly, but put you in an environment that fits your mood and allows you fruitful growth of your own special abilities.

A variety of activities will easily bring you into contact with the general public, where you have an instinctive responsiveness to the public pulse. You can meet with groups in a home environment, with music, with interracial or intercultural exchange, on committees or teams, or you can be active in mass production or marketing of commodities or foods.

Pluto sextile Moon: You can set more unified, better and happier patterns in your domestic and family relationships at this time. By taking the opportunity to show responsive sympathy to others you can elicit cooperation for the greater good of the whole.

With intuitive insights into your own attitudes and automatic emotional responses that have been shaped by past conditioning, you can give up self-destructive habits and reform a better private life. You can reconcile any differences with your parents, dependents or kin. Women exert a potent force and easily gain cooperation and attention. A specific woman could become a close friend.

A variety of activities can bring you into contact with many people, where you have an instinctive feel for their attitudes.

Pluto semisquare Moon: You are apt to be emotionally restless as a variety of activities and people make demands on your cooperative sympathy. Dependents may be pulling at you; there can be occasional pressures and upsets connected with family relationships and domestic affairs. You may suffer the removal of one of your kin or undergo a revision of the family structure.

An indecisive emotional reaction to someone in your private life can bring up some of your own covert material and unresolved conflicts. As a result of this friction you could go underground with passive resistance. Psychological or metaphysical groups could test your discrimination; you may feel manipulated by the force of other people's mental attitudes, and unsure of your own attitude. You can meet with groups on a fluctuating basis.

Pluto sesquisquare Moon: Your home and family life may be variable and unstable; you may feel coerced by the emotional needs of dependents. Women tend to exert a subtle force, and if you feel manipulated your tendency is to go underground with passive resistance.

Inconsistent, heavy emotional pressures and upsets in your relationships and domestic affairs put you in an uncooperative mood and stimulate compulsive or covert reactions. There can be the removal of one of your kin, or a revision of the family structure.

A variety of intermittent activities brings you into public contact. If you have a compulsive responsiveness it may seem impossible to say no; you can be divided into a dozen pieces by committees, clubs, and teams. Cooperate with those for whom you do care, but detach yourself from impossible demands.

Pluto conjunct Mercury: The external events of this time may not reveal the extent and intensity of your thinking. With a sense of solitude and isolation, a repetitive compulsive driving train of thought can be directed toward the search for answers within yourself, toward solving problems, looking for direction, mulling over plans, or reaching for the answer to imponderable mysteries.

You are swayed by the attitudes and force of others; your rational attempts to communicate are swept into collusion or compromise. You seem to be forced to arbitrate and negotiate for your own position and for the unity of your group or team.

You could be privy to secret plots or grave information. You may even be aware of the thoughts of others telepathically. Your study and correspondence could include contracts, papers or data about taxes, insurance, legacies, negotiable funds, or group programs. You could speak before groups or function as the representative of a collective.

Areas of study and education intensify with the will and awareness that can take you into profound investigation of advanced fields. The solutions you find are the natural result of prior conditioning and education, as refined by your discrimination.

There will be at least one person to whom you can communicate in depth. Encounter groups or psychological counsel could hit you hard in covert areas, but it requires effort through the duration of this period to complete the cycle and transmutation that you seek.

Pluto opposite Mercury: The external events of this time seem to impel you toward a given destination. With a sense of solitude and isolation, you may go over and over matters in your thoughts, looking for direction, mulling over plans, searching for answers.

A certain situation may offer you no other choice but to cooperate, as you are swayed into collusion by the attitudes and force of others. Someone who exerts a powerful influence on you could give you advice or counsel that puts you in a bind. If you deliver an ultimatum, you must be prepared to let go, to quit, to leave the situation. If you're not ready or able to do that, then you must compromise.

Dogmatic and opinionated views make rational communication difficult, and dictatorial methods arouse your passive resistance. You'd best guard against your own compulsion to reform others; they are simply not ready to make the changes you want.

Secret plots or grave information could stir up your own covert areas. Encounter groups or psychological counseling would require your maximum involvement, and may leave you drained. When this period is finished you will have completed a certain cycle and transformed much of your own potential into stronger capacity.

Areas of study and education intensify with the will and awareness that take you into advanced fields. Your correspondence could include contracts, papers or data about taxes, insurance, legacies, negotiable funds, or group programs. You could speak before groups as the representative of a collective.

Pluto square Mercury: There are obstacles to cooperative communication at this time. Your environment may include people who are not your intellectual peers, or who do not have the same interests or background. This can give you a sense of solitude and isolation, as the barriers are frustrating; you can't make yourself understood nor grasp the realities of other people. Dogmatic and opinionated views make rational communication difficult, and dictatorial methods arouse an uncooperative passive resistance.

You may be working out a problem in your mind, going over and over it with a repetitive, compulsive train of thought, looking for solutions and direction. You may experience the shock of seeing many of your ideas and concepts shattered under the impetus of new data. This forces you to change your way of thinking, and to readjust your plans and methods in your work and approach to life.

You could be swayed into collusion and compromise by the attitude and force of others. Someone who exerts a powerful influence on you could give you advice or counsel that puts you in a bind. A relationship with a person who has hidden power drives or concealed plans could be permanently broken.

Secret plots or grave information could stir up your own covert areas. Encounter groups or psychological counseling would require tense involvement and would leave you drained.

Unprecedented situations demand that you transmute your potential into stronger capacity, with intensified study and education in the school of hard knocks. Your correspondence could include contracts, papers or data about taxes, insurance, legacies, negotiable funds, or group programs. You could speak before groups, or as the representative of a collective.

Pluto trine Mercury: External events of this time may not reveal the extent and intensity of your thinking. As a result of prior experience, you now can bring a decision into conscious awareness. That repetitive, compulsive, driving train of thought that comes out of your solitude can be directed toward solving a problem, setting a direction, formulating a plan, or finding an answer.

You can focus your mental acuity and insight into a regenerative study of advanced fields or research. Special courses or programs can help increase your mental powers and ability. Your literary work or communications hold a powerful sway. Your correspondence could include contracts, papers or data about taxes, insurance, legacies, negotiable funds, or group programs. You could speak before groups, or as the representative of a collective.

You are in an excellent position to be effective in reforms and negotiations. By being privy to secret information, you can be the arbitrator between differing factions in order to maintain unity. You can conceal your own covert plans until the timing is right for a successful power play.

Encounter groups or psychological counseling would bring out more of your potential. A former cycle has been completed, and the transmutation of this time will affirm your plans for the future.

Pluto sextile Mercury: The events of this time will lay the groundwork for new directions in your thinking, making decisions, and finding solutions.

A repetitive, compulsive train of thought in your moments of solitude and isolation will gradually intensify a deep drive to increase your conscious awareness.

Study, research, special courses or programs give you the opportunity to increase your mental powers and ability to sway others. Encounter groups or psychological counseling could bring out more of your potential. You could have an occasion to speak before groups, or as the representative of a collective.

Your correspondence could include contracts, papers or data about taxes, insurance, legacies, negotiable funds, or group programs.

By compromise and negotiation with others, you can be the arbitrator between differing factions in order to maintain unity. You can conceal your own secret or covert schemes until the time is right to make plans for the future.

This period is, in a sense, an hiatus between a cycle of the past and a cycle of the future. A subtle inner transmutation is going on that will lead to new opportunities.

Pluto semisquare Mercury: Your decisions, plans, and directions tend to vacillate. In moments of isolation you may direct your thinking toward an intense search for answers within yourself, but the solutions remain indecisive until more data and information filter out of the shifting variety of experience. Some of your cherished ideas and concepts may shatter under the impact of new realities, which will force you to change your way of thinking and your methods of operation.

You must compromise and adjust to indecisive conditions that keep giving you new information and experience. Unprecedented situations demand that you cooperate for the good of all concerned. You can be swayed by the force of someone who exerts a powerful influence on you. Dogmatic or opinionated views will cause friction, and dictatorial methods arouse passive resistance.

This period is an unstable hiatus between the past and the future, during which you must learn a greater depth of understanding.

Your correspondence could include a variety of contracts, papers or data about taxes, insurance, legacies, negotiable funds, or group programs.

Pluto sesquisquare Mercury: This is an inconsistent period; your directions, plans, and decisions tend to fluctuate. You may have a repetitive and compulsive drive to make an intense search for solutions or answers, but you seem unable to come to a conclusion. The breakup of old conditions is gradually completing a cycle of the past, but your present instability requires more understanding of the educational value of experience as applied to shifting conditions and unprecedented situations. Your tendency is to conceal your own secret or covert plans.

You may be swayed by the force of someone who has a powerful influence on you. Rather than resorting to passive resistance or mental and verbal manipulation, try to cooperate in order to maintain unity. Weed out the nonessentials to allow your own core of reality to grow.

Your correspondence could include revisions of contracts, papers or data about taxes, insurance, legacies, negotiable funds, or group programs.

Pluto conjunct Venus: Your social life will cover a much broader range during this period, with a greater variety of people and activities. You may involve yourself in the fields of art, fashion, culture, music, entertainment, or social work. Psychological or metaphysical groups could foster deep friendships and could have considerable impact on your life.

With the people you love, and those with whom you live, it is necessary to compromise and cooperate to keep your unity. An intense involvement could bring out all your latent feelings, from possessiveness to longing for the ultimate union that raises you to spiritual and creative heights. A romance or love affair at this time would be all-consuming. You may well meet someone whose emotional impact remains with you for your lifetime.

Your feelings could be deeply stirred by a loss or emotional crisis involving a family member or a friend. Some matter will bring up long-buried feelings from the past for you to reexamine and release, or purge.

As your values are transformed and tempered you can come out of this cycle with a greater sense of peace, beauty, serenity, and understanding.

Pluto opposite Venus: Circumstances thrust you into a much broader range of social involvements, with a greater variety of people and activities. You must extend yourself to learn more about love, life, art, fashion, culture, music, entertainment, or social work. Psychological or metaphysical groups could make insistent demands on your social development.

Your marriage or family relationships could exert inexorable pressures that make it necessary for you to compromise and cooperate if you wish to keep unity. All your latent feelings could surface, from jealousy and possessiveness to intense longing, from long-buried resentments to emotional passions. A secret affair or close relationship would be either degrading and debasing or would raise you to new spiritual heights. A matter from the past must be encountered and resolved now, in order to purge your life and yourself of collusion, emotional manipulation, or coercion.

Your feelings could be deeply stirred by a loss or emotional crisis concerning a family member or a friend.

As your values are tempered and transformed you can exit this cycle of stress with a greater sense of peace, beauty, serenity, and understanding.

Pluto square Venus: You may have a more intense longing for companionship, love, care, gaiety, and fun; but there are obstacles to a fulfilling social life. Your family, mate, or friends, are not being too cooperative, and the people with whom you do have social contact can't fill your needs.

Marriage or family relationships could engender inexorable conflicts; it may be necessary for you to compromise for the sake of unity, and you could find yourself bending over backwards to placate someone with a stronger will and force. Ultimatums, or attempts to reform, will only bring resistance or emotional outrage. A certain situation could bring out your feelings of resentment, jealousy, and possessiveness, or could strengthen your passive compliance in lonely isolation.

A secret affair or close relationship could put you through compulsive changes, emotional heights and depths.

Your feelings could be deeply stirred by a loss or emotional crisis regarding a family member or a friend.

You can gain satisfaction from working with groups in the areas of art, fashion, culture, music, entertainment, or social work. You appreciate psychological or metaphysical groups that bring up matters from the past for you to confront, resolve, and release, though there are certain group factions that disturb you.

As your values are tempered and transformed you can emerge from the emotional isolation of this cycle with a greater sense of peace, beauty, serenity, creativity, and understanding.

Pluto trine Venus: Your social life will cover a much broader range during this period and will encompass a greater variety of people and activities. You can be active with groups in art, fashion, culture, music, entertainment, or social work. The impact of psychological or metaphysical groups could result in the formation of deep friendships.

You tend to be more intensely involved with the people with whom you live; working and playing together with companionable cooperation.

An intense emotional and romantic experience could evoke the whole gamut of latent feelings from all-absorbing possessiveness to a longing for the ultimate union. A love affair or close relationship could take you to the heights and the depths.

If your feelings are touched by a loss or emotional crisis with a family member or friend, you can be helpful, considerate, and caring.

You can bring up buried feelings from the past to reexamine, release, and purge. As your values are transformed and tempered you can come out of this cycle with more creativity and a greater sense of peace, beauty, serenity, and understanding.

Pluto sextile Venus: Your social life provides more opportunities to enjoy a variety of people and activities during this time. You can be involved with groups in art, fashion, culture, music, entertainment, or social work. Deep friendships may form as a result of the impact from psychological or metaphysical groups.

Though one of your loved ones may not be too cooperative, you can compromise and placate for the sake of peace; for the most part you can work and play together companionably.

Some situation could bring out latent or covert feelings of jealousy and possessiveness, or a lonely longing for greater unity. If your feelings are touched by an emotional crisis or loss of a family member or friend, you can be helpful and caring.

Buried feelings from the past may boil up to be reexamined, released, and purged, bringing you more peace and understanding.

Pluto semisquare Venus: Your social life tends to vacillate with a wider variety of people and activities. You can be involved with groups in art, fashion, culture, music, entertainment, or social work. Psychological or metaphysical groups could shift their emphasis with a change in membership of their various factions.

Occasionally you want to withdraw into lonely isolation—to get away from the friction and demands of family relationships, mate, or friends. Someone may not be too cooperative, and you feel irritated, resentful, and coerced by the need to compromise.

A secret affair, or close relationship, could put you through compulsive changes and emotional heights and depths. Your feelings could be stirred by an emotional incident or loss of a family member or friend. Buried feelings from the past may come up to be reexamined, released, and purged, giving you more peace and understanding.

Pluto sesquisquare Venus: Your social life tends to be highly inconsistent and scattered during this time. You may long intensely for companionship, love, care, and fun, but a breakup of patterns can give you a sudden emotional jolt. At times you may withdraw into lonely isolation, as your family, mate, or friends are embroiled in some inexorable conflicts that you cannot seem to reconcile or reform. You could be bending over backwards to placate someone with a stronger will and force, but ultimatums only invoke passive resistance.

A secret affair or close relationship could put you through compulsive changes and emotional heights and depths. Your feelings could be deeply stirred by an emotional crisis or the loss of a family member or friend.

You can gain satisfaction from involvement with groups in art, music, culture, entertainment, or social work. Psychological or metaphysical groups may include disturbing factions that you are in no position to reconcile.

As your values are tempered and transformed you can come out of the emotional agitation of this cycle with a greater sense of peace, serenity, creativity, and understanding.

Pluto conjunct Mars: During this period you may have a compelling desire for productive action. Your covert drives and passions surface with intense desire. According to your basic nature that desire can be either constructive or destructive.

On the constructive side, you can work with a group or team in mass production for the welfare of people as a whole. Your efforts can sway or influence others to improve their conditions, and with the force of your own conviction you can gain cooperation for a common goal.

On the destructive side, any latent criminal tendencies can surface to involve you with underworld persons or groups. Someone in your environment may exert a coercive force that demands your collusion. You may be swayed by intense sexual drives that overrule any cool judgment. A festering physical or psychological area can come to a head, where it must be lanced, purged, or surgically removed in order to heal.

Face up to your own power drives, your hidden passions—jealousy, possessiveness, competitiveness, and hostility—in order to resolve and transmute these into tools and weapons to fight injustice, to tackle problems in your physical environment, or to drive toward a goal. You can be more aggressive, courageous, resourceful, and decisive.

Pluto opposite Mars: During this period there seems to be an inexorable repression by uncooperative circumstances that block your efforts to achieve. In that attempt to better your objective environment, you must persevere, with research, investigation, and resourceful aggression. In both objective and subjective areas, your covert drives and passions can surface with intense desire. According to your basic nature that desire can be either constructive or destructive.

On the constructive side, you can work with a group or team in mass production for the welfare of people as a whole. If there are factions in the group, it may be necessary for you to define your own position, or even to deliver an ultimatum. There can be counter-forces within the group that are playing power games in an ateempt to undermine you. Someone close to you may be using manipulative tactics or passive resistance that demands your compromise.

You could be swayed by intense sexual extremes of either excessive lust or repressive denial.

On the destructive side, you must face up to your own power drives, resentment, fury, hostility, jealousy, possssiveness, or violent compulsions. If you have any criminal tendencies, or are involved in underworld dealings, this too can surface. A festering physical or psychological area will come to a head, where it can be lanced, purged, or surgically removed, in order to heal.

With courageous action, resolve and transmute your hidden passions into weapons and tools to fight injustice. Be decisive; maintain the force of your own convictions, and you can better your conditions.

Pluto square Mars: It's very difficult to be constructive during this period. People around you are uncooperative, and counter-forces in your group are playing power games that undermine your position. Someone close to you may be using manipulative tactics, offering you either passive resistance or ultimatums.

Your own hidden areas can surface with intense desire. According to your basic nature that desire can be either constructive or destructive. On the constructive side, you can work with a group or team in mass production for the welfare of people as a whole.

You could be swayed by intense sexual drives that lead you to either extremes in practice, or repressive denial.

Face up to your own power drives, resentment, fury, hostility, jealousy, possessiveness, or violent compulsions. If you have any criminal tendencies, or are involved in underworld dealings, this too can surface. A festering area will come to a head, where it can be lanced, purged, or surgically removed, in order to heal.

Resolve and transmute your hidden passions into weapons and tools to fight injustice and to remove deep destructive areas. Use courageous action to improve conditions and to gain achievement.

Pluto trine Mars: You can put your energy, will power, and initiative into constructive action. You can work with a group or team to manifest improved conditions. Your efforts can sway or influence people, and with the force of your own convictions you gain cooperation for the common good. Go after what you want.

Within your own psyche you can face up to your deeply hidden passions, possessiveness, competitiveness, hostility, and power drives. Convert these energies into tools or weapons of decisive action to fight injustice or to tackle problems in your physical environment. If there is a festering area in your life, it can come to a head and be resolved cooperatively.

You could be influenced by intense sexual attractions at this time; however, if there is repression, you have the resolution with which to transmute that energy into other forms of gratification.

You can take a massive step of growth in the achievement of a goal that leads to further development of your capacities.

Pluto sextile Mars: This time is opportune to make constructive changes that will put you into a position of improved circumstances. Use your will power and initiative to work for constructive action. In a group or team, your efforts can sway or influence people, and with the force of your convictions you gain cooperation for the general good.

You could be influenced by intense sexual attractions; however, if there is repression, you have the resolution with which to transmute that energy into other areas of gratification.

Within your own psyche you can face up to your deeply hidden passions, possessiveness, competitiveness, hostility, and lust for power. Convert these drives into tools or weapons of decisive action to fight injustice or to solve problems in your physical environment.

If there is a festering area in your life it can come to a head to be resolved cooperatively.

Pluto semisquare Mars: You may vacillate between periods of repression or withdrawal and periods of intense desire to remake your life with constructive action. Certain people around you seem manipulative or uncooperative, and you may be indecisive about whether to make a compromise or deliver an ultimatum.

At intermittent periods you are compelled to look at your own areas of passion, your jealousies, possessiveness, competitiveness, hostility, sexual impulses, and power drives. Gradually root out the nonessentials and purge the festering areas in order that you may heal and move ahead. As your resolution takes form, direct that decisive action toward improving your conditions.

Pluto sesquisquare Mars: This is a period of intermittent repression and passionate desire to break up old patterns. At times it is difficult to be constructive, as others are uncooperative, manipulative, or playing power games. Though you feel a hostile resistance you may not be ready nor able to take a decisive action, or you may not be in a position to make an ultimatum. You may be swayed by intense sexual drives that are inconsistently overwhelming and repressive.

As your hidden areas surface, face up to your own power drives and your passionate jealousy and possessiveness. Gradually resolve and purge the festering areas in order that they may heal. Use ingenuity to gain constructive satisfaction, and direct your restless energy to make constructive improvements in your physical environment.

Pluto conjunct Jupiter: This is a period of growth for your faith and optimism; you will acquire a new sense of joy and freedom. You can take a massive step by expanding your education, teaching or travel, religion or philosophy, or business and financial areas.

You can be attracted to group procedures that range from formal pomp and circumstances to buoyant and gay camaraderie. As your tolerance horizon is broader, your experiences can include people of other cultures, races, and nationalities. You may even be more indulgent and extravagant.

This is an excellent time for financial investment. Former matters can pay off, and new ventures will prove to be lucrative. Professional or business matters could develop through group investments or cooperative programs dealing with mass production, publications, legalities, insurance, or inheritance.

There could occur a religious conversion, or the awakening of deep urges to spiritual consciousness. Your changing ethical values could launch you on a campaign to reform yourself, others, and the world. The secrets of nature and the universe could lead you to deeper studies and radiant insights, even to clairvoyance or mystical experiences. With faith in the ultimate order, and with confidence about your own capacities, you can cooperate with others for the general good.

In all, as former repressions are removed, a new cycle is set into motion that is fortunate for your position of honor, prestige, and financial return, as well as for your deeper understanding and self-integration.

Pluto opposite Jupiter: Circumstances at this time put you in a position to take a massive step of growth. By cooperating with others for the general good, you can extend your own capacities in fields of education, teaching or travel, religion or philosophy, or in business and finance.

However, opposing factions can sorely try your self-confidence and faith in others. Certain people in your group are pompous or ostentatious, or they demand formal procedures that you find threatening to your personal freedom. You must compromise as you continue to expand your world of experience.

As your tolerance level is broader, your environment can include people of cultures foreign to you. There are certain elements with which you can identify, but on the whole you do realize that this identification is merely a stepping stone on your path, not the path itself.

You may even be caught in a period of indulgence – "going along with the gang" in areas of growth that are not in your best interests. A strong-willed person may hold a powerful sway over you; though you want to cooperate, your position makes it difficult to do so, or you are torn between conflicting loyalties.

Professional or business matters can develop through group investments or cooperative programs dealing with mass production, publications, legalities, insurance, or inheritance. Though the red tape is time-consuming, you can make steps of lucrative growth. If you're put on a spot where you must lend or invest money, there is a risk unless you have a formal irrevocable contract.

If there is a religious conversion it may be with a note of fanaticism, in obeisance to ritualistic codes. Religious groups tend to operate under the auspices of an "inner circle," and a lack of compliance could subject you to anathema.

Through intense heights and depths, and with faith in the ultimate order and the integrity of your own honor, you can set a new cycle of deeper understanding and self-integration, as well as acquire a mundane position of prestige.

Pluto square Jupiter: Though you have an intense urge to expand, there are obstacles to overcome in your growth of education, teaching or travel, religion or philosophy, or in business and financial areas.

Formal procedures can involve you in a great deal of red tape. As you have a compelling urge for freedom you may resist cooperating with the program; the greatest danger you face is a rampant penchant for self-indulgence. A strong-willed person may have a powerful effect on you, or you may go along with the gang in areas of growth that are not in your best interests. Your own self-confidence and your faith in others can be sorely tried.

As your tolerance level is broader, your environment can include people of cultures foreign to you. There are certain elements with which you can identify, but on the whole you do realize that this identification is merely a stepping stone on your path, not the path itself.

In professional or business matters you could be drawn into collusion on group investments or cooperative programs, mass production, publications, legalities, insurance, or inheritance. If you're put on a spot where you must lend or invest money it's risky unless you have a formal irrevocable contract. There could be a compulsion to extravagance that accumulates bills.

If there is a religious conversion, there can be a note of fanaticism in the required obeisance to ritualistic codes. Religious groups tend to operate under the auspices of an inner circle, and a lack of compliance would subject you to anathema.

You can hit intense heights and depths. If you are striving for self-integration in the scheme of the whole, you can work through surface problems to a deeper sense of faith and contentment. If you are striving for compulsive gratification at the cost of others, you can leave a trail of financial and moral waste.

Pluto trine Jupiter: During this time, certain conditions that repress your freedom can be resolved, to make an easy and natural step of growth. This can be the turning point, at which you take a massive step of expansion in your education or teaching, travel, religion and philosophy, or in business and financial areas.

There may be a deeply moving experience, removing or purging you of a handicap, that you handle with faith and understanding, and through which you are given supportive care by a person eternally dear to you.

Your enthusiasm elicits cooperation from others in your group, and you can feel a joy and contentment in the camaraderie of loyal compatriots. With your new tolerance level, you can encompass foreign environments and peoples with ease.

Professional matters of the past may be consummated with satisfactory negotiation. A move or business expansion can set a cycle into operation that involves group investment or cooperative programs dealing with mass production, publication, legalities, insurance, or inheritance. Purchasing power, combined with a turnover in sales, reaches a peak that is lucrative. You may be cautioned to observe some restraint in overextending your credit; you do have a tendency to extravagant judgment and action through which you could squander your increases by overdevelopment.

With a natural acceptance and philosophical understanding you may draw on your religious faith for peace and insight. In your spiritual consciousness you can be touched by an intimate awareness of the cycles of life and death in the harmony of the ultimate order.

Pluto sextile Jupiter: You have the opportunity at this time to take a turn in your expansion of education or teaching, travel, religion and philosophy, or business and finance. There is a way out of a repressive area or situation that you can resolve with the cooperation of others. A handicap to your freedom may be removed.

Your enthusiasm sways others in your group to camaraderie. A business program in mass production, group investment, publication, legalities, insurance or inheritance tends to expand. Purchasing power, sales and financial negotiations tend to be on a productive up-cycle. You may be cautioned to not overextend yourself, as extravagances could squander your advantage.

In your religious life, there is faith and serenity in your philosophical understanding of the natural order.

Pluto semisquare Jupiter: During this time you may vacillate between an understanding tolerance of your present situation and a restless, compelling urge for more freedom. Though you are expanding in gradual steps you tend to be indecisive about the way to resolve an area of repression.

If you take a step of rampant indulgence, extravagance, or overextended credit, it seems that you must backtrack to renegotiate. In your education or teaching, travel, business and finance, formal procedures occasionally involve you in red tape, and tend to be inconclusive. Business or professional matters of group investments or cooperative programs, mass production, publication, legalities, insurance, or inheritance meet with varied delays and risks.

In your philosophy you may have cause to question your own faith, as the inner circle in your religious group can be divided into factions.

Though certain steps of growth can make a turning point about which you are optimistic, on the whole this tends to be an indecisive period of starts and stops.

Pluto sesquisquare Jupiter: This tends to be an inconsistent period of growth, during which your contentment and tolerance are spiced with sudden compelling urges for freedom. With rebellious extravagance you could suddenly lay waste to the formal order of your life.

Abrupt changes in your education or teaching, travel, business or financial areas could involve you in red tape, or in the need for collusion or compromise. In business and finance, overexpansion or overextension of credit can be risky with your group investments in cooperative programs, mass production, publications, legalities, insurance, or inheritance.

An unexpected disruption of unity could cause you to question your own religious faith. As your philosophical views are changing and reforming, you may feel a compelling urge to break with the order of ritual and obedience. In all your group contacts, there seems to be a disturbing diversity of factions.

Reach out for those unprecedented steps of growth that can remove areas of repression, but be careful of erratic or compulsive, indulgent extravagance.

Pluto conjunct Saturn: Out of your experience with restrictive conditions you can formulate an intense ambition. As you gain some taste of the power that comes with control, you learn the deep satisfaction of working to your full capacity.

This is not a period of success, but rather a period of training. In group activities you can work with discipline, endurance, enterprise, and resolution that will gradually put you in a key role in your organization, and will establish certain fundamental abilities that will always be useful to you. With methods that are conscientious and thorough, you gain more security in your worldly position. Each step of responsibility that you take increases your potential.

It is necessary that you conform to certain group standards. If you try to manipulate or control your group, team, or party, you'll be subject to disapproval, coventry, or exclusion. However, cooperation and team effort, in which you place your personal drives secondary to the good of the whole, can involve you in a finished product that is efficient and accomplished.

You may have a problem with someone in your life who is repressive, coercive, poor, worried, grievous, overworked, or dependent on you. Be supportive, but don't get pulled into their depression or their debts.

By being frugal and calculating with your money, you can increase your savings for an important long-term investment of a practical nature. Pay off old financial and moral obligations in order to rid yourself of impediments that could handicap your future.

You may have periods of intense solitude, of feeling alone even in a crowd. Out of this you will tap your deepest reservoirs of strength. Certain old forms are being completed; within the year ahead you can find in yourself a stronger resolution of purpose and direction.

Pluto opposite Saturn: During this period, circumstances can be highly restrictive to your personal control, and repressive to your ambitions. It is necessary that you cooperate with your group, team, or party for the good of the whole, in spite of insubordination and lack of cooperation from opposing factions. You may be thrust into a key role of arbitration, of dealing with negotiations for which you have full responsibility but limited authority. If your methods are conscientious and thorough, disciplined, enduring, enterprising, and resolute, you can fulfill your obligation.

Some person in your life who is poor, worried, grievous, ill, depressive, overworked, or dependent on you can present a problem. That person can be highly coercive with overt compliance and passive resistance, but you are unwilling or unable to break that bond just yet. Be supportive and honest in your duties and work it out. Pay off old financial and moral debts now, or else you'll have that handicap for years to come.

Obligations can be discharged if you are frugal and calculating. Practice self-denial, place your personal drives secondary to the good of the whole and gradually overcome the impediments of this period. There is a subtle breakdown of old forms, and the responsibilities you take with resolute purpose will determine the extent of personal power in your future direction. The way in which you cooperate and get the job done will set a precedent for greater efficiency and accomplishment.

You may have periods of intense solitude, of feeling alone even in a crowd. Out of this you tap your deepest reservoirs of strength.

Pluto square Saturn: During this time, obstacles, restrictions, and stringent problems test your patience and fortitude. As a result of former repressions and errors you could make a compulsive decision that you feel will resolve an impediment to a conclusion. On the contrary there is no instant resolution; through the period you must work out to conclusion a responsibility of the past. Don't jump from the frying pan into the fire, but let your own ambitions simmer. A new sense of direction will emerge with compelling force as you discharge old debts and obligations.

You may have periods of intense solitude, of feeling alone even in a crowd. Out of this you tap your deepest reservoirs of strength. As you gradually begin a new course, formed by your discipline, endurance, enterprise, and resolution, you begin to set that precedent for the future. Each step of responsibility that you take increases your capacity.

You may have a problem with a person in your life who is poor, worried, grievous, ill, depressive, overworked, or dependent on you. Be supportive and honest to the extent of your duty; and if you're in a bind, compromise for now as you work it out.

It is necessary that you cooperate with the group, team, or party for the good of the whole, in spite of insubordination and lack of cooperation from opposing factions. You may be thrust into a key role of arbitration, of dealing with negotiations for which you have a responsibility but limited authority. You could be exposed to scheming or dishonest power plays, corruption, collusion, passive resistance, or coercive ultimatums.

With frugal, calculating self-denial, you can pay off financial and moral debts. If your methods are conscientious and thorough, by the time this period is completed you can overcome great obstacles to a massive step forward—a step of greater strength, capacity, control, and security.

Pluto trine Saturn: This is a period of powerful accomplishment, during which you have greater control and responsibility in the advancement of your ambitions. If you have encountered former repression or error, restriction or obstacles, now is the time to correct or resolve it. Old forms are being completed, financial and moral debts and obligations can be discharged, and a new sense of direction will emerge with compelling force.

You can have the deep satisfaction of working to your full capacity to achieve results relative to the discipline, endurance, enterprise, and resolution you put into your goals. In your group activities you can elicit cooperation in favorable negotiations. As you hold a key role in your organization, the impact of your drive will sway the group or party to work as a team for the good of the whole program.

If there is a problem with someone who is dependent or dragging on you, you can easily work out the relationship now, with no further obligation. Impediments that could handicap your future tend to drop away, and commitments you make at this time are supportive and enduring.

Though there is greater financial security, your attitude tends to be practical and calculating. An investment at this time tends to be solid with a long-term gradual return of capital gain.

Out of your periods of solitude you tap your deepest reservoirs of strength and resolution. The precedents that you set now will establish a form and pattern for years to come.

Pluto sextile Saturn: During this period you have the opportunity to discharge old debts and obligations, as many old forms are being completed in your life. A former repression or error, restriction or obstacles, can be resolved or corrected to remove an impediment to your future control.

Out of your periods of solitude you can tap your deepest reservoirs of strength and determination to gain a firmer resolution of purpose and direction.

In your group activities you can work with the team or party in cooperation that is opportune for your own ambitions as well as for the good of the whole program. You can be supportive of your dependents and can have a deeper unity with your peers. A new sense of direction and responsibility will establish your long-term goals.

Pluto semisquare Saturn: You may vacillate between a resolve to keep your security status quo, and a restless compelling urge to advance your ambitions in a new area. Intermittent obstacles and restrictions test your patience,

156

and a repressive situation seems a handicap.

Work it out. Old debts and obligations, financial and moral, can cause friction until they are completed and resolved.

There can be a problem with someone who is poor, worried, grievous, ill, overworked, depressive, or dependent on you. At odd times that person may be uncooperative or unstable; be supportive and honest in your responsibilities, and compromise to the extent of your duty.

In your group activities you can work with enterprise; however, your own indecision weakens your control. You may be exposed to passive resistance, collusion, corruption, or power plays. If you are pressed to take a side, withdraw until you can gain more information; ultimatums are untimely.

In your moments of solitude, of feeling alone even in a crowd, you can tap your deepest reservoirs of strength and fortitude. Out of the fluctuations of this period, a new direction can emerge that will lead to greater stability and security.

Pluto sesquisquare Saturn: Old forms are breaking up; the usual stable conditions are inconsistent, and there are subtle obstacles to your ambitions. You may be erratic in your responsibilities.

Occasionally you suffer an intense solitude, a feeling of being alone even in a crowd. Out of this you can tap a deep potential of strength to find a stronger resolution of purpose in your life.

With frugal calculation, old debts and obligations can be discharged. In your work you can gain greater control as you learn to handle a shifting variety of duties and demands. Discipline, endurance, and enterprise are required in your group activities.

There can be a problem in your life with someone who is poor, worried, uncooperative, overworked, or dependent on you. Be supportive and honor your commitments, but don't get pulled into debt or depression.

As new conditions emerge with compelling force, regenerate your directions for long-term goals.

Pluto conjunct Uranus: Not applicable to persons born in the twentieth century.

Pluto opposite Uranus: This is a massive and compelling period of change in your life, not from one specific incident or situation alone, but as a gradual turnaround. Matters of the past are coming to a conclusion; when you release compulsive attachments that demand your unwilling compromise, repressive situations or people will be reconciled or eliminated. A replacement is there and waiting. Reach out for greater potential possibilities. Open new doors of idea and experience. Enter into new situations and environments. You may even diametrically change your life style.

There can be a sudden, unexpected sweeping incident or circumstance that calls for maximum cooperation and unity with others. Circumstances can push you into looking with harsh clarity at your own attitudes in order to find your priorities in terms of direction, potential, and values. In your moments of detached isolation, look deeply within your own hidden areas in order to cleanse

157

and purge yourself of the nonessentials. As you gain the insight of greater awareness, a new path will begin to shape your future. Though some compromise is necessary, do not yield your independence to a situation or person in your life that is coercive, manipulative, covert, or frustrating; keep your right of choice and your own resolution.

In your highly eclectic group situations there can be a remarkable diversity of people united under one common banner. You could be drawn into, or even be a key factor in, changes of the power structure. Counter-factions, who seem unenlightened, are giving you passive resistance in the form of isolationism or inflexible uncooperation. There can be unpleasant incidents of insubordnation, rebellion, or insurrection.

For the good of the whole program, contribute your full measure of inventive original ideas. If you should be forced out, it is certainly time for you to follow an alternative independent course. The group, team, or party can be a powerful vehicle for you only so long as you maintain your own individuality.

Change is not always comfortable. It may even be necessary to go back to the past to repeat an old pattern, or to finish up old attitudes before you can move forward in this transition. The period marks a resurgence of vital identity, with individuation based on your inner awareness of personal strength and purpose.

Pluto square Uranus: Circumstances that repress your individuality tend to cause obstacles to the unfolding of your singular potential. Though unconventional situations or manipulative people can cause you a high tension of rebellion, you are expected to cooperate for the benefit of unity.

Within your group, team, or party, there are subtle counter-factions that can foment a crisis of insubordination or insurrection. The group may split, or certain members may detach, in isolationism, passive resistance, or inflexible uncooperation. As the team is a powerful vehicle for you, you tend to compromise your own priorities for the good of the whole program. Do contribute your own inventive original ideas and reach solutions to unprecedented experiences and unexpected problems with ingenuity. However, do not yield your independent realities to a situation or person that is coercive, covert, or unenlightened. If you should be forced out, it is certainly time for you to strike out on an alternative independent course.

Compelling forces within you are germinating changes in your own attitudes. As a matter from the past is coming to a conclusion, you may question deeply your own direction, potential, and values. In your moments of detached isolation, look within: cleanse and purge yourself of nonessentials. As you let go of compulsive attachment to frustrating limitation, the matter, situation, or person will be resolved or eliminated.

In this period you can move from repression, to isolation, to a more powerful awareness of your own individuality and independence. You may even change diametrically your life style and direction.

Pluto trine Uranus: Sudden and unexpected events and new experiences can bring you massive changes during this period. Unprecedented situations and environments are not only interesting and stimulating but even open up greater possibilities. You can either touch upon, begin, or move into, your own area of capacity potential, depending on your age and former awareness of priorities.

As your individuality and resolution are greatly increased, with progressive independence you can achieve greater goals. You can break former records and set precedents for your future directions.

In your group situation you have the force of magnetic identity with which you can sweep others along to cooperation for the good of the whole program. The group, team, or party, is a powerful vehicle through which you can express inventive ideas, or can even influence the masses. Though the group can work as a coordinate team, you tend to stand out as an individual with an original contribution. Any uncooperative factions yield to, or compromise with, your position.

As matters of the past are resolved and concluded, this can mark a new chapter in your life—one that you'll always remember. You may even change your life style in an increase of scope and direction.

Pluto sextile Uranus: There are opportunities for you to make massive changes in your own attitudes. Sudden and unexpected events and new experiences can put you into situations that you haven't known before. New people and new ideas are interesting and stimulating.

Group situations, involving highly diverse people, will require your cooperation for the good of the whole team. You can stand out as an individual with an original contribution.

With an increase of will power and resolution you can achieve goals of progressive independence and positions of leadership.

Matters of the past are coming to a conclusion; this next chapter of your life will offer chances to change your life style with greater scope and direction.

Pluto semisquare Uranus: A nervous and compelling independence could make you quite restless. Unconventional situations or manipulative people could occasionally cause you a high tension of rebellion. For your own good, and for the benefit of others around you, you're expected to cooperate.

New people or unexpected problems that bring friction require your ingenuity in order to reach original solutions. Your attitude may be changing; you may be reluctant to yield your independence to a situation or person who is coercive, covert, or frustrating. Compromise for unity, but keep your right of choice and your own resolution.

Your group situation with a variety of diverse people may vacillate. Though you have a unique position of originality or leadership, a counterfaction could be working underground with power plays.

A matter from the past is coming to a conclusion for you to resolve. Rather than adapting an attitude of erratic compulsive independence, throw out the nonessentials and cooperate in areas of value.

Pluto sesquisquare Uranus: Certain matters of the past are being completed. Sudden, inconsistent changes and unusual circumstances are breaking up your present attitudes. As a result of present repression, there can be a reformation of changes in many of your opinions and deep convictions.

A willful and compelling independence could be explosive, but will be more constructive if you reach out for new ideas, new experiences, and new doors to open.

Unconventional situations or manipulative people cause you a high tension of rebellion. Rather than utilizing erratic compulsive independence, throw out the nonessentials and cooperate in areas of value.

In your group situations there can be occasional agitation over subtle counter-factions of highly diverse people. Erratic power plays, coercion, or insubordination can split the group; certain members may resist in isolationism, subtle manipulation, or inflexible uncooperation. Though you may compromise your priorities for the good of the whole program, your tendency is to detach your involvement. With the force of your independent resolution, you can reconcile the shifting changes and gradually make the transition to a new chapter.

Pluto conjunct Neptune: At some time, usually later during this period, you can go into a communal group within which you feel that you belong. Either the group itself, or a single strong member, can have so powerful an influence on your realities and directions that out of this era there may evolve a subtle change in your life path.

If you have a dream or an ideal, you can bring that vision into a forceful reality. The circumstances may be such that you were not even consciously aware of that inner need or hunger until you moved into the new situation and gradually realized, "This is what I was searching for."

You can have some wonderful times in group situations, where each contributes voluntarily to the democratic good of the whole, with unity and comraderie.

There may be an anxiety in your life, from vague situations in your career or personal life, or from repressions to your own creative striving. You may be able to see through the manipulative promotional schemes, but you are still swept into collusion. As you have high hopes for the outcome, you may compromise under the illusion that you have the power to resolve the conflicts into cooperative unity.

Someone in your community is devious, covert, or hiding insubordinate attitudes, or at the least is lazy and uncooperative. This is difficult to meet directly; you can't quite put your finger on an elusive problem or bring it into the open. Trust your own instinct and secretely investigate or research the hidden factors. Keep your own feet firmly on the ground in order to avoid exaggeration or overdramatization.

Anxiety can be engendered by a specific incident or person. A festering area must be purged and removed from either your environment, your psychology, or your body, in order for you to be healed and well again. If you are into compulsive drugs or booze, or rampant homosexuality, there is a greater proportional chance of hidden infections, overdoses, deception or fantasy, hospital or jail. In any event, there could be some time of compulsive retirement, either from unemployment or from a personal need to withdraw and regenerate.

If you are a highly imaginative and sensitive person, you can have poignant experiences of insight. Memories of the past can resurface from the depths of your unconscious. Sort out your priorities in meditation and contemplation. Psychological, psychic, or metaphysical groups can help you tap your vision and resources, but your deepest awareness comes from your moments of dreamy solitude.

If you are a highly practical, pragmatic person, or are strongly involved in mundane affairs, this period is less apt to have the bittersweet intensity; rather, it will tend to be more innocuous. There will be cooperation with others to gain common goals and advance your own striving directions.

Pluto sextile Neptune: During this time there are some ideal opportunities to cooperate with communal groups, where each person contributes voluntarily to the democratic good of the whole, with unity and comraderie. Through team work, the group can present a finished product or program that is of benefit to the community.

If you are anxious about a person or situation that is vague, devious, covert, manipulative, lazy, or uncooperative, it may be difficult for you to confront it directly. You can't quite put your finger on a certain elusive problem to bring it into the open. Trust your own instinct and plant your feet firmly on the ground; the underground factors will come out where you can either purge or resolve them.

There can be short periods of retirement, where you withdraw from activities in order to regenerate. Psychological, metaphysical, or psychic groups can help you tap your vision and resources, but in your moments of dreamy solitude you can have flashes of deep insight.

Cooperate with others during this time to gain common goals and to advance your own dreams and ideals.

Pluto semisquare Neptune: During this time you may feel an occasional urge to escape reality, tending to withdraw in semi-retirement. Though promotional schemes and community involvements may seem vaguely incompetent, your compromise is required for the good of the program. An elusive problem is hard to pin down, or a promise may fall through, but you are indecisive about whether to cooperate or to use the undercover information that you have in order to manipulate the situation.

You may feel anxiety about a person or situation that is covert, devious, coercive, or lazy. You may vacillate from helpless compliance, to compulsive resistance, to sensitive cooperation.

There is some group situation where you feel that you belong, with idyllic consideration and camaraderie. Teamwork can coordinate with unity and democracy. Psychological, metaphysical, or psychic groups can help you tap your vision and resources, but your deepest awareness comes from your moments

161

of dreamy solitude.

That slight nagging indecision will resolve into a clearer vision of your direction if you keep your feet on the ground with your own resolutions.

Pluto conjunct and opposite Pluto not applicable.

Pluto square Pluto: (Persons born in 1900 have Pluto square Pluto at approximately age 66, persons born in 1950 have the aspect at approximately age 40. As Pluto takes eleven to thirty-one years to go through a sign, there is not a consistent time span for the Pluto-to-Pluto aspects.)

Question and reevaluate your life. Are the same things still meaningful? Are there matters that you have to go back to finish? What do you want to do?

It's time to put away an area that is no longer essential and to bring out a resurgence of force into an area that has been dormant. Some deep interest, for which you've had no time, may now be developed. It's the end of a phase in your life and, with good health and mental vigor, you have the power to pursue latent potentials. You may possibly even start a new career.

Certain matters are completed; there could be the death of an old companion, or the dissolution of a relationship that is no longer cooperative. If there is a repressive condition, it is a matter of the past. Tie up the loose ends and let it go.

Do put your financial affairs in order. Update business and partnership matters - your will, taxes, insurance, legacies, negotiable funds, or group programs. It is definitely not the time to lend or invest money; any partnership agreements that you enter into now could be a direct loss, or there could be an insidious power struggle for control at a later date.

There could be subtle insubordination from a younger, stronger power structure within your group that will be difficult to meet on any direct terms, as it tends to manipulative politics. A strong-willed person could hold sway over you, forcing you into collusion against your will and better judgment. You may try reasonable negotiation, but find yourself drawn into compelling power plays. Use your resourcefulness, and compromise with tactical maneuvers.

You can reevaluate your own deep attitudes of life and death and your own place in the universal scheme. You could investigate or research material of a psychological or metaphysical nature in order to effect a personal metamorphosis.

Pluto trine Pluto: (Persons born in 1900 have Pluto trine Pluto at approximately age 78; persons born in 1950 have the aspect at approximately age 52.) A matter which you thought finished may regenerate at this time with vigor and resolution. As a repressive situation is resolved, a resurgence of an old interest, long dormant, gives you a new lease on life. Financial matters are comfortable and you may even reach a lucrative peak. Negotiations with powerful people effect cooperative programs.

Pluto sextile Pluto: You have the opportunity to start a new life during this time. A certain phase is completed; a matter or relationship that is no longer cooperative may be resolved.

It's time to rid your life of nonessentials and to bring a resurging force into an area that has been dormant. There can be creative opportunities to apply your resolution along lines of deeper mental activity and creative research.

Pay attention to your financial affairs of business and partnership, and update your will, taxes, insurance, legacies, negotiable funds, or group programs. Investments at this time could give rise to some subtle power plays that would be difficult to meet on direct terms, as they tend to manipulative tactics. A strong-willed person could hold sway over you against your will and better judgment, but with resourcefulness you can compromise and keep your individual control.

In group activities you can elicit cooperation for the good of the whole, and team efforts are productive with the strength of unity.

Pluto semisquare Pluto: During this time there can be a shift of emphasis in your directions. A certain phase of your life may be reaching completion, so you thrust out into new areas and experiences but without the confidence and assurance of which precise step to take.

A specific matter or relationship that is no longer cooperative may be abruptly removed or dissolved. However, it will be necessary for you to go back at intermittent times to tie up loose ends. A strong-willed person could hold sway over you, causing you to be indecisive, but you feel impelled to cooperate.

Pluto sesquisquare Pluto: (Persons born in 1900 have Pluto sesquisquare Pluto at approximately age 84; persons born in 1950 have the aspect at approximately age 60.) Cooperative goals and transitions tend to break up and reform in alternate patterns which may even be an improvement on the original plan when approached with flexibility and insight.

163

QUICK REFERENCE GLOSSARY

Sun conjunct Sun   Make your New Year's resolutions!
Sun opposite Sun   Set better goals.
Sun square Sun   Don't make a fool of yourself.
Sun trine Sun   Take the lead.
Sun sextile Sun   Open a new door
Sun semisquare Sun   Take it easy; the matter is shaky.
Sun sesquisquare Sun   Crazy goals go nowhere.

Sun conjunct Moon   Center with home and family.
Sun opposite Moon   Family comes first, take care of home needs.
Sun square Moon   It's a poor day to start something, relax and take care of yourself.
Sun trine Moon   Matters work out well.
Sun sextile Moon   Consider a new offer.
Sun semisquare Moon   Take care of family and home; outside areas bring restless indecision.
Sun sesquisquare Moon: You're in a dozen scattered pieces; goals hit snags.

Sun conjunct Mercury   Talk about yourself, your goals and plans.
Sun opposite Mercury   Communications are strained.
Sun square Mercury   Talks and plans meet blunt obstacles and bring bad news.
Sun trine Mercury   Pleasant visits and good news clear the air.
Sun sextile Mercury   If talk and plans are strained, ease off—another person offers an open ear.
Sun semisquare Mercury   Talk and plans are inconclusive.
Sun sesquisquare Mercury   Sudden poor news and change of plans are upsetting.

Sun conjunct Venus   Favors, love, and approval surround you if you're calm; overemotional scenes are touchy.
Sun opposite Venue   A social affair is strained, as an emotional scene lurks just

164

under the surface.

Sun square Venus   A social exchange doesn't work out well.

Sun trine Venus   Someone agreeable wants to please you.

Sun sextile Venus   Though you feel touchy, a favor or approval can cheer you up.

Sun semisquare Venus   One nice friend or favor comes out of a touchy day.

Sun sesquisquare Venus   Social matter overlap with unexpected highs and lows.

Sun conjunct Mars   Work, drink, fight, or make love with vigor.

Sun opposite Mars   Robust excess can be rash.

Sun square Mars   Crude, harsh, or uncomfortable conditions cause stress.

Sun trine Mars   Wade through obstacles to a constructive outcome.

Sun sextile Mars   Vigor and charm clear the way.

Sun semisquare Mars   Sudden impulse tends to be rash.

Sun sesquisquare Mars   Demands and desires are hectic.

Sun conjunct Jupiter   Protection, leisure, and favors abound.

Sun opposite Jupiter   Expansion and excess can go to extremes.

Sun square Jupiter   Your own discontent could push you overboard.

Sun trine Jupiter   With confidence and contentment, you can appreciate your benefits.

Sun sextile Jupiter   Tensions ease and relax.

Sun semisquare Jupiter   Restless excess challenges your poise.

Sun sesquisquare Jupiter   The expectation is greater than the realization.

Sun conjunct Saturn   There is satisfaction in your work, and strength and stability in your mature responsibilities.

Sun opposite Saturn   Work through restrictions and delays to catch up; set a new ambitious goal.

Sun square Saturn   Work, worry, and imposition are a strain.

Sun trine Saturn   Wade through obstacles and delays to push for ambitious projects.

Sun sextile Saturn   Maintain responsibility for your own security.

Sun semisquare Saturn   Varied pressures and worries are a strain.

Sun sesquisquare Saturn   Sudden upsets and job changes have to be tackled one at a time.

Sun conjunct Uranus   Sudden changes and new people stand out.

Sun opposite Uranus   Matters are as unstable and volatile as you are.

Sun square Uranus   Unexpected changes bring tension.

Sun trine Uranus   Make changes for the better.

Sun sextile Uranus   Changes are opportune if you can keep stable.

Sun semisquare Uranus   People and situations are erratic.

Sun sesquisquare Uranus   Ups and downs are sudden and crazy.

Sun conjunct Neptune   The day is a bit strange—either mellow or weird.

Sun opposite Neptune   Goals are unrealistic and unfirm.

Sun square Neptune   It's a vaguely low-tone day.

Sun trine Neptune   An ideal ease, favor, or camaraderie comes to you.

Sun sextile Neptune   Yield—and give a little.

Sun semisquare Neptune   Matters are not quite as they seem.

Sun sesquisquare Neptune   Ideal situations hold nebulous undercurrents.

Sun conjunct Pluto   Go along with the gang for cooperative results.

Sun opposite Pluto   Yield and cooperate where you must—but resist tyranny or imposition.

Sun square Pluto   Keep your reservations to yourself, as strong people around you deflect you from your goals.

Sun trine Pluto   Cooperate with others eighty percent for the greatest benefit.

Sun sextile Pluto   Cooperate to be agreeable, even if you are aware of the undercover conflicts.

Sun semisquare Pluto   Coordination pulls scattered activities together.

Sun sesquisquare Pluto   Go along with a sudden change of plans for the best results.

Mercury conjunct Sun   Have a good, deep talk.

Mercury opposite Sun   It's not cool to say all that you're thinking.

Mercury square Sun   Understanding is lacking, so be quiet and listen.

Mercury trine Sun   Meet with people you like for a mellow visit.

Mercury sextile Sun   Work out conflicts through a good talk.

Mercury semisquare Sun   Ideas are unstable; plans are up in the air.

Mercury sesquisquare Sun   Activities and talk are both scattered.

Mercury conjunct Moon   An understanding talk goes to the heart of the mood.

Mercury opposite Moon   Lack of understanding can bring a low-tone mood.

Mercury square Moon   Empathy is lacking, and agreements are shaky.

Mercury sextile Moon   Communications are helpful and agreeable.

Mercury semisquare Moon   Plans may change or bring a shift of mood.

Mercury sesquisquare Moon   Moody temperament brings unstable agreements.

Mercury trine Moon   A pleasant call or visit lifts your spirits.

Mercury conjunct Mercury   Pay attention; rambling talk can hold an important piece of information.

Mercury opposite Mercury   If you don't understand what's being said, listen; you may learn something—or teach another something.

Mercury square Mercury   Listening to another can be a bore until you break through to real communication.

Mercury trine Mercury   Communications are agreeable, as they hold promise and interest.

Mercury sextile Mercury   A talk can lead to plans ahead.

Mercury semisquare Mercury   A talk is inconclusive; plans are changed.

Mercury sesquisquare Mercury You may change your mind or your plans.

Mercury conjunct Venus Visit with a friend.
Mercury opposite Venus Smile through touchy feelings or a social dilemma.
Mercury square Venus A social visit takes some effort to reach warm understanding.
Mercury trine Venus A friend is warmly eager to visit or to please you.
Mercury sextile Venus Be polite—even if you feel touchy.
Mercury semisquare Venus Keep peace with give and take.
Mercury sesquisquare Venus Scattered social plans bring strain until you relax.

Mercury conjunct Mars Be careful of temper, trauma or tickets—or of fever.
Mercury opposite Mars If a matter you desire is blocked, keep a cool head.
Mercury square Mars Meet challenge with direct honesty; watch that grouchy temper!
Mercury trine Mars Tackle an interesting challenge; assert yourself to win.
Mercury sextile Mars Meet challenge with initiative.
Mercury semisquare Mars Impatience can bring irritation.
Mercury sesquisquare Mars Many activities and sudden changes bring tension.

Mercury conjunct Jupiter Your tolerance and hospitality gain respect.
Mercury opposite Jupiter Big expectations are overrated.
Mercury square Jupiter Take that big bite only if you can digest it; it could be overrated.
Mercury trine Jupiter People are mellow, helpful, and agreeable.
Mercury sextile Jupiter Be tolerant rather than overoptimistic.
Mercury semisquare Jupiter A matter you hope for can be unstable.
Mercury sesquisquare Jupiter Scattered activities and plans take patience and tolerance.

Mercury conjunct Saturn Work and discreet conservative plans give satisfaction; social extensions tend to drag.
Mercury opposite Saturn Work demands your attention with a cold self-sufficiency.
Mercury square Saturn Duties and impositions can exhaust or depress you.
Mercury trine Saturn Make ambitious or responsible moves; older persons are stable and helpful.
Mercury sextile Saturn Handle work or restrictions with quiet discretion.
Mercury semisquare Saturn A disappointment limits your options.
Mercury sesquisquare Saturn Work affords a change of pace.

Mercury conjunct Uranus There's a change of pace in work, ideas, talk, and news.
Mercury opposite Uranus Plans tend to undergo revision, or to put you into

unusual circumstances.

Mercury square Uranus You receive unusual news or communication, or you see different people and places.

Mercury trine Uranus Talk or news is interesting, and different activities are stimulating.

Mercury sextile Uranus Handle a change of pace with a different approach.

Mercury semisquare Uranus Sudden changes of activity could rattle you.

Mercury sesquisquare Uranus Plans are open to sudden changes or new information.

Mercury conjunct Neptune You may feel spaced-out as a result of vague or elusive communications.

Mercury opposite Neptune Communications can be dramatic, elusive, evasive — or even untrue.

Mercury square Neptune Matters tend to be inconsummate or vaguely disappointing.

Mercury trine Neptune A matter of ease, luxury, or thoughtful consideration is mellow.

Mercury sextile Neptune Talk and news are delightful, even though incomplete.

Mercury semisquare Neptune A talk is inconclusive.

Mercury sesquisquare Neptune A plan is unconsummate or falls through.

Mercury conjunct Pluto A talk can have impact, even though you repress some of your deepest thoughts on the matter.

Mercury opposite Pluto Cooperation is easier if you repress your true attitude and compromise; an ultimatum brings deep resentment.

Mercury square Pluto Communication is blocked by uncooperative resistance or lack of understanding.

Mercury trine Pluto Cooperative activities go well; a talk or news can have impact.

Mercury sextile Pluto If a talk digs into deep attitudes with give and take, it is cooperative.

Mercury semisquare Pluto Talk or news that seems shallow may contain some deep notes.

Mercury sesquisquare Pluto Keep heavy opinions to yourself until the talk or news shifts to a cooperative tone.

Venus conjunct Sun A pleasant person seeks your agreement.

Venus opposite Sun Feelings are vulnerable, as you long for more tenderness.

Venus square Sun People may not be as agreeable as you'd like.

Venus trine Sun Someone comes through with interest and approval to cheer you up.

Venus sextile Sun Social affairs may have a divided interest.

Venus semisquare Sun Feelings are indecisive, and social plans vacillate.

168

Venus sesquisquare Sun   Social plans shift along with your feelings.

Venus conjunct Moon   People are helpful and loving.

Venus opposite Moon   Family and emotional pressures require your responsible adaptation.

Venus square Moon   Family or social matters can be awkward.

Venus trine Moon   Matters stay serene with an easy, low profile.

Venus sextile Moon   Hold an easy calm for serenity.

Venus semisquare Moon   Yield and keep it easy to hold your poise.

Venus sesquisquare Moon   Don't get excited, keep adaptable and serene.

Venus conjunct Mercury   Seek familiar friends for pleasant, loving visits.

Venus opposite Mercury   Observe propriety and avoid emotional discussions in order to keep peace.

Venus square Mercury   A social matter may drag or lack understanding.

Venus trine Mercury   Visit friends with loving poise.

Venus sextile Mercury   Feelings are friendly if you stay pleasant.

Venus semisquare Mercury   Unsteady feelings cause touchy talk.

Venus sesquisquare Mercury   Social plans tend to be up in the air, as feelings are volatile until you stabilize.

Venus conjunct Venus   Love, beauty, and harmony are desirable.

Venus opposite Venus   You long for more closeness with a loved one.

Venus square Venus   Feelings hold a note of muted tension.

Venus trine Venus   Appreciate your benefits with serene content.

Venus sextile Venus   Pleasant social opportunities hold promise.

Venus semisquare Venus   A social matter may be touchy, until you relax.

Venus sesquisquare Venus   Hold your poise through a vulnerable moment.

Venus conjunct Mars   A social or romantic matter takes a little charm and effort to keep it smooth.

Venus opposite Mars   Sparks can fly in a social or romantic exchange.

Venus square Mars   Emotional temperament or social excess can be lusty and impulsive.

Venus trine Mars   You have charm, zest, and appeal.

Venus sextile Mars   A social exchange holds promise of further action later.

Venus semisquare Mars   Social exchanges vaccilate between serenity and irritation.

Venus sesquisquare Mars   Social matters are subject to change of plans and varied activities.

Venus conjunct Jupiter   Whatever you do tends to be excessive or expensive — but classy!

Venus opposite Jupiter   A matter may be overrated or excessive.

Venus square Jupiter   An excessive response is indiscreet; observe moderation.

Venus trine Jupiter   Appreciate your benefits with serenity and good faith.

Venus sextile Jupiter   Observe calm discretion and tolerance to keep serene.

Venus semisquare Jupiter   Varied social exchanges shift in time and tempo.

Venus sesquisquare Jupiter   Social plans tend to change from hectic to serene.

Venus conjunct Saturn   Approach your responsibilities with a poised, serene maturity.

Venus opposite Saturn   If there is lack, loss, or cold feelings with a loved one, keep your emotional world serene with patient responsibility.

Venus square Saturn   As social matters tend to drag, and loved ones are either cold or worrisome, keep serene with the work that pleases you.

Venus trine Saturn   Your social and emotional lives tend to be stable and secure, though none too romantic.

Venus sextile Saturn   Familiar social exchanges are more comfortable than are innovations.

Venus semisquare Saturn   Social exchanges vary from serene to gloomy.

Venus sesquisquare Saturn   Your social and emotional lives are touchy and unstable.

Venus conjunct Uranus   New people and sudden social changes are stimulating, though unstable.

Venus opposite Uranus   Sudden changes in your feelings and social life can stimulate erratic reactions.

Venus square Uranus   Unexpected social changes tend to be hectic and unstable.

Venus trine Uranus   Social exchanges are interesting and stimulating, though without endurance.

Venus sextile Uranus   Emotional changes or new activities bring mixed feelings.

Venus semisquare Uranus   Shifting matters and feelings bring a sudden tension that is hectic until you relax.

Venus sesquisquare Uranus   Sudden changes and emotional tension can be volatile; keep your poise.

Venus conjunct Neptune   Act with consideration to gain loving camaraderie.

Venus opposite Neptune   Don't exaggerate an emotional drama; keep your *own* integrity in relationships.

Venus square Neptune   Put your efforts into thoughtful consideration and hospitality rather than into anxiety or exaggeration.

Venus trine Neptune   With mellow consideration, aspire to your highest ideals in love and camaraderie.

Venus sextile Neptune   Stay mellow and low-key; yield graciously.

Venus semisquare Neptune   Your feelings may vacillate between anxiety and a dreamy calm.

Venus sesquisquare Neptune   Social changes can give you a sudden anxiety until you relax into mellow calm.

Venus conjunct Pluto   Cooperate with friends and loved ones to gain the greatest unity.

Venus opposite Pluto   Under the circumstances you have to cooperate; do so graciously.

Venus square Pluto   Though you may long for deeper unity, be prepared for give-and-take in relationships; compromise.

Venus trine Pluto   Social matters have more depth and unity when you extend yourself gently and firmly.

Venus sextile Pluto   Be discreet about your deep feelings in order to keep unity in a social situation.

Venus semisquare Pluto   If a social matter trembles in the balance, don't push— let it take shape.

Venus sesquisquare Pluto   Shifting social situations could bring uncooperative tension until you relax into calm unity.

Mars conjunct Sun   Take the bit in your teeth and go—for action toward constructive goals.

Mars opposite Sun   Meet problems and conflicts with energy and constructive decisions.

Mars square Sun   Use that energy constructively, rather than in rash, impulsive acts of hostility or temper.

Mars trine Sun   Meet challenge and constructive goals with zest.

Mars sextile Sun   Act with decision.

Mars semisquare Sun   Varied activities or obstacles can bring irritation; count to ten.

Mars sesquisquare Sun   Inconsistent drives scatter your forces; a sudden impulse could be rash.

Mars conjunct Moon   Keep busy on multiple odd jobs to relieve moody temper; care for those who need you.

Mars opposite Moon   Temperamental attitudes bring stress and conflict.

Mars square Moon   Moody tension and multiple pressures bring stress that can be relieved with constructive action.

Mars trine Moon   Put your effort into nurturing care for others in order to relieve moody tension.

Mars sextile Moon   A touchy mood cries out for tender nurturing.

Mars semisquare Moon   Your mood tends to be restless and touchy.

Mars sesquisquare Moon   Sudden mood shifts and restless temperament scatter your activities.

Mars conjunct Mercury   Harsh news or blunt talk makes impact.

Mars opposite Mercury   Demands of hard work, disputes, or car problems take practical action to meet head-on.

Mars square Mercury Busy activities are a challenge, but can also hold an insult, dispute, or harsh news.

Mars trine Mercury Meet challenge and busy activities with zest.

Mars sextile Mercury Turn a challenge into constructive action.

Mars semisquare Mercury Varied busy activities can include a brief challenge or irritation.

Mars sesquisquare Mercury Sudden news, challenge, or changes in a busy schedule add stress.

Mars conjunct Venus Put charm and energy into gaining more social satisfactions.

Mars opposite Venus Volatile feelings are aroused, urging you to seek more social outlets.

Mars square Venus A physical outlet is satisfactory to restless feelings.

Mars trine Venus Seek pleasurable social activities with charm and vigor.

Mars sextile Venus If you feel emotional tension, seek relief through social action.

Mars semisquare Venus As feelings are unstable, there may be touchy moments.

Mars sesquisquare Venus Feelings can range from frivolous to volatile instability.

Mars conjunct Mars Use that energy drive in positive action that is constructive—not destructive.

Mars opposite Mars Restrain a smoldering desire to strike out at harsh obstacles; use that energy constructively.

Mars square Mars Volatile energy can be expressed in meeting a challenge constructively, rather than in rash combat.

Mars trine Mars Meet busy activities and interesting challenges with zest and initiative.

Mars sextile Mars Challenge or strife can be turned to your advantage.

Mars semisquare Mars A spark of irritation can be erratic, respond with rational, constructive action.

Mars sesquisquare Mars An unexpected irritant could disrupt your disposition.

Mars conjunct Jupiter You can expand your activities with busy zest, energy, and robust enthusiasm.

Mars opposite Jupiter With rash enthusiasm, you may overestimate.

Mars square Jupiter Busy activities are constructive if they stop short of rash overindulgence.

Mars trine Jupiter You have the zest, passion, and energy to run wild and free.

Mars sextile Jupiter Meet busy activities with eagerness and confidence.

Mars semisquare Jupiter Restless indecision can trigger a rash indulgence.

Mars sesquisquare Jupiter You have a varied range of restless, busy activities.

Mars conjunct Saturn   Trauma or stress is in your environment; maintain control with responsible action.

Mars opposite Saturn   Busy, driving ambition must be used with constructive control, or it can turn into hostile depression.

Mars square Saturn   Put in hard work and long hours to overcome obstacles of competition, trauma, or stress.

Mars trine Saturn   You have the energy and ambition to act upon constructive decisions.

Mars sextile Saturn   Work through a time of busy stress to advance an ambitious opportunity.

Mars semisquare Saturn   Meet a moment of stress with self-controlled action.

Mars sesquisquare Saturn   An unexpected stress or imposition can rattle you until you regain control.

Mars conjunct Uranus   You have the courage and initiative to make independent decisions, as you're ready for a change.

Mars opposite Uranus   Though you'd like to make independent decisions for change, caution and responsibilities give you a monitor.

Mars square Uranus   Sudden changes or rash decisions at this time are impulsive and unstable.

Mars trine Uranus   New people, different attitudes, and changing conditions give you greater independence.

Mars sextile Uranus   New situations range from being tense and unstable to being exhilarating.

Mars semisquare Uranus   Restless rebellion stirs you to hunt for a different activity.

Mars sesquisquare Uranus   Erratic activities and unexpected attitudes shift from volatile to exhilarating.

Mars conjunct Neptune   A strange brooding restless discontent stirs you to seek an elusive ideal.

Mars opposite Neptune   Desires are tremulous and unrealistic; passions and anxieties are exaggerated.

Mars square Neptune   A brooding anxiety or deception can enervate you.

Mars trine Neptune   Your actions tend to take the path of least resistance.

Mars sextile Neptune   Act with discrimination as your footing is not quite firm.

Mars semisquare Neptune   If you feel restless, bored, or anxious, act with discretion rather than impulse.

Mars sesquisquare Neptune   A matter doesn't turn out as you expect; the alternative may be better.

Mars conjunct Pluto   An action at this time reaches well into the future.

Mars opposite Pluto   If you cannot consummate the matter you desire, the timing is premature; don't force it.

Mars square Pluto You may find that you can't rule or ruin, but have to compromise to work things out.

Mars trine Pluto Honest action lays a constructive groundwork for the future.

Mars sextile Pluto Current action and decision have later repercussions that may call for renegotiation.

Mars semisquare Pluto Work out a compromise before you make a rash decision.

Mars sesquisquare Pluto Selectively eliminate nonessential activities and attitudes.

Jupiter conjunct Sun Good luck and protection make this a time to shoot for big goals. Honorable men are generous.

Jupiter opposite Sun Reach out for big goals that you're prepared to grow up to, but don't bite off more than you can chew.

Jupiter square Sun Extravagance, indulgence or overrated promises can hurt.

Jupiter trine Sun Be happy and content; there are richly rewarding satisfactions.

Jupiter sextile Sun Opportunities surface to make important contacts with influential people, and to raise your position or income.

Jupiter semisquare Sun Good luck can vacillate with indulgence or extravagance.

Jupiter sesquisquare Sun Don't overrate your good luck; indulgence or extravagance can waste it.

Jupiter conjunct Moon There's contentment and an increase in your home, family, or income.

Jupiter opposite Moon Your gain is balanced by an extravagance. Family or home expansion is costly.

Jupiter square Moon A gain is paid for in a different coin. Domestic expansion is fruitful but expensive.

Jupiter trine Moon Financial decisions bear fruit. Honor, peace, and favorable attentions abound.

Jupiter sextile Moon Opportunities are favorable for business or domestic growth and increase.

Jupiter semisquare Moon Your domestic or financial expansion is unstable.

Jupiter sesquisquare Moon Sudden expenses are costly; your faith in another is shaken.

Jupiter conjunct Mercury A trip, move, or restless expansion is brewing.

Jupiter opposite Mercury Don't overrate that trip, move, or big step—it can be delayed or disappointing.

Jupiter square Mercury A trip or move is untimely, expensive, or overrated. A promise falls through.

Jupiter trine Mercury With faith in the future and confidence in yourself, make that expansive move ahead!

Jupiter sextile Mercury A person you meet is important and/or generous.

Jupiter semisquare Mercury You may shift from serene optimism to misplaced confidence.

Jupiter sesquisquare Mercury Your faith in another is shaken, or your own indulgence is costly.

Jupiter conjunct Venus Underneath that serenity, an emotional profusion brews. A love affair, increased social life, or a pleasure trip is in the near future.

Jupiter opposite Venus Your social life increases with a restless profusion of longing for more fun, romance, or affluent pleasures.

Jupiter square Venus Your social life increases but presents obstacles to the emotional satisfaction for which you long.

Jupiter trine Venus Your life style and social affairs increase with rich satisfaction and serene content.

Jupiter sextile Venus Your financial or social expansion is more rewarding with moderation and serenity rather than with flamboyance or misplaced trust.

Jupiter semisquare Venus Social and romantic feelings bounce between serene trust and a loss of faith.

Jupiter sesquisquare Venus An emotional relationship is trembling on the edge of breakup. Feelings are unstable.

Jupiter conjunct Mars With rowdy, lusty enthusiasm you can tackle extra busy activities. A lot can happen.

Jupiter opposite Mars Restless frustration pushes you into extra busy action.

Jupiter square Mars It's a busy period of stress and lusty, restless action. There is danger of extravagance, of loss, theft, or other trauma.

Jupiter trine Mars With lusty robust enthusiasm and confidence you can start a new affair, job, school, or social expansion.

Jupiter sextile Mars Bursts of energy and overrated confidence can misguide you into rash action.

Jupiter semisquare Mars A reckless zest can bring hectic activities or rash losses; take one step at a time.

Jupiter sesquisquare Mars You break up old conditions with enthusiasm and energy under this aspect.

Jupiter conjunct Jupiter If you are planning a big step, *now* is the time. You have the confidence and the wind at your back.

Jupiter opposite Jupiter Faith and trust can move mountains, but don't promise more than you can deliver.

Jupiter square Jupiter New areas burst into your life.

Jupiter trine Jupiter Your life will never seem more pleasing.

Jupiter sextile Jupiter If you take the chance afforded by this aspect, it will lead to new paths of growth.

Jupiter semisquare Jupiter Any expansive undertaking will be based on insufficient information. Watch out.

Jupiter sesquisquare Jupiter This step will be a detour—perhaps a step of growth—but keep your eye on your main goal.

Jupiter conjunct Saturn If your freedom is restricted, remember there is honor and contentment in your duty. An indulgence at this time exacts a heavy price.

Jupiter opposite Saturn For an indulgence or freedom you'll pay a heavy price in loss of faith, honor, or capital.

Jupiter square Saturn A step of growth takes a lot of work. As you finish old debts you move forward.

Jupiter trine Saturn A step of growth that you work for will pay off. Expand your ambitions.

Jupiter sextile Saturn Each old debt you complete opens a new opportunity.

Jupiter semisquare Saturn Win a few, lose a few. You can vary between increase and expense, high hopes and a handicap.

Jupiter sesquisquare Saturn The price of expansion is a breakup of old conditions. There is an inconsistent battle between freedom and security.

Jupiter conjunct Uranus A new beginning is fortunate. Break out of that rut, make that big change *now!*

Jupiter opposite Uranus Break away from the past; put everything you've got into that next big step—and grow up to it!

Jupiter square Uranus An unexpected change can throw you for a loop. It's a time of flux and a new step of growth.

Jupiter trine Uranus *There is no better time to make a change than now!*

Jupiter sextile Uranus That big step of change is opportune if you're ready to let go of the past.

Jupiter semisquare Uranus Try on that new pattern before you make it your own; it may not fit nor last.

Jupiter sesquisquare Uranus Sudden changes are unstable; they may stop and start before you gain confidence.

Jupiter conjunct Neptune Big dreams inspire you to believe in a better future. Is it real, or is it a fantasy?

Jupiter opposite Neptune Great expectations are unrealistic. Be careful; it may be a pipe dream.

Jupiter square Neptune A matter for which you long with high hope is neither firm nor realistic. Come back to earth.

Jupiter trine Neptune A dream can come true; a wondrous door can open to a new world.

Jupiter sextile Neptune An opportunity knocks to start a wondrous new affair, adventure, or promotional expansion.

Jupiter semisquare Neptune   You swing from optimism to anxiety, as you walk through patches of fog over the solid ground.

Jupiter sesquisquare Neptune   Conditions that are vaguely unstable hold moments of unexpected and ideal enchantment.

Jupiter conjunct Pluto   With faith and self-confidence, let go of the past and welcome the future.

Jupiter opposite Pluto   You're at a transition point. A decision that you must make now points the direction of the future.

Jupiter square Pluto   A moral decision that you make now will influence the shape of your future—productive growth through the breakup of old patterns.

Jupiter trine Pluto   You have the wisdom and protection now to make a decision that eliminates a past problem, and to move forward freely.

Jupiter sextile Pluto   An opportunity to step into the future is balanced by the loss of a past pattern.

Jupiter semisquare Pluto   An old condition is not yet finished, and the future not yet formed. In this period of flux, explore various avenues.

Jupiter sesquisquare Pluto   This is an inconsistent period of growth and transition, in which you can release certain old patterns in order to try on new ones to test the fit.

Saturn conjunct Sun   Work is heavy and progress slow, but the responsibilities you take on now can stabilize your ambitions into a cold, clear direction.

Saturn opposite Sun   This is a cold, poor, or worrisome period that's a hard test to your character.

Saturn square Sun   Obstacles, restrictions, and hard work block your ambitions. Money is tight and progress slow.

Saturn trine Sun   Work hard for that responsible ambition; that which you achieve will endure with stability and will advance your status.

Saturn sextile Sun   There are opportunities to advance your ambitions and status if you're prepared to work hard against obstacles and delays.

Saturn semisquare Sun   An obstacle, delay, or tough problem creates a setback to work through.

Saturn sesquisquare Sun   A nagging obstacle, problem, or delay restricts you, until you break up an old condition by working it out.

Saturn conjunct Moon   Your home or family takes work and responsibility to keep a serene safe harbor. Even if money is tight, improvements are needed. Get a health or dental checkup.

Saturn opposite Moon   A move is untimely; even if money is scarce, improvements are necessary. Make the best of it and organize what you have to keep your family secure. A health or dental checkup may be needed.

Saturn square Moon   Worries about home, family, health, and money depress you. Keep a firm responsibility toward your work and duty in order to hold a safe harbor.

Saturn trine Moon If your home and family are restrictive, you can work hard to improve conditions gradually and to be supportive of those who need you.

Saturn sextile Moon Plan moves and take steps now to improve home and family conditions, and to overcome restrictions and delays.

Saturn semisquare Moon Occasional home and family worries take time and effort to clear up.

Saturn sesquisquare Moon Sudden hectic home and family worries take work and responsibility. An old pattern is breaking up.

Saturn conjunct Mercury Plan and schedule a serious program of self-improvement in your studies, job, and ambitions. What you learn now will gradually pay off.

Saturn opposite Mercury Any ambitious move forward is blocked by routine limitations, poverty, or a loss. Make long-range plans and start a program of self-improvement.

Saturn square Mercury Routine responsibilities that block your ambitions to improve are depressing. You must work through a restriction or handicap with persistence.

Saturn trine Mercury With work and responsibility you can gradually overcome a handicap or restriction in order to organize a secure routine.

Saturn sextile Mercury An ambitious plan of improvement is opportune, if you are willing to work to its completion.

Saturn semisquare Mercury If intermittent setbacks depress you, you must work through the handicaps and restrictions that are your responsibility in order to improve conditions.

Saturn sesquisquare Mercury An unexpected setback or restriction breaks up your sense of security. Work on an improvement plan to stabilize future ambitions.

Saturn conjunct Venus As your feelings are cold, lonely, or restricted at this time, your social or emotional life is stilted, or even grievous. Work to make your environment more beautiful and secure.

Saturn opposite Venus A loss, grief, or problem with a loved one causes you worry, loneliness—or dull boredom. Work through it to keep your life secure.

Saturn square Venus Restrictions and duties block the social and emotional satisfactions for which you long.

Saturn trine Venus Stabilize your environment to maintain emotional security. A loved one is supportive in time of need.

Saturn sextile Venus This is an opportune time to stay with old secure patterns rather than to start a new social program or romance.

Saturn semisquare Venus A minor conflict, loss, or neglect can upset your emotional security.

Saturn sesquisquare Venus Disruptive changes that upset your emotional security take work to stabilize.

Saturn conjunct Mars Hard work, trauma, depression, or rejection requires your disciplined energy to control a constructive ambition.

Saturn opposite Mars Restriction, rejection, loss, or trauma takes maximum hard work and tough courage.

Saturn square Mars A restriction, loss, or trauma calls for hard work and disciplined energy.

Saturn trine Mars It feels good to get in and tackle a tough demanding job.

Saturn sextile Mars Competitive challenge or a tough job is satisfying to tackle.

Saturn semisquare Mars You may feel rash and restless under the present restrictions.

Saturn sesquisquare Mars Your energy is scattered by inconsistent jobs, duties, or restrictive changes.

Saturn conjunct Jupiter Work hard for that next step of advancement or freedom. It's a long slow pull—uphill all the way!

Saturn opposite Jupiter Work is heavy and freedom restricted; you can't bust out until you've paid all your dues.

Saturn square Jupiter With cautious optimism, pay old debts and finish obligations to make that next advance.

Saturn trine Jupiter You can take a responsible but cautiously optimistic step of advancement.

Saturn sextile Jupiter Work hard for an expansive opportunity—and carry it through with responsibility.

Saturn semisquare Jupiter You vacillate between a desire for freedom and a desire for security. Which will you choose?

Saturn sesquisquare Jupiter Each step of expansion breaks up your present restrictions into an inconsistent growth pattern.

Saturn conjunct Saturn Conditions at this time are just reward for your actions, in either the deep satisfaction of hard-working security, or in debt, poverty, and loss of reputation.

Saturn opposite Saturn Conditions of restriction and loneliness at this time are a hard test of character; as you persevere through obstacles, a cold clear ambition takes form.

Saturn square Saturn Coping with restriction and poverty takes perseverance, character, and hard work to overcome.

Saturn trine Saturn The effort you put into responsible ambitions pays off in deep satisfactions and greater security.

Saturn sextile Saturn You have the opportunity to take a mature and responsible step that advances your ambitions and security.

Saturn semisquare Saturn Your work vacillates between restrictive delays and calm responsibility.

Saturn sesquisquare Saturn Your work breaks up and shifts to another level, with inconsistent jobs that are alternately restrictive and deeply satisfying.

Saturn conjunct Uranus Work or an unexpected problem leads to a new step of original ambition.

Saturn opposite Uranus Ambition for independence emerges out of restriction.

Saturn square Uranus Secure patterns are subject to drastic changes.

Saturn trine Uranus There are sudden exciting changes in your work and responsibility.

Saturn sextile Uranus Take responsibility and work for that sudden opportunity or original step.

Saturn semisquare Uranus Your work or security pattern is subject to erratic change.

Saturn sesquisquare Uranus Independent ambitions tend to break up and reform in a different pattern, as your work changes inconsistently.

Saturn conjunct Neptune The past is dissolving; work for a better future, to attain an ideal in which you believe.

Saturn opposite Neptune With self-discipline and responsibility strive to create a new form out of chaos; the past is dissolving and becoming less secure.

Saturn square Neptune As a formerly secure position dissolves, a new life takes shape.

Saturn trine Neptune Work to make a dream come true; strive to give form to your highest ideals.

Saturn sextile Neptune You have the opportunity to attain a dream, if you take the responsibility to work for it.

Saturn semisquare Neptune Security vacillates with anxiety, as the past blurs and shifts to a new form.

Saturn sesquisquare Neptune Out of dissolving security, a new pattern emerges.

Saturn conjunct Pluto A powerful ambition emerges out of present restrictions to long-range goals.

Saturn opposite Pluto Work through the present handicaps that repress your ambitions; complete a cycle of the past to prepare for the future.

Saturn square Pluto Repressive disciplines give form to deeper ambition for long-range goals.

Saturn trine Pluto You can work through the repression of the past to plan future goals with powerful ambition.

Saturn sextile Pluto Detour around obstacles in order to gain greater control of your long-range goals.

Saturn semisquare Pluto   Despite handicaps, each faltering step gets stronger as you struggle for control of your long-range goals.

Saturn sesquisquare Pluto   Your security can suffer some devastating breakups, but with each one you strengthen your long-range goals for the future.

Uranus conjunct Sun   During this unstable period new people, ideas, experience — even a new life — is exciting!

Uranus opposite Sun   During this period of volatile instability, changes press insistently in conflict with restriction.

Uranus square Sun   With independent rebellion, you can break loose from a former pattern to make a big step of change.

Uranus trine Sun   Interesting and exciting changes are opening new doors, now and ahead of you.

Uranus sextile Sun   There are opportunities to make progressive — or unstable — changes.

Uranus semisquare Sun   Unstable changes vacillate and fluctuate, keeping you in a state of nervous tension.

Uranus sesquisquare Sun   This is an unstable period of flux, change, and turmoil.

Uranus conjunct Moon   Changes in your home and family life fluctuate from day to day.

Uranus opposite Moon   Your home or family life may turn upside down with dynamic changes.

Uranus square Moon   Domestic changes put you in an unstable state of flux.

Uranus trine Moon   Home and family changes give you more independence and add excitement to your life.

Uranus sextile Moon   Unexpected opportunities for home and family changes are exciting.

Uranus semisquare Moon   Changes in your home and family life waver and fluctuate before they come to rest.

Uranus sesquisquare Moon   Inconsistent changes in your home and family life break up and reform in unstable patterns.

Uranus conjunct Mercury   Unconventional changes in your studies or work, travels or moves give you greater independence.

Uranus opposite Mercury   Unexpected changes in your job or studies, travels or moves alter your routine and attitudes drastically.

Uranus square Mercury   With restless independence, you can make erratic or drastic changes in your studies or job, travels or moves.

Uranus trine Mercury   Independent decisions open new doors of fortunate change in your studies or job, travels or moves.

Uranus sextile Mercury   Take advantage of that opportunity to take a step of change in your studies or job, travels or moves; a new door opens.

Uranus semisquare Mercury   Restless changes are brewing in a state of flux that will affect your studies or job with a trip or move.

Uranus sesquisquare Mercury   Erratic changes are trembling in an inconclusive state of flux at this time.

Uranus conjunct Venus   Social and emotional changes are dynamic. An unconventional friendship or love affair is exciting.

Uranus opposite Venus   An unexpected change has emotional impact. A friendship or love affair tends to be unconventional, indiscreet, and volatile.

Uranus square Venus   Unexpected changes in your social life and emotional relationships are unstable and volatile.

Uranus trine Venus   With greater independence and sparkle, you can make unconventional changes in your social life, and have an exciting friendship or love affair.

Uranus sextile Venus   Unexpected changes in your social life give you the opportunity to form a dynamic friendship or romantic liaison.

Uranus semisquare Venus   Intermittent changes in your social and emotional lives are unexpected and unstable.

Uranus sesquisquare Venus   Inconsistent changes in your social and emotional lives are varied and highly unstable.

Uranus conjunct Mars   You tend to detach yourself from an unexpected problem in your objective environment, to direct your energies into an independent thrust of action.

Uranus opposite Mars   Though you'd like to walk away from it, the stress of circumstances demands that you handle abrupt changes, trauma, or a problem in your objective environment with courageous and independent decisions.

Uranus square Mars   Though you'd rather take an independent stand, a sudden problem or unexpected stress or trauma demands constructive decision.

Uranus trine Mars   Radical changes in your life are constructive, as they open new doors to insight and practical experience.

Uranus sextile Mars   Radical changes in your life are stimulating; one unexpected opportunity leads to another.

Uranus semisquare Mars   Vacillating changes bring tempestuous restlessness and rash, erratic decisions.

Uranus sesquisquare Mars   Inconsistent changes of direction put you in an unstable state of stress and flux. Look for ingenious detours.

Uranus conjunct Jupiter   A sudden or unexpected change is fortunate, as it gives you more independence, insight, and personal growth.

Uranus opposite Jupiter   Unexpected changes go to abrupt extremes — extremes of good fortune or loss of faith, of honor or disgrace, of affluance or extravagance. Put your trust only in formal contracts and honorable dealings.

Uranus square Jupiter   Sudden changes exact a heavy toll before they finally work out to your advantage.

Uranus trine Jupiter   A great change falls into place that gives you a new life of independence, freedom and growth.

Uranus sextile Jupiter   Sudden expansive changes give you the opportunity for more freedom and independence.

Uranus semisquare Jupiter   Your changes and growth move in fits and starts that are for the most part inconclusive.

Uranus sesquisquare Jupiter   Sudden inconsistent changes bring you both gains and losses.

Uranus conjunct Saturn   You can work for a structural change in your job or routine to advance your independent ambitions.

Uranus opposite Saturn   To gain those independent ambitions you must work hard. Unexpected problems and unusual responsibilities take time and ingenuity to solve.

Uranus square Saturn   Independent ambitions meet with delays, unexpected obstacles, and radical problems.

Uranus trine Saturn   Changes in your life structure give you more self-reliance to handle independent responsibilities.

Uranus sextile Saturn   A variety of changes helps to develop your self-reliance, but the changes tend to be neither secure nor enduring.

Uranus semisquare Saturn   Erratic and unstable changes take work to maintain stability through a period of flux.

Uranus sesquisquare Saturn   Sudden radical changes and restless ambition break up the secure order of your life.

Uranus conjunct Uranus   (Age 83-85) You are in the unique position of standing between the past and the future, belonging to neither.

Uranus opposite Uranus   (Age 41-43) This is an unstable transition period between the past and the future.

Uranus square Uranus   (Age 20-21, age 61-63) You have a rebellious urge to break conventional patterns, but your independence is blocked.

Uranus trine Uranus   (Age 26-28, age 55-57) This is a fortunate and progressive period of change that opens doors to the future.

Uranus sextile Uranus   (Age 13-14, age 68-70) There are opportunities to make progressive changes that give you more independence.

Uranus semisquare Uranus   (Age 10, age 72-74) Unstable changes bring nervous independence.

Uranus sesquisquare Uranus   (Age 31-32, age 50-52) Conditions break up and reform in erratic patterns of change that give you nervous tension.

Uranus conjunct Neptune   A new chapter begins that can be ideal if you strive for independent, progressive aspirations.

Uranus square Neptune With sensitive detachment or erratic discontent, you feel your way through a nebulous period of change.

Uranus trine Neptune Tension areas ease and give you the time to pursue independent aspirations.

Uranus sextile Neptune Independent aspirations bring opportune advantages; however, erratic discontent opens strange doors.

Uranus semisquare Neptune Changes are elusive and unfirm; avoid crazy schemes.

Uranus opposite Neptune Changes are vaguely disturbing. Explore alternate choices for the best solution.

Uranus sesquisquare Neptune Sudden changes tend to be unstable and elusive, and they seldom endure the test of time.

Uranus conjunct Pluto A chapter in your life is reaching a conclusion. Through the experience of this time there is a subtle transition of your perspective.

Uranus square Pluto An area in your life can reach a reluctant, wrenching conclusion, out of which you gradually change your perspective and try to resolve compulsive attitudes.

Uranus trine Pluto From this period emerges a subtle transition of direction that sets the standard of future directions.

Uranus sextile Pluto An opportunity you pursue at this time leads to a subtle transition of direction.

Uranus semisquare Pluto As you resolve a repressive situation, you gradually gain more independence.

Uranus opposite Pluto Let go of old attachments as you move into the next chapter of experience.

Uranus sesquisquare Pluto Disruptive changes remove old patterns to clear the way for new directions.

Neptune conjunct Sun Rather than being evasive, aspire to the idyllic goals in which you believe.

Neptune opposite Sun Are your aspirations realistic? Keep your eyes on idyllic goals with integrity, as a person or situation in your environment is nebulous.

Neptune square Sun Deception, confusion, and unrealistic aspirations threaten your goals.

Neptune trine Sun A dream can come true, if you have been aspiring to idyllic goals with integrity.

Neptune sextile Sun An idyllic goal to which you've aspired is opportune.

Neptune semisquare Sun You may aspire to an idyllic goal that wavers on a nebulous note just now.

Neptune sesquisquare Sun Vague, disruptive, or dramatic changes are disturbing.

Neptune conjunct Moon Even if the future seems cloudy and unformed, home and family conditions evidence more sensitive empathy. There is consideration and camaraderie with loved ones.

Neptune opposite Moon Your sense of direction in the future is nebulous as a home or family situation causes vague unrest or anxiety.

Neptune square Moon With vague unrest and nameless hunger you push against indistinct obstacles toward an unformed future.

Neptune trine Moon This is an idyllic domestic period, with more ease, camaraderie, and fun.

Neptune sextile Moon You have the opportunity to improve your domestic life with more consideration and camaraderie.

Neptune semisquare Moon A nebulous future gives you restless anxiety.

Neptune sesquisquare Moon Shifting, unstable, and hazy conditions give you a vague sense of rebellion.

Neptune conjunct Mercury Though you can promote your plans, products, or services, with sensitive imagination, this tends to be a retiring period.

Neptune opposite Mercury Though there can be a dramatic, even idyllic, incident or move, this tends on the whole to be an obscure period in which your plans are nebulous.

Neptune square Mercury Even though restless dreams and ideals stir you, this tends to be a shadowy period in which you are blocked by nebulous obstacles.

Neptune trine Mercury This tends to be a seclusive or retiring period; even if there is a dramatic move or incident it is accompanied by mellow camaraderie and good luck.

Neptune sextile Mercury A dramatic move or incident gives you the opportunity to promote your idyllic plans.

Neptune semisquare Mercury Obscurity causes vague restless anxiety, but nebulous obstacles block your idyllic plans.

Neptune sesquisquare Mercury A dramatic move or incident may shake you up and leave you vaguely discontent or anxious.

Neptune conjunct Venus Communal social life holds camaraderie and gentle consideration. You may idealize a platonic friend or romantic lover.

Neptune opposite Venus In your communal social life there are some idyllic exchanges of camaraderie, even though you are more passive and retiring than usual. A romance can be unrealistic, fascinating, but unstable.

Neptune square Venus Even though you have a vulnerable longing hunger for more camaraderie or love, a romance can be vaguely unstable, or it may even dissolve.

185

Neptune trine Venus Love relationships based on sensitive commitment are ideal. Cultural or communal social exchanges flourish.

Neptune sextile Venus There are opportunities to build cultural and communal social exchanges. A romance is nebulous, unless you're willing to make a commitment.

Neptune semisquare Venus Though you are restless with a lonely hunger, social and romantic exchanges seem vaguely unsatisfactory.

Neptune sesquisquare Venus Cultural and social aspirations tend to break up or dissolve, unless you can change them into a firm commitment. You could be vulnerable to an unrealistic romance.

Neptune conjunct Mars Your imagination is stimulated to high ideals—or exotic drama; to constructive promotions—or erotic scandal; to intricate problems and schemes—or busy community activities.

Neptune opposite Mars Discontent with present conditions pushes you to bigger and better aspirations. With pragmatic. integrity you can make an ideal move, but on the whole you are walking through a field pitted with beds of quicksand.

Neptune square Mars This is a potentially tricky or dangerous time that takes integrity and self-control to keep your ideals.

Neptune trine Mars A matter into which you have put passion and energy can be ideal. Communal activities have camaraderie and zest.

Neptune sextile Mars Advance your community activities with energy and enthusiasm, integrity and passion to promote the opportunities.

Neptune semisquare Mars You may feel a vague discontent with your community activities as you vacillate between restlessness and an aspiration to better your conditions.

Neptune sesquisquare Mars A matter you'd counted on could collapse, while an unexpected alternative is ideal. Disruptive conditions can bring confusion as you sort out your priorities.

Neptune conjunct Jupiter Your communal life expands in scope during this period of contentment, reward, and growth. There is a gain in camaraderie and trust.

Neptune opposite Jupiter Expand your community life with faith and integrity in your high aspirations. A deceptive area can collapse with confusion, or there can be financial and legal muddle.

Neptune square Jupiter In your visions of expanded community life there are vague obstacles and nebulous directions.

Neptune trine Jupiter This is a period of mellow and gentle rewards, in which you are insulated from harshness in your community growth.

Neptune sextile Jupiter There are opportunities to expand your communal life with mellow ease, if you don't overrate your expectations.

Neptune semisquare Jupiter Your growth areas vacillate between confused anxiety and high hopes for a better condition.

Neptune sesquisquare Jupiter There are inconsistent steps of dissolution and growth in your communal life.

Neptune conjunct Saturn Though money and prestige are modified, you can attain ideal working conditions in which long hours devoted to your own interests give you stimulation and satisfaction.

Neptune opposite Saturn Perfecting your creative aspirations takes long hours of disciplined practice in overcoming resistance to complex problems and responsibilities.

Neptune square Saturn Your work and responsibilities at this time encounter vague obstacles and frustratingly nebulous problems.

Neptune trine Saturn You can perfect a creative aspiration, or modestly strive to gain a secure ideal.

Neptune sextile Saturn There are opportunities to gain certain aspirations if you're willing to work toward perfecting your goals.

Neptune semisquare Saturn Certain secure patterns dissolve, as you search for deeper meaning in the structure of your ideals.

Neptune sesquisquare Saturn A matter in which you hope to find security may dissolve or be inconstant.

Neptune opposite Uranus This is a vague period of unstable changes, during which there are both unexpected problems or losses, and exceptional or ideal gains.

Neptune square Uranus You may feel that you are neither fish nor fowl during this unstable period of flux. The past dissolves; the future is forming in unexpected patterns.

Neptune trine Uranus This can be a major period of dynamic transition in your life. As the past dissolves, you can take a step forward that benefits you for years to come.

Neptune sesquisquare Uranus During this rare period of inconstant flux, it takes your highest idealism to avoid making crazy moves.

Neptune conjunct, sextile, semisquare Uranus are aspects not applicable to persons born in the twentieth century.

Neptune conjunct Neptune Occurs only every 167 years.

Neptune opposite Neptune (Age 82-84) Your area of focus becomes vague.

Neptune square Neptune (Age 40-42) This is a strangely unstable period, as you may feel vaguely discontented with what you have, and may pursue an unformed or unrealistic idea of what you want. Idyllic incidents can vary with weird dissolutions or anxieties.

Neptune trine Neptune (Age 54-56) Though this period is muted and insulated, you can gain an ideal condition or inspiration.

Neptune sextile Neptune (Age 26-28) Out of this generally retiring period,

187

have an opportunity to gain an ideal.

Neptune semisquare Neptune (Age 19-21) A certain ideal can be realized, out of a period that is for the most part vaguely anxious and obscure.

Neptune sesquisquare Neptune (Age 61-62) Vague, inconsistent changes bring a measure of anxiety, as you're unsure of how they will conclude.

Neptune square Pluto This tends to be a period of limbo; you are in a transition cycle when your power to control your own destiny is blocked. Strive to attain communal teamwork.

Neptune trine Pluto With communal teamwork and striving you can gradually come out of a period of limbo, to gain greater control of your own destiny.

Neptune sesquisquare Pluto As certain matters dissolve, strive to attain deeper insight into your own destiny.

Neptune opposite Pluto Decisions feel pressing but elusive. Move toward a transition only if it improves your general position.

Neptune conjunct, sextile and semisquare Pluto are not applicable to persons born in the twentieth century.

Pluto conjunct Sun A situation or attitude of the past is being resolved and completed to give you more powerful awareness and greater capacity to perceive the future.

Pluto opposite Sun Inexorable conditions demand cooperative teamwork to bring out your deeper potential for, and clearer perspective on, the new cycle into which you are moving.

Pluto square Sun As you conclude and resolve repressive or compelling obstacles you can acquire a more powerful insight into the direction of the cycle you're now beginning.

Pluto trine Sun In this important transition period you can establish a powerful pattern of direction in a new cycle of perspective.

Pluto sextile Sun As one area of your past is resolved or concluded, a door opens that is opportune to a new cycle.

Pluto semisquare Sun This transition period requires more time, information, and experience to shape into a firm direction.

Pluto sesquisquare Sun This is an inconsistent period of transition when you need to shape, discard, and integrate varied conditions in order to gain a new perspective.

Pluto conjunct Moon Family or close relationships are compelling, with a concern for health or welfare, or a change in the household structure.

Pluto opposite Moon You are thrust into a fluctuating variety of activities that could include a move or a change in the family structure.

Pluto square Moon A fluctuating variety of activities can include moves, changes in the family structure, or a concern for health and welfare.

Pluto trine Moon A shifting assortment of activities opens new areas of scope and influence. Moves, or changes in the family and domestic structure, are highly advantageous.

Pluto sextile Moon Opportunities to move or make a change in the domestic structure give you a wider range of varying activity.

Pluto semisquare Moon Restless, fluctuating changes in your home or family situation bring you concern and resistance.

Pluto sesquisquare Moon Inconsistent and varied activities scatter your forces and oscillate your moods. A move or change in the family structure can be unexpected and unstable.

Pluto conjunct Mercury As you search for guidance within yourself as to what to do, you can conclude and abandon an old pattern, in order to plan and begin a powerful direction.

Pluto opposite Mercury Powerful influences pull you in several directions. Negotiate and compromise, until you feel you are sure of the right answer.

Pluto square Mercury Your plans meet with powerful resistance and barriers you must overcome before finding the right answer to a problem or direction.

Pluto trine Mercury If you've been working out a firm direction of plans, you can now set them into powerful motion.

Pluto sextile Mercury This is an opportune time to set your plan into motion in a firm direction.

Pluto semisquare Mercury Your plans meet with vacillating resistance that keeps you restless and indecisive, as your directions tend to stop and start.

Pluto sesquisquare Mercury Your direction, plans, and decisions tend to be in a state of flux, as you discard, negotiate, compromise—and finally move ahead.

Pluto conjunct Venus Emotional relationships are intense and compelling; they could include both loss and gain, resistance and unity. Your social life acquires greater scope and wider experience.

Pluto opposite Venus The emotional pressure of uncooperative resistance can cause a separation or loss. To gain maximum unity with loved ones you must negotiate and compromise.

Pluto square Venus Though you may long for closer companionship, there are obstacles in your social and emotional lives that bring loss, isolation, or unfulfilling contacts. Compromise to keep unity for now and the future.

Pluto trine Venus Your social life covers a broader and more varied range of involvement. A friendship or possible love affair can be deep and compelling.

Pluto sextile Venus In your social life there are opportunities to meet a variety of people, that can bring you a deep friendship or emotional impact.

Pluto semisquare Venus Your social life tends to vacillate with a greater range of people, and a possible loss as well as gain.

Pluto sesquisquare Venus Inconsistent changes, gains, and losses in your social life can take you to emotional heights and depths.

Pluto conjunct Mars   A powerful drive impels you to take constructive action — or to act on disastrous impulse — according to your own deep-rooted patterns. If there is a festering area, it comes to a critical head.

Pluto opposite Mars   Inexorable pressure forces you into a powerful drive to constructive action — or demands that you cope with disastrous events.

Pluto square Mars   Intense stress, anger, and competition under heavily repressive conditions require constructive courage. If there is a festering area, it reaches a crisis.

Pluto trine Mars   Under stress, competition, and repression you can transmute your passion into constructive action.

Pluto sextile Mars   Under stress or repression, you have the opportunity to direct your energies into positive action.

Pluto semisquare Mars   You could vacillate between a desire for constructive action and a penchant for disastrous impulse. Purge the festering areas in order to heal and move ahead.

Pluto sesquisquare Mars   With inconsistent and rash impulses alternated with constructive moves, you struggle to break up repressive areas.

Pluto conjunct Jupiter   You come out of repression into freedom, joy, and expansion with which you can make a powerful move in the areas of career, money, or personal indulgence.

Pluto opposite Jupiter   You can take massive steps of growth in teamwork for a high ethic in expanding goals; however, the education of this period is only a steppingstone to your growing capacity.

Pluto square Jupiter   In your urge to be free of a condition that is repressive or passé, you could take a step that is expensive, but that nonetheless opens up the next cycle of your growth.

Pluto trine Jupiter   This can be a turning point, during which you move through a repression or crisis in your next step of growth.

Pluto sextile Jupiter   There is the opportunity to turn from repression to growth in an area into which you have put prior hopes and preparation.

Pluto semisquare Jupiter   During this period you vacillate between repressive conditions and steps of growth and freedom.

Pluto sesquisquare Jupiter   During this inconsistent period of growth, you take short and sudden steps of extravagant freedom out of a repressive area.

Pluto conjunct Saturn   This is a period of training. Work to full capacity; what you learn or establish now will give you powerful control over future ambitions.

Pluto opposite Saturn   Circumstances are highly repressive of your ambitions. The way you handle present responsibilities sets a precedent for future security.

Pluto square Saturn Obstacles, repression, poverty, or loss pressure you to either take desperate moves to hang onto your security, or to risk that security for the resolution of a powerful ambition.

Pluto trine Saturn You have the force and determination to take powerful control of your own ambitions, for either selfish or responsible directions.

Pluto sextile Saturn The responsibilities you take now give you the opportunity to resolve old repressions, and to increase your control of personal ambitions.

Pluto semisquare Saturn You may vacillate between the security of a repressive condition and a restless urge to take on greater ambitions.

Pluto sesquisquare Saturn As a repressive condition breaks up, you must take on more responsibility toward your future ambitions.

Pluto conjunct Uranus Not applicable to persons born in the twentieth century.

Pluto opposite Uranus This is a massive and compelling period of transition from the past to the future.

Pluto square Uranus You could make a diametric - but inconclusive - change during this period, as it is a period of flux between the past and the future.

Pluto trine Uranus As a prior situation is concluded you move into a new chapter in your life with powerful impetus.

Pluto sextile Uranus There is an opportunity to start a new chapter in one area of your life.

Pluto semisquare Uranus You may waver between cooperation and rebellion during the fluctuating changes of experience in this period. You could discard old patterns to try on a new life style for a tentative fit.

Pluto sesquisquare Uranus As certain matters of the past are concluded, you can make erratic changes in searching for future directions.

Pluto conjunct Neptune During this period you find where you belong, and your life path turns toward new ideals.

Pluto opposite, square, trine, sesquisquare Neptune Not applicable for the rest of the twentieth century.

Pluto sextile Neptune In your life path, there is an opportunity to find a certain ideal.

Pluto semisquare Neptune During this period, there can be false starts that alternate with repression, before you find that ideal niche where you belong.

Pluto conjunct and opposite Pluto not applicable.

Pluto square Pluto (Persons born in 1900 have Pluto square Pluto at approximately age 66; persons born in 1950 have the aspect at approximately age 40.) It's time to close a cycle, tie up the loose ends and let it go. Bring out the full force of your potential in a resurgence of powerful direction, for which you are equipped by past experiences and present interest.

Pluto trine Pluto A regenerative vigor stimulates your interests into a stimulating cycle.

Pluto sextile Pluto As you conclude a repressive situation or phase in your life you have the opportunity to take those first faltering steps into a new cycle.

Pluto semisquare Pluto This interval is a bridge - a steppingstone between the person you were and the person you will be as you gain more resolute direction.

Pluto sesquisquare Pluto Goals and transitions shift to a different level.

As Pluto takes twelve to thirty-one years to go through a sign, there is not a consistent time span for the Pluto-to-Pluto aspects.